AN

EYEWITNESS

TO

HISTORY

AN AUTOBIOGRAPHY

BY

FRANK ELDON GRAVES

Christmas 2013

Remembering Frank Eldon Graves:

Wife

Frank and I were married December 17, 1942 in San Diego, California. At that time the saying was "Young marriages never last". I would say we proved them wrong because we were married for seventy-one years, seven months and twenty-two days.

We moved every two to three years while Frank served in the Marine Corps. The moves were trying but I found something to enjoy in each place we lived. Everywhere was interesting for me because I had never been out of Texas until I went to California to be married.

After Frank retired from the Marine Corps, we moved back to Texas so he could attend College. He graduated and after two more moves we settled in Denison, Texas where we finished out our years together.

Frank was a gentle and caring man. He had great respect for women so I always felt cherished. Over the years we had disagreements as all married people do, but we reached a compromise agreeable to both of us.

Together we brought up three wonderful children who have lead exemplary lives and made us proud. Frank made me very happy as a wife and Mother. I enjoyed all our years together and I hope I made him happy also.

Christene Graves

Children

This is the story of the life of Frank Eldon Graves; son, husband, father. He was a man whose early years were spent in abject poverty and family conditions that can turn people to lives of dishonor. Frank chose another path and found every way he could to improve his life—whether it was answering his country's call to duty, education, the love of a good woman or just plain old hard work. He was a perfect example of the American Success Story: Someone who pulls himself out of a loss-filled childhood and a world war, and rises to become a role model for his entire family.

When he reached "a certain age", Frank decided that he needed to share his story with his descendants. He felt that we should know of the life he led and how we got to where our family is today. His memory was remarkable. He wrote of childhood experiences that are funny & poignant. He wrote of his war experience with a recall and accuracy that amaze.

He wrote it for us. We would like to share it with you.

Sharon Graves-Mulrey (daughter)
Wade Graves (son)

Friend

I had not known Captain Graves until late in his life. He went to the same Church that we attended when we first moved to Denison, Texas.

Like many older people at church, you would greet them and move on.

Following his retirement he came to see me seeking my professional help. I am a Podiatrist by trade and have had the great pleasure to visit in depth with people during office visits.

Captain Graves and I were both in the Marines Corps and were immediately connected. Once a Marine, always a Marine. It is a brotherhood. Our visits quickly turned to where we served and when.

This was when I promptly quit speaking of my career for I quickly recognized I was in deep water. Being a history buff I was amazed at his life experiences.

His life was a classic Horatio Alger story. Although before my time, my mother would always speak of young underprivileged boys that thru hard work and determination could succeed.

Frank had told me of an autobiography he had written and was gracious enough to allow me to read it. It was riveting to me and I immediately believed this is a story that should be published.

After a lot of convincing, Frank being a very humble man, he agreed to have it published.

This is a story of how privileged we are to be born Americans. Truly something that is taken too lightly by those of us fortunate enough to be born here.

He was a man of pride, backbone, hard work, and "never quit"; a deeply devout Christian, husband, father, educator, soldier and Patriot.

This book is a tribute to the man.

Dr. Coyle DeMoss

Publisher's note:

After the demise of Frank Eldon Graves, a friend of his, Doctor Coyle DeMoss, asked me to publish his autobiography. The pages presented to me were apparently an exact copy of the manuscript that had been prepared by Mister Graves. After reading only a few pages, I recognized that the style in which it was written should be preserved. Therefore, I have tried not to change the punctuation, methods of emphasis, spelling or sentence structure.

PHOTOGRAPHS and then an EPILOGUE
follow the
AUTOBIOGRAPHY
Back-of-Book

Beon Besott Publishing Company

Copyright © 2015 Christene Graves

ISBN: Paperback 978-0-9891502-9-3

FOREWORD

Events discussed on these pages were written as I remember them. There may be passages that are not politically correct by today's standards. For this, I make no apology. All English purists may find the grammar and syntax in need of additional work. As I approach my 75th year I can find more interesting things to do than to labor over grammar and syntax. This document has been written over a period of six years for family information. There have been many occasions when I have been forced to walk away for weeks at a time. The memories brought back emotions that were so painful I could not continue. Many dates used have been firmly burned into my memory. Other dates that were vague have been taken from Pacific War Diary by James J. Fahey a Sailor on the MONTPELIER who kept an illegal secret diary. After World War II, he published his book. The proceeds of his book permitted him to live comfortably on Sanibel Island, Florida until his death. Some of the dates of minor operations on the U.S.S. ENTERPRISE were taken from The Big 'E' by Commander Edward P. Stafford, U.S.N.

The events on both ships are described as I remember them.

AN EYEWITNESS TO HISTORY
An Autobiography
by
Frank Eldon Graves

I was born September 17, 1922 at the home of my Great Grandfather George Freemont Tyler 5 miles Southwest of Honey Grove, Texas in the McCraw's Chapel Community. My parents were John Campbell and Ida Ethel (Culbreath) Graves. My mother died of Tuberculosis when I was about 3 1/2 years of age. Most of my childhood was spent in the home of my paternal Grandparents, John William and Jennie Barbara (Fields) Graves. My father also lived in the home until his remarriage in 1934. My Grandfather was a Share Cropper Cotton Farmer and Lay Baptist Preacher in the Flag Springs Community 4 1/2 miles south of Windom, Texas. My Grandparents were extremely poor (so was everyone else in the community). There were no Sociologists or Welfare workers to tell us how poor we were so everyone in the community made do with what they had, or in most cases, did without. My Grandparents treated me as one of their own children, and what they lacked in financial resources were more than made up in love and caring. A more loving home life would be difficult to imagine. Also in the home were my Aunt Pauline and Uncle Dewey, both teenagers. They were a great help in caring for me, especially my Aunt Pauline. She and I enjoyed a special relationship until her death in 1974. Little is known about my Great-grandparents Graves, except that they were subsistence farmers in Tennessee (near Lawrenceburg). My Grandfather Graves decided to look for greener pastures when he was 17 years old. He rode a small boat down the Mississippi to New Orleans then a ship to Galveston and eventually found his way to Ladonia Texas.

There he met his future bride Jennie Barbara Fields. Her parents Rufus and Tennie Fields had migrated to Texas from "middle Tennessee" (according to my Grandmother) in a covered wagon after the Civil War (they called it the War Between the States since there was nothing civil about it). They settled in Bowie County, near Texarkana. They later moved to Hopkins

County for a few years and then settled 2 miles west of Ladonia in Fannin County. They raised Cotton and Corn and established a comfortable home for that period. I visited their home many times as a child. The house could best be described as based upon the earlier double log cabin. There were two large rooms in front, a living room and a parlor, separated by a breezeway, commonly called a "dog trot". A wing led off of the living room and consisted of a dining room and a kitchen. Bathing facilities consisted of a washtub (water heated on the wood burning cook stove) and an "Outhouse" about 50 yards out back. One of the things I remember about my Great-grandmother Fields was that she smoked a corncob pipe at times. My Great-grandfather Fields would not chop wood for the woodburning cookstove in advance. He would get up early and chop wood for breakfast preparation. His reasoning was he might die in his sleep and would be spared the hated chore of chopping wood.

After falling in love with Jennie Barbara Fields, my Grandfather returned to Tennessee and convinced his family to move to Texas. They traveled by wagon and crossed the Mississippi by Ferry. I am sure he told me how long the journey lasted, however I am unable to recall. They settled on a farm 2 miles west of Ladonia near Rufus and Tennie Fields. They also raised cotton and corn. This was during the time when cotton was in great demand and was the main cash crop in most of the south. My Grandfather and Jennie Barbara Fields were married in 1895. They raised five children of their own: Leonard, John, Namon, Pauline and Dewey. They had a daughter Maudie who died as a teenager and another child who died as an infant. After the death of my mother, they took me and my infant brother Durward in. My brother died when he was 6 months old. In retrospect, I am sure my grandparents had their hands full.

Very little is known of my Grandmother Culbreath. In addition to my mother, she and my Grandfather Carrol Frank Culbreath had two other children (twins) who died in infancy. My Grandmother Culbreath died soon after at an early age. My Grandfather Culbreath migrated to Oklahoma Territory when it was opened for settlement. He homesteaded 160 acres 17 miles southeast of Frederick and lived in a Sod Hut for several years. He eventually remarried and had one son, Marion Joe Culbreath. He grew wheat and cotton until shortly before his death at age 68. I did not know my Grandfather Culbreath. In 1939, just prior to joining the U.S. Marine Corps, I went to Oklahoma and found him. We maintained relatively close contact until his death.

One of the great events of my childhood was to visit my Great Grandfather Tyler. I am sure my lifelong fascination with machinery and mechanical things can be traced to my visits to the home of Great Grandfather Tyler. He came to Texas as a young man and met and married my Great Grandmother Nannie McGraw. Her family had been in Texas for several generations, some said prior to the Republic. He became a successful farmer and businessman. He owned a cotton gin and store northeast of Honey grove and also a store at his home. His home was a large 2-story house with running water, an indoor bathtub and electric lights! This was the only home in the community with such facilities. The water was pumped by a windmill into a large metal tank mounted on a tall platform. Electricity was provided by a gasoline powered Delco Power plant attached to the side of the store.

One of the more interesting farm machines was one that would grind green corn and blow it about 50 feet up into the air into a Silo to be used later for cattle feed.

Among the many buildings at the Tyler home was one about the size of an airplane hangar called the warehouse. In this building were stored two large Threshing Machines and two Steam Powered Engines used to power the threshing machines. These were huge machines with rear wheels about ten feet in diameter. They burned coal in the firebox to generate steam that turned a large wheel on the side of the engine. The engine would be placed about 50 feet from the Thresher and would be connected to a large wheel on the Thresher by a large belt to run the Thresher. This equipment remained in the warehouse except during harvest time. I spent many hours sitting in the cab of one of the engines, pretending to drive it by working the handles and knobs. The Threshers were as large as a present day mobile home. There was an access door on one side and I would frequently crawl into one of them and inspect the augers, gears and large fans that removed the straw and chaff blowing it through a large pipe about 18" in diameter and about 20 feet long into a straw stack as large as a house. You can see many of these threshers today in North and South Dakota usually parked on top of a hill looking like some ancient animal surveying his kingdom. It took 18 or 20 good men to run this equipment. First the grain had to be cut with a machine called a Binder which cut the grain and tied it into bundles. The bundles were dropped on the ground and would be picked up and stacked into a shock of about 30 bundles. After curing for a few days they would be loaded onto a wagon and hauled to the Thresher where they would be tossed into the intake jaws of the Thresher where the grain would be separated from the straw. The straw would be blown into a large stack in the field and the grain would be loaded into a grain wagon to be hauled to a storage area. Every time I see some lone farmer running a combine harvesting grain all by himself, I cannot keep from thinking about watching my Great-grandfather Tyler and his crew of 20 men harvesting grain when I was a youngster.

We read and hear a lot about child abuse today, however we can be thankful adults do not tease children as much as they once did. When I was a youngster, it seemed the favorite pastime of most adults was to tease children. During my many visits to my Great Grandfather Tyler's home, I would visit a neighbor by the name of Mr. Ilie. Mr. Ilie was a fascinating man. He had a workshop where he was always making something. One of the things he was working on was a wind powered generator to charge the batteries of his Atwater-Kent Radio. The neighbors could not understand (or did not care to understand) what he was up to so they called his device a "Thunderpump". A Mr. Blackwood, one of the workers for Granddad Tyler was always teasing me. Since I hung around Mr. Ilie's workshop Mr. Blackwood accused me of helping him develop the "Thunderpump". The next stage was to call me "Thunderpump". I did not like the name and the more I protested the greater his delight in calling me "Thunderpump. After a period of time that seemed forever, one day Mr. Blackwood was sitting down leaning against a building smoking his pipe, he started his usual teasing calling me "Thunderpump". There was a large leg bone from a cow on the ground nearby. I picked up the bone and hit him on the head with it. The blow knocked him out cold. My father heard the commotion and came up to see what was going on. He removed his belt to give me a good whipping. Just as he started to work on me, Mr. Blackwood opened his eyes, rubbed his head and insisted my father stop the whipping. He said "I had that coming to me for a long time". I must have been about six years of age at the time. Mr. Blackwood moved away but almost every time I went to Honey Grove I would run into him. He would call me "Thunderpump" and would regale anyone that would listen with the story of how I knocked him out with a cow bone when I was a little guy. Mr. Ilie's "Thunderpump" worked quite well. He did not know about obtaining a patent on the device, but the machine was a great success. Someone in the Midwest produced them commercially and prior to President Roosevelt's Rural Electrification Program in the late 1930's many rural homes were equipped with a Windcharger that looked very much like Mr. Ilie's "Thunderpump".

Grandfather Tyler died in 1927. My Great Uncle Eugene Beasley and Great Aunt Myrtle (Tyler) Beasley moved into the home to take care of Grandmother Tyler and to manage the home place. Great Uncle Brock Tyler managed the other businesses.

Uncle Eugene and Aunt Myrtle had two children, twins Louis and Lois. They were about ten years older than I, however we enjoyed a good relationship and they always looked after me to see that I did not get hurt or get into any serious mischief.

I don't know what happened, but a few years later, the Beasleys moved to a farm East of Honey Grove and Brock Tyler moved into the home place. The depression played havoc with the Tyler enterprises and by the time of Great grandmother Tyler's death in 1933, she and the Tyler estate were living in poverty. Brock Tyler and his family continued to live at the old homeplace until his death, after which, his son T. B. Tyler and his family lived there for many years. I did not see the Tyler home for more than 20 years. When we returned to Texas in 1962, we lived in Commerce. One day we decided to visit the old Tyler home. The view was most depressing. The house was falling down. All of the many outbuildings were gone. We went into the house. It appeared vandals had been there ahead of us. We salvaged a few family pictures from an upstairs room, which had been torn from their frames and thrown on the floor. Some were repaired and now occupy a prominent position in our home. Today, a hay barn stands near where the house was located, the only evidence of human activity. When I drive by, I do not see the haybarn, but instead see the once beautiful estate, surrounded by many well maintained outbuildings and lots of human activity. I am sure my wonderful wife and children have difficulty understanding why I become emotional when I visit that area.

My great Uncle Eugene Beasley, with little formal education, knew more about Psychology than some PhD types I have known. The fact I never smoked can be attributed to a bit of Psychology he used on me when I was visiting his home when I was 12 or 13 years of age. I had somehow managed to save enough money to buy two packages of Lucky Strike Cigarettes. I was out in his Blacksmith Shop smoking a cigarette when he caught me in the act. He said "Boy what are you doing?" I told him I was smoking. He said "Don't you know only women smoke readymade cigarettes. If you want to be a man, you need to smoke a man's smoke. Roll your own, or smoke a pipe. Tell you what I will do, you remind me tomorrow before breakfast, and I will let you smoke my pipe, that is a real man's smoke, it will put hair on your chest, if you want to be a real man, you need to smoke a pipe." I should have been smart enough to realize he was setting me up, however no one ever accused me of being exceptionally bright. He had apparently forgotten the promise, so before breakfast - I said "Hey, Unk Eugene how about that pipe." I should have recognized the twinkle in his eye, but it went right by me. He smoked a corncob pipe. The tobacco was called Kentucky Twist it was all twisted into a loop and he used a knife to cut some of it off to put into his pipe. This he did very carefully. I was becoming more anxious by the moment. He took his time and finally lit the pipe and passed it to me. I took a couple of puffs and he said, "Oh no, a woman smokes like that. Let me show you how to smoke like a man. You are supposed to inhale, like this". He took a deep drag on the pipe, sucked the smoke deeply into his lungs, held it for a few seconds, then exhaled. He said "now that is how a man smokes. That will put hair on your chest" He passed the pipe back to me. I took a couple of drags like he had demonstrated. All at once, the room started spinning, I became so sick I thought I would surely die. I lost my supper from the night before and went back to bed. The room continued to spin and Uncle Eugene sat in his chair laughing and slapping his legs. I was unable to eat for a couple of days and had a weak stomach for a week. Over the years, I have been offered a cigarette more times than I would care to count, however I always declined. When I think about the incident, to this day I call still see that old man sitting in his chair, laughing at the top of his lungs and slapping his legs. That was one Psychology lesson I will always remember.

SCHOOL DAYS

In the fall of 1929, I started school in the First Grade at Flag Springs School. In those days, there was an Elementary School within walking distance of every child. The schools were located within 4 miles (more or less) so no child would have to walk more than 2 miles. My Grandparents (Graves) lived on the line between Flag Springs and Brawley Pool Schools. I could have attended either, however since both Pauline and Dewey had attended Flag Springs School my grandparents decided it was more appropriate for me to attend Flag Springs School.

The school consisted of two rooms, four grades in each room. The rooms were separated by a large partition that could be raised into the attic, creating one large room for special programs or activities. Training aids consisted of a chalk board (blackboard) and a series of large cards arranged end to end across one wall, showing the Alphabet in both block letters and cursive. Each room was adorned with a large picture of George Washington, a single Aladdin Lamp and a large, coal burning stove in one corner of the room. There were 5 or 6 children in each grade. My Teacher was Miss Mildred Herriage. We all called her Miss Mildred. She was very pretty and I immediately developed a deep affection for her. We had only one textbook. It was a beginning reader called The Baby Ray Book. We were drilled on the alphabet and quickly learned the alphabet and mastered the Baby Ray Book. In retrospect, I think there was a great deal of wisdom in having 4 grades in one room. When we had finished our reading assignment, we had to be quiet. I quickly learned to stay awake and listen to what was taking place in the other three classes. I think we learned more by osmosis, listening to the other classes than by formal instruction. If someone in one of the lower grades was having difficulty, Miss Mildred would assign a Mentor from one of the higher grades to assist the slow learner. We also learned to spell, starting in the first grade. Every Friday afternoon, the first four grades would move into the big room (actually the rooms were the same size, but this was the 5th, 6th, 7th and 8th grades). The big room teacher (he was also the Principal), would select two of the students from the 8th grade to choose the participants for the weekly Spelling Bee. First one then the other would choose a student. Students chosen would line up against the wall. One group on the north side the other on the south side. The procedure would continue until everyone in the school was lined up against the wall. The teacher would choose a word, the student at the head of the line would spell the word. The process would continue until all students had participated. If the student did not spell the word correctly, he or she would be seated. The younger students would be assigned easier words, but the system worked well and was an excellent teaching tool. The last person standing at the end of the day was the winner and received a gold star by their name. We all studied our spelling words during the week and listened carefully during the spelling contest every Friday. Modern teachers would look down their nose at this teaching method, however I cannot recall ever having difficulty with spelling or reading. Miss Mildred left after my second year at Flag Springs and was replaced by Miss. Robin Little. She was an excellent teacher and we all loved her almost as much as Miss. Mildred. I had a most pleasant experience 56 years later when Mrs. Mildred Burnett (Miss Mildred) walked into my office at Grayson College. I knew who she was immediately. She was in her late 70's but still attractive and mentally alert. We had a good visit and I could not resist asking her how she taught us to read and spell in the 1st and 2nd grade when we had college students enrolled at Grayson College who could barely read and could not spell Grayson County College. Her comment was, "I don't remember, but we learned, didn't we?" I commented that the education at Flag Springs had served me well all my life. Athletics played a minor role at Flag Springs. We had an outdoor basketball court (sort of) and one basketball. Across the road, in Ford's pasture was a baseball field with a chicken wire backstop. The school owned two bats and one baseball. Bathroom facilities consisted of a two-holer for the girls on the west side of the school and one for the boys on the east side of the school. Near the end of the school year, they always put on a play. This was THE EVENT for the community. The School Board would borrow rough sawed, oak bridge lumber from the Road Commissioner to build a stage. The people in the community would provide (on loan) their wagon sheets (cover for the wagon) to provide walls for the outdoor stage. Rehearsals would be conducted during daylight, however on the night of the play, people would take the batteries out of their Model T and Model A Ford cars, about a dozen batteries would be connected in series and hooked up to a number of 40 watt light bulbs to provide lights for the stage. This provided a very impressive setting for the play. Usually there would be more than 100 people show up for the play. In the darker shadows one could frequently see young couples hugging each other and young men frequently lifting a brown paper bag to their lips. I later learned the brown paper bag contained a jar filled with a liquid (called "White Lightening"). The young men would take a gulp, hold their breath for a long time, cough and wheeze and then announce, "boy is that good stuff." If it was so good I wondered why it took them so long to get their breath after taking a drink. A few years later, I learned the truth. That stuff would just about take your tonsils out and burned like fire!

FARMWORK -
RAISING COTTON AND CORN

I was introduced to the world of work at an early age. All of the children in the community worked on the farm after school and on weekends and during the summer months when school was not in session. Until about 1940 almost 50% of the population lived on farms or ranches. It was therefore expected that children would help with the various farm chores. There were animals to be fed and watered, fences to be repaired and lessons to be studied at night by the light of a kerosene lamp (not quite as bright as a 10 watt night-light). The process of growing cotton was much different from today.

In late November (weather permitting) the fields would be plowed into furrows. In some years cotton would not be harvested until late in the year because of bad weather. In this case the fields would be plowed in January or February. In April, cotton would be planted by a mule drawn planter. This device would open a small furrow on top of the previously plowed row, deposit the cottonseed and would cover the seed two inches deep. In May after the cotton plants were about two inches tall, we would go through a process known as "chopping cotton". This involved going up each row with a hoe (commonly called a gooseneck) and chopping some of the cotton plants, leaving a space the width of the hoe. It was also necessary to cut the ever present weeds and grass so the cotton plants would have room to grow. The weeds and grass needed to be hoed out every two or three weeks until the cotton plants were large enough to shade them from the sun. This would stop most of the weeds and grass. You always hoped to be through with the hoeing and plowing by the 4th of July.

In addition to hoeing, it was necessary to plow the fields as often as you could, in order to put dirt up to the plants, to cover or plow up the weeds and grass. This was accomplished with a Walking Cultivator, (commonly called a heelburner) drawn by two mules. There was a long tongue made of wood, a doubletree at the front (piece of wood about 4 feet long with hooks to connect the front harness of the mule to the plow) at the rear of the mule there was a singletree (similar to the doubletree at the front, but this device was attached to the plow and connected to the mule by trace chains connected to the harness around the neck of the mule). Before starting to plow, the first job was to catch the mule, put his bridle on by putting the bit between his teeth and then the top part over his ears, then fasten the strap under his neck to keep him from throwing the bridle off. This accomplished, put the collar around his neck (this was to cushion the mule from the hames). The hames were wood devices made to conform to the collar and contained metal parts to attach the trace chains. Once both mules were harnessed, you would then hook them to the plow by connecting the harness and chains to the plow. If everything went well, this procedure would take 15 or 20 minutes. Things seldom went well. Granddad Graves had two mules, one an old deadhead, that had fully accepted his lot in life and was gentle and easy to catch and harness. The other one "Old Red" was a different story. I am not sure I truly hated anything in my life, however if I did it was "Old Red". I remain convinced to this day, "Old Red" was the meanest, sorriest stubbornnest mule that ever lived. I would lure the mules from the pasture into the lot by giving them a few ears of corn. While they were eating, I would close the gate leading to the pasture. The lot was about 50 by 100 feet in size. You would expect that in this small area it would be no problem to harness the mules. The "deadhead" was no problem. "Old Red" was a different story. About the time you thought you had the bit in his mouth, he would pull his head back, throw his tail in the air and run around the lot going haw haw. It would frequently take 15 or 20 minutes to catch the mule! By the time I had them hooked to the plow I was pretty well worn out. Once in harness and hooked to the plow "Old Red" acted like he was half dead! He could not be persuaded to pull his share of the burden; as a result the "deadhead" mule pulled most of the plow and "Old Red". This would go on all morning until my Grandmother hung the dishtowel on the clothesline to signal me it was time for lunch. At this point, "Old Red" would come alive and drag me and the other mule to the barn. When I turned the mules loose for their noon feeding of corn, "Old Red" would run by me kicking up his heels and going haw! haw! I could have gladly killed that mule! After lunch when it was time to go back to the field, the entire procedure would be repeated. After finally getting "Old Red" hooked to the plow he would drag all afternoon, letting the other mule do most of the work. Near sunset when it was time to go to the back, "Old Red" would again drag me and the other mule along to the barn in a hurry. Once the harness was off, "Old Red" would then kick up his heels and run around going haw! haw! I was convinced he was giving me the raspberry for putting it over on me once again. I tried to talk my Grandfather into getting rid of that mule, but he thought he was a great mule.

As the cotton plants grew to maturity, when about knee high, they would start to bloom.

First white blooms, then after a few days the white blooms turned pink then red. The red bloom would wither and fall off; leaving a small cotton boll.

During the bloom stage, cotton produces marvelous nectar for bees. My Grandfather kept about 80 beehives and the bees produced a lot of honey during the bloom season. We would rob (harvest) the beehives almost every Saturday during the cotton bloom stage. Cotton honey is probably the best type of honey. It is almost the same consistency as Karo Syrup with a slight amber color. We would obtain many gallons each season. There was no market for honey so most of it would be given to the neighbors and we practically lived on it during the winter. Honey is nature's perfect food. It will not spoil and in winter it will turn white and become thick, but placed on a hot biscuit it is even better than when fresh. Chemically it is about the same as the Glucose they feed into your veins when you go into the Hospital. If one does not like the honey after it has turned to sugar, by placing it in a pan of water and heating it for about an hour, it will return to its original state.

The hot summer sun increases the growth of the cotton bolls. When they mature (about golf ball size) usually about the middle of August or early September, the bolls pop open exposing the soft white cotton. In early August, my Grandfather would go to town and purchase a large roll of heavy canvas. From this, my Grandmother would make several large sacks, about 10 feet long, open at one end, with a large strap at the open end. When enough of the bolls had opened, we would proceed to the field with our individual sacks and pick the cotton from the bolls and place the cotton in the sack. We would drag the sack along behind us as we placed the cotton into the open end. When the sack was full, we would take it to the cotton wagon to be weighed and then emptied into the wagon.

When all of the weights totaled 1800 to 2000 pounds we called that a bale. It would usually take 3 or 4 days to pick enough cotton to make a bale. At this point, the cotton contained the lint and the seed. The next step was to hitch the mules to the wagon and take the cotton to Ladonia to the Cotton Gin. The mules would be fed and hitched to the wagon before daylight so we could be home before dark. It was 7 miles from home to Ladonia and the mules moved at a rather slow pace pulling the wagon loaded with 2000 pounds of cotton.

On the dirt road to Ladonia there were several culverts that crossed small creeks. These culverts did not have banisters and at this point "Old Red" showed one of his more serious mean streaks. He was really nervous and skittish (or pretended to be). As you approached one of the culverts, it was necessary to stop and place a "blind fold" on "Old Red" otherwise as he approached the culvert, he would shy and push the deadbeat mule to the culvert on its side with disastrous results. I wanted to hit "Old Red" between tie ears with a 2X4, but Granddad insisted he was just a little shy and we had to be gentle with him. Upon reaching the Cotton Gin, the wagon would be placed under a shed that contained a large metal pipe. The cotton would be sucked up the pipe and into the Cotton Gin. the ginning process consisted of separating the lint from the seed. A 2000 pound bale would result in approximately 1500 pounds of seed and a 500 pound bale of cotton. At times the seed would be used to pay for the ginning process. At other times the seed would be loaded into the wagon and taken home to be used as feed for the milk cow or for seed for the next year's crop. The bale of cotton would be sold to a Cotton Broker for whatever price he was paying at the time, usually a few cents per pound. In the early 1930's cotton was selling for 10 cents per pound. Some songwriter (yes we also had them in those days) wrote a song called "Ten Cent Cotton and 40 Cent Meat, How in the World can a Poor Man Eat". This was a big hit and was played by all of the Radio Stations. The next year was a disaster. We had the best cotton crop ever. The fields turned white with the stuff. We made more cotton than we could pick and haul to the gin. The only trouble was cotton brought 4 cents per pound! A bale of cotton and the cotton seed barely paid the expense of the ginning. This was what was commonly called the great Depression of the 1930's.

In retrospect, I am sure what made the Depression bearable was the fact that everyone was in the same predicament. Jobs were not available and fortunately about half of the people in the country lived on small farms. While money was scarce to non-existent, most people had a cow that provided milk and butter, chickens that furnished fresh meat and eggs. A garden provided fresh vegetables in season and the surplus was canned for use in the winter. The corn crop, which required almost as much work as the cotton crop, provided fresh corn for eating and canning. At harvest time the rest of the ears were pulled from the stalk and stored in the barn to be used as feed for the animals in winter.

The finest ears of corn were shucked and shelled by hand (grains removed from the cob) and taken to a Grist Mill (there was one in most towns) to be ground into corn meal. Everyone had 2 or more hogs that were butchered in the fall, usually during the first freeze. It was necessary to do the entire operation in one day since the only way to preserve the meat was to place it into a large box and completely cover it with salt for several weeks until all of the moisture was removed. This was called "cured". When cured, the meat would be hung in a small building called a "smokehouse" Later, a commercial preparation called "Sugarcured" became available that made the meat more palatable. I never cared for salt cured pork and ate it only when there was nothing else available. One of the highlights of "hog killing time" was the pork sausage. The less desirable cuts of meat would be placed in a container and ground into sausage by means of a hand cranked grinder. The women in the community would always supervise the sausage making. They all grew sage in one corner of the yard. The leaves would be gathered and crushed and placed into the sausage meat along with red pepper, salt and black pepper. The contents would be thoroughly mixed and put through the grinder. When ground, the sausage would be stuffed into small sacks made from a worn out sheet, pillow case or flour sack. When filled, the sacks would be hung in the smokehouse. The sausage was cured by the red pepper and sage (no self-respecting bacteria would dare enter a contest with the red pepper and sage). I never heard of spoiled sausage. After a few days the sausage would become hard and could be sliced with a knife and placed into the skillet to be fried. Sausage cured in this fashion would keep indefinitely, however most people would consume all of their sausage before Christmas.

It was delicious with fresh eggs for breakfast. My school lunch usually consisted of biscuits containing a sausage left over from breakfast and a third biscuit containing honey that had gone to sugar. I was always sad to see the sausage consumed, since that meant salt pork for the remainder of the year. This of course would be supplemented quite often by fried chicken. The really fat part of the hog would be cut into small pieces and placed into a separate container. The next day, my Grandmother would have me gather wood and place it under the cast iron washpot. After the fire was going she would place the fat meat into the washpot. After several hours, the fat would turn to a liquid and be drained off and placed into large containers, usually about 20 gallons. It would cool and solidify and was called "lard". Lard was used in all fried food as well as pastry. (Talk about cholesterol - the nice part about it was no one knew there was a thing called cholesterol.

The people in the community did not waste anything that might serve a useful purpose. After the hog fat had been boiled into a liquid and turned to lard, what was left was called "cracklins" (much like what is left when fat bacon is thoroughly cooked and the fat drained off). The "cracklins" were left in the iron kettle, Lye (sodium hydroxide) was added and the cooking process renewed. The mixture was stirred with a wooden paddle for several hours and then permitted to cool. When cooled, the mixture became a solid and was called Lye Soap. The soap was used for washing dishes and laundry purposes. Most people used it to wash their hair and dandruff was unknown by those who used Lye Soap as a shampoo.

The Grocery Stores had a wooden barrel in the back room containing cooking oil called "Cotton seed Oil". This was a by-product of the process where cottonseed was crushed to make cattle feed. The people in the community who did not raise hogs had a gallon jug they would take to town and the grocer would fill the jug from the barrel of cottonseed oil. Today cottonseed oil is no longer dispensed from a barrel in the back room, but is a prime ingredient in no cholesterol margarine. In those days however, the women in the community all looked down their nose at the women who used cottonseed oil to cook with rather than hog lard. I elaborate on these items, not to necessarily describe how tough things were during the depression but to describe instead the resourcefulness of the people. There was no welfare or Social Workers to tell the people how bad off they were so they made the best of a every situation. Many people bartered or sold surplus chickens, milk and butter as well as eggs for items they could not produce themselves. Granddad frequently traded Honey for flour (a 48 pound bag of flour cost 98 cents), coffee and sugar (I am unable to recall the price of coffee, but sugar was always 20 pounds for $1.00). A good pair of shoes cost $1.98, a shirt was 49 cents and a pair of trousers was 98 cents. If I could raise 25 cents I could have a good time in town on Saturday afternoon. The Movie was 10 cents including the main features a continuing feature (always a cliffhanger so you would be back the next Saturday) and a cartoon. A pint of ice cream was 10 cents and the remaining 5 cents usually went for a Candy Bar. Milky Way, Baby Ruth and Three Musketeers were always available in 1/4 pound bars for 5 cents. If you did not care for candy you could frequently land a Hamburger for 5 cents.

My Grandmother always raised a flock of Turkeys every year. She would feed them stale cornbread for a few days after they hatched and then they were on their own with the mother turkey. They roamed the pastures, cotton fields and corn fields and survived on bugs and grasshoppers. We would round them up every year in late October and sell them to an itinerant turkey buyer. This along with the cotton crop was the cash income for the family for the year. (Would you believe I never tasted Turkey until I enlisted in the Civilian Conservation Corps in 1937). Granny always said the turkeys were not fit to eat, they were too tough according to her.

MY FATHER

Even at this late date, in my twilight years I find it extremely difficult to discuss my father. I was told that after the death of my mother, my father started hitting the bottle. This was no doubt the truth because my earliest memory of my father was seeing him in a drunken state. I loved my father deeply. At times he was capable of returning my love, however these sessions were extremely rare. When he was sober, he was the nicest man, pleasant to be around and could always find a job when others could not. When he had a few nips from the bottle, he was as mean as a "junk yard dog". At the slightest infraction of his rules, he would box my ears or use his belt on me.

In 1932, my father came into a windfall of money as back pay for an injury incurred in the Army during World War I. The total of $2,200.00 was a lot of money in 1932. He bought a farm at McCraw's Chapel, a Model A Ford and married Juanita James. Granddad was concerned about the wedding because Dad was 34 years old and Juanita was about 19. Granddad did not kick up a fuss, but I overheard him tell Granny there was too much difference in their age and his boozing, that Juanita thought was funny would soon create problems. I moved to McCraw's Chapel with Dad and Juanita and attended the 4th grade at McCraw's Chapel School. Things would have gone quite well except that Dad began to hit the bottle even more than before. During the summer after completing the 4th grade, Dad and Juanita and new baby Billie Juanita were visiting the James family in Honey Grove. I was visiting Granny and Granddad Graves. Early the next morning, a neighbor rode up on his horse with the news that the house at McCraw's Chapel had burned during the night. There was nothing to salvage. I had on a shirt and pair of trousers, no shoes (I was saving them to wear to school in the fall). This was my complete wardrobe for several weeks. The cause of the fire was undetermined, however Granddad surmised Dad had set the fire to obtain the $500.00 insurance on the house. Granddad may have been correct because he had remarkable perception.

After the fire, we moved into the home of the James (Juanita's parents) family. This was a large two story house in Honey Grove. The arrangements were less than desirable since the James family consisted of Juanita's parents, an older sister, two younger sisters and two younger brothers as well as Dad, Juanita, baby Billie Juanita and myself. The balance of the summer Dad and I helped the James family cut wood for sale. We would cut trees in Bois D'Arc bottom, haul them to the back yard in Honey Grove and cut them into proper lengths to sell to the public. In the fall, Dad purchased a 2-pump gasoline station near the Square in Honey Grove and I started to school in Honey

Grove. All of my school records were burned in the fire and when I presented myself to the Principal in Honey Grove for assignment to the 5th Grade, I was told that since I last attended a country school (much inferior) to the Honey Grove School, I would be assigned to the 4th Grade. Even at the age of 12, I recognized arbitrary action when confronted with it. I protested that I had completed the 4th Grade, but was told the decision had been made and if I wanted to attend school in Honey Grove, I would be in the 4th Grade. The entire school year was a disaster. I resented having to repeat the 4th Grade and as a result my homework was sloppy. I did not pay attention in class and was frequently required to remain after school for a minor infraction of some rule. My grades changed from A's and B's the previous year to C's and D's, mostly D's. After school and on weekends, the James boys and I would take turns working at the Gas Station. The pumps were hand operated and it was necessary to keep the large 10 gallon bowl on top of each pump filled, since putting gasoline into a car was by gravity flow. White gasoline was 10 cents per gallon and Red gasoline was 12 cents per gallon. I soon learned the quality of the gasoline was the same when I observed the delivery man put gasoline into the underground storage tanks from the same hose. He then proceeded to dump a small package of red dye into the Red gasoline tank. The work was not difficult except when a big Buick pulled in and said fill her up. This often required that the 10 gallon bowl on top of the pump had to be pumped full twice.

It soon developed that one of the James boys or myself were in charge of the Gas Station most of the time. Dad was out chasing down a "Bootlegger" to get himself a fresh bottle of booze. They were not hard to find since he had no difficulty in locating one whenever he had the money. On several occasions, he was thrown into the City Jail for public drunkenness. This would really upset the James family and I never did figure out the rationale of their thinking but their resentment appeared to be directed toward me as well as Dad. Sometime during the summer their frustration peaked. They kicked Dad and myself out of the house. Our few belongings were placed into a cardboard box. We, along with the box, were put onto the back of the truck and taken to a spot a short distance from the home of Granny and Granddad Graves and unceremoniously dumped into the middle of the road. Dad did not go to the house, but instead went to the home of an old friend Earl Perry and persuaded him to take him to Honey Grove. Somehow he persuaded the James family and Juanita to take him in. I picked up my few belongings from the road and proceeded, crying all the way to the home of my Grandparents. They welcomed me with open arms and sat quietly while I explained what had happened. A few days later Dad came in the James truck to take me back to Honey Grove with him. Granddad said, "the boy stays with me, as long as I am able to wiggle, no one is ever going to dump him into the middle of the road again." That was the way it was. In the fall I again entered Flag Springs School in the 5th grade. Things went well, my grades improved and I developed a keen interest in History and Geography. I continued to do my share of the farm work. Although I still had difficulty with "Old Red" we learned to tolerate each other. The Sociologist would say the balance of my childhood was quite normal and well adjusted.

In 1937, my Great Grandmother Tyler died. The balance of the Tyler estate was divided and my share consisted of 26 Acres of good farmland, a small house and barn. Dad was appointed Trustee, the farm was sold and Dad made off with the proceeds!

My remaining years at Flag Springs School passed quickly. I had no difficulty with my classes, except Algebra was a complete mystery to me and remains so to this day. I tried Algebra a couple of times many years later in college and always ended up dropping the course because it was still a mystery to me. The only redeeming virtue of my problems with Algebra is the fact that in almost 68 years I have never found a need for it. I seriously doubt I will do so in my remaining time on Earth.

During the summer of 1937 at the age of 14, my childhood came to an abrupt halt. President Roosevelt, in an attempt to get the country moving out of the Great Depression created, among other things, the Civilian Conservation Corps (CCC). Camps were created in about every state. Many states had numerous camps. The camps were like an Army Camp and the day to day operation of the camp was under the command of a Reserve Army Officer. The work performed during the day was under the supervision of an official of the Forest Service, Park Service or Department of Agriculture, depending upon the mission of the particular camp. The idea was to provide meaningful work for unemployed young people. The enrollee would be paid $30.00 per month. The enrollee would receive $8.00 and $22.00 would be sent home to his parents.

My good friend Mervin Cagle was going to enroll in the CCC and prevailed upon me to fudge on my age (I was large for my age) and join up with him. I thought it was a good ideal since I would do almost anything to get away from those mules. Grandmother did not like the idea, however Granddad did not protest (he confided in me later, the reason he did not object was he was sure I would not be able to pass the physical examination). Both Mervin Cagle and myself passed the physical examination and were sent to the CCC Camp at Wolfe City, Texas for processing.

At Wolf City, we were issued World War I Army uniforms, heavy wool uniforms for after work and weekend wear and Blue Denim work uniforms. Two pair of the best shoes I had ever owned, two wool blankets, underwear and socks. We stayed at Wolfe City a few days and were joined by about 20 other new recruits. We were then sent to White Rock Lake Camp near Dallas where we were assembled with about 300 other new recruits and were told we would be sent to various camps in California.

At the appointed day for departure, we were loaded into trucks along with our new baggage and taken to the Railroad Station in Dallas. The train was delayed and we spent several hours in our woolen uniforms sitting in a large open area in front of the Railroad Station in the hot July sun. The train eventually arrived and we were loaded aboard. I had never been on a train before and was assigned to all upper berth in the sleeping car. I couldn't figure out how I was supposed to sleep with two other guys on the small seats that were assigned to us. I was amazed when the Porter came in with a little crank about dark and opened the overhead area containing a bed. He put sheets on the upper berth and turned the seats over to make a double bed for the lower berth. He put sheets on the lower berth and enclosed both with a privacy curtain. My reaction was; what are they going to think of next!

The eating arrangements left something to be desired. There was nothing wrong with the food. It was served in Army Cafeteria Style with the main item meat or stew, followed by vegetables and dessert. The Dining Car was located in the center of the train. Everything worked fine for those in front of the Dining Car. We ate from our Army Mess Kits. Those of us located in rear of the Dining Car were served in reverse order going through the serving line. Bread first, then dessert followed by vegetables and then meat or stew. The dessert being on the bottom was somewhat soggy with an unusual taste by the time you got down to it. Some of the new recruits became sick from the motion of the train. I managed to retain my food and was fascinated by the scenery since I had only seen mountains in the movies.

The train trip was uneventful until we crossed the Colorado River and crossed from Arizona into California. We stopped at Needles, California to unload some of the new recruits for assignment to camps in the area. Mervin Cagle and I both agreed this must surely be the Hell the Preachers used to warn us about at Church. Here we were, off the train, in wool uniforms at Needless California in the middle of July! The temperature was 110 degrees in the shade and the hot wind was like it was coming out of a blast furnace. We decided if this is what California was like we were in big trouble.

We spent the next two days on the train, finally stopping at Redding, California. Redding is located at the northern end of the Sacramento Valley. After getting out of the train, our group was assigned to various camps in Northern California. Mervin Cagle and myself were sent to a camp high up in the Cascade Mountains called Halls Flat. This is about midway between Westwood and Bieber, 60 miles from the nearest town. The trip to Halls Flat by truck was quite an experience. After leaving the city of Redding we started to encounter large pine trees. I learned the trees were called Ponderosa Pine. They were beautiful trees at least 100 feet tall and 2 to 3 feet in diameter. The trucks had to labor as we climbed higher and higher into the mountains. We finally turned off of the paved road onto a gravel road. After some time on the gravel road, we entered upon a more or less flat plain surrounded by mountains and the entire area was covered by the same beautiful Ponderosa Pine trees. I was fascinated. We had nothing like this in Fannin County Texas. The camp was located at an altitude of more than

7,000 feet. The air was clear and I could breathe clear down to my toes. The mountains appeared to be about a mile away. I was told the closest one was more than 10 miles! At night the stars were so bright it looked as if you could reach up and touch one. Camp routine was well organized. We were assigned to a barracks and put in charge of a Leader who wore three stripes on his sleeve (like a Sergeant, but he was called a Leader). The Camp was commanded by an old World War I Army Captain who was assisted by a much younger First Lieutenant. There was also a six striper called a First Sergeant. He pretty well ran the camp, getting his orders from the Captain and Lieutenant.

For our work routine, we were assigned to the Forest Service. It turned out the senior Forest Service Official was a World War I Fighter Pilot. He flew Spads in France and was an interesting individual. Our first job was to build roads into the mountains in order to harvest the mature Ponderosa Pine trees. A Bulldozer was used to rough out the road. My assignment was to roll granite rocks down a long wood chute to a Rock Crusher. Here the large rocks would be crushed into gravel to put on the roads. The Forestry people had a theory that trees were like any other crop and should be harvested on a selective basis. The Forest Rangers would mark the mature trees that were ready for harvest and we would cut the trees trying to avoid damage to nearby trees. Once the tree was cut, one team would remove the limbs, another team would saw the tree into 3, 30 foot sections. The logs would be skidded to the road with a bulldozer and then loaded onto a truck to be hauled about 10 miles to a railroad siding. At this point the logs would be loaded onto a Narrow Gauge Railway Flatcar and hauled to the sawmill in Westwood. I worked on several of the teams and was then assigned to a group to build a house for the Forest Rangers. My job was to push a wheelbarrow from the Cement Mixer up a wooden ramp and then dump it into concrete forms to provide a foundation for the house (talk about work). After dumping the cement into the forms, we would take a stick and punch the wet cement to fill all of the cracks and crevices and remove any air bubbles. (Today when I see someone drop a vibrator into wet cement and watch the cement flow like water, I think boy, would that have come in handy when we were building the Ranger Home in 1937. The problem was the cement vibrator had not been invented in 1937. As I recall there were no disciplinary problems. If two guys couldn't get along, the First Sergeant would march them to the supply room, outfit each of them with a pair of boxing gloves, march them to the boxing ring (every camp had a boxing ring) and tell them to go at each other and to keep at it until they could shake hands and be friends. Of course they would be cheered on by the rest of the enrollees. This system was the most effective method I have ever observed for controlling dissension between two individuals.

My duty assignment was changed and I was given the job of assisting the mechanic that serviced the heavy equipment. After we had finished servicing the equipment, the mechanic would teach me how to operate the equipment. I was extremely interested in the D-8 Caterpillar Bulldozers and the logging trucks. Our job was to change the oil, filters, and grease the equipment as well as clean and add fresh oil to the oil bath air cleaners. After leaving Halls Flat, I never set foot on a bulldozer until some 15 years later while serving as a Lieutenant in the Marine Corps.

One day the Colonel was upset because there was no bulldozer operator available and he wanted an area leveled for a parking area. I told him I would do it for him, he said "you are a personnel officer, what makes you think you can operate a bulldozer?" I said "nothing to it". We went down to the area to be leveled, fired up the bulldozer and leveled the area while the Colonel stood around with his mouth open. When the job was finished, he wanted to know where I learned to operate a bulldozer, I told him in the CCC. He had heard of the CCC but had no idea what they did.

My friend Mervin Cagle fell into what he thought was a nice cushy job. He was assigned duties as a Radio Operator. When the trucks took the men out to work in the mountains, they would drop Mervin off on one of the mountains. He would pack the radio part way up the mountain to an observation point and be on the lookout for smoke. If he observed smoke, he would report to the Ranger Station the direction and his best guess as to the distance. One day, his nice cushy job changed! For some reason, he was not at the pickup point for the return to camp (I suspect he went to sleep). The truck driver thought he had been picked up by another truck and proceeded to camp. No one noticed that Mervin was missing. His Radio would not work at the pickup point because of the mountains. He proceeded to pack the radio back up the mountain and try to raise the Ranger Station. By the time he had moved the radio back up the mountain and set up to operate, it was dark and the Ranger Station was not manned after dark. At an altitude of more than 7,500 feet in the Cascade Mountains, as soon as the sun sets, it starts to get cool. As the night wears on, it becomes downright cold!

Mervin was about to freeze and the coyotes yipping did not help him one bit. Suddenly he realized the noises he was hearing were bear and mountain lions. Mervin became panicky at this point and started an emergency C. Q. on his radio. Around 2:00 a.m., some Ham Radio Operator at Grass Valley, California (about 300 miles south) heard his emergency call. He telephoned the Camp at Halls Flat and a truck was dispatched to bring Mervin back to camp. They arrived at daylight. A very distressed Mervin turned in his radio and announced he would do permanent K.P. or anything else they wanted him to do, but he was not ever going into those mountains alone.

In early October, everyone was assigned the job of cutting Quaking Aspen trees and hauling them to camp. The trees were placed in each building to brace the roof supports, since it was reported that snow would be

6 to 10 feet deep in the winter and it would cause the buildings to collapse unless they were properly supported to handle the weight of the snow.

Our weekends at Halls Flat were our own time. Recreation trucks would frequently go to Bieber or Susanville. We also had recreation trips to Lassen National Park. This was a very interesting place. The remains of a Volcano that erupted in 1914 were still in evidence. Enrollees from another CCC Camp had built a narrow trail up to the summit of Mt. Lessen. Several of us decided to climb Mt. Lessen (10,400 feet). The trip up and back consumed most of the day. We had to rest as we approached the summit due to a lack of oxygen. The view from the summit was something to behold. You could see for at least 100 miles. The trip down the mountain was as difficult as the climb because the gravel would slide under your feet and was very dangerous.

One of the many things about Northern California that impressed me was the clear streams teeming with Rainbow Trout. I did not know there were any fish except Perch and Catfish. Some of the streams would only be 2 to 3 feet wide and about a foot deep, but many of them would have some guy casting and catching Trout.

In late October, the camp at Halls Flat was closed. I was sent to a camp at Whitmore, California, 30 miles east of Redding. My job at Whitmore was to work with a crew stringing telephone wire back into the mountains to the Fire Lookout Stations. The work was easy. The survey crew would mark the route with stakes. We would dig holes and put up the poles, add an insulator and then string the wire on the poles. I never knew why, but the poles were square. We used climbing spurs and a safety belt looped around the pole. The climbing spurs would hold us in place while we worked. The dangerous part was not setting the spur properly and "burning" down the pole.

I enjoyed the stay at Whitmore and was sad to hear the news that the camp would be closed in December and we would be moved to a camp in Colorado. (In 1950, while stationed in San Francisco we decided to rent a trailer and visit Northern California. We went to Whitmore, and much to my surprise, the Camp looked about like it was in 1937. The big difference was a Chain Link Fence around the entire camp since it was now part of the California Youth Authority, a detention center for young criminals).

In early December the camp at Whitmore was closed and we were sent to Colorado. My introduction to Colorado was a stop at Grand Junction. There was an outdoor thermometer and the temperature was 10 degrees below zero. This was quite a contrast to the balmy weather in California. Little did I realize there was more to come.

The towns along our route were decorated for Christmas. We stopped for fuel and water at Glenwood Springs, Colorado. The town was covered by a blanket of snow, just before dark, all of the Christmas lights came on. My thoughts were this was the prettiest town I had ever seen. It was like something out of another world. We did not have anything like that in Fannin County, Texas.

At Walsenberg, Colorado the train was side tracked. It was announced the several cars in the rear of the train would remain in Walsenberg for assignment to a camp in the area. Mervin Cagle was in this group. The rest of us would go on to another camp at Fork, Colorado. The train continued on to Alamosa Colorado, the end of the rail line. My thought at the time was that they must be planning to send us back into the mountains if there was no Railroad into the area. How true! At Alamosa we were met at the Railroad Station by a group of long wheelbase automobiles. They looked like small busses. The trip to South Fork took several hours. We passed through Monte Vista and Del Norte and finally the village of South Fork. We continued on beyond South Fork to the Camp that was located near the Wolfe Creek Pass at an elevation of about 8,000 feet, There was snow about a foot deep at the camp and much deeper on all of the mountains. All the trees were covered by a heavy blanket of snow and were very pretty. It looked just like a picture post card. The temperature was 22 degrees below zero. Pretty or not, I decided I was not very happy at the thought of working in snow at 22 degrees below zero!

The Camp at South Fork was like the other camps from a construction standpoint. They were made of 2x4's, one wall thick and covered by rolled roofing (a little thicker than tar paper), and no insulation. There was a "Pot Bellied" coal burning stove in each end of the barracks. The barracks were arranged in an East West location with windows on the North and South side. At 10:00 p.m. each night the Camp Doctor would walk through each barracks and make sure all south windows were open! He claimed we needed the fresh air for health reasons. The Latrine (toilet and showers) were located about 200 feet in rear of the barracks. This was no problem in the warm weather in California, drape a towel over you and have a leisurely stroll to the shower. Not so at South Fork in the 22 below zero temperature. One soon learned to move rapidly!

The mountains around South Fork were covered in Ponderosa Pine and Fir trees. We were told our work assignment was to inspect the Ponderosa trees to see if they were infested by "Black Hills" Beetles. The beetles would bore through the bark of the tree and eat the Cambium layer right under the bark (this is the life sustaining part of the tree). The following Spring, the tree would die and the beetles would move out of the dead tree and the colony would infest 10 more trees. The Forest Rangers taught us how to recognize an infested tree. When we discovered an infested tree, we were to cut it down, burn it and peel the bark from the stump in order to expose any remaining beetles to the frigid temperature.

We were issued woolen mittens and additional wool socks. For our work assignments we were told to wear woolen long handle underwear (these were issued when we enlisted but had never been worn), woolen trousers and shirt, then cotton khaki trousers and shirt, then cotton (dungaree) shirt and trousers. This was then topped off with a wool jacket and wool cap. (During the Korean War the military thought they had invented the layer principle of clothing to keep the troops warm). We were using the layer principle in the Civilian Conservation Corps at South Fork in 1937.

We were loaded into trucks and taken back into the Mountains for our work assignment. About ten o'clock the sun would come up over the mountain and it would get warm. We would start taking off coats and would be hot until about 2:00 p.m., when the sun dropped behind the mountain. This would be about like walking into a large refrigerator. The temperature would drop back to 20 below zero in a few minutes. Except for the cold temperature, the weather was beautiful. At 8,000 feet, the sky was a deep blue and at night it was so clear the stars sparkled and seemed so near it was difficult to believe they were millions of miles away.

After about a week, we got up one morning and there was a small cloud in the northwest. One of the guys who had been at South Fork for about a year, said "oh oh, we are going to have snow". I thought we already had snow since it was still about half knee deep. At around 8:30 a.m., the sky became overcast, the wind ceased and it became very still and started to snow. I thought I had seen snow in Texas but this was different. The snowflakes were about the size of your index finger and drifted down ever so slowly, just like in the movies. By noon, we were wading in snow waist deep. I thought the trucks would not be able to pick us up, but the snow plows kept the snow off of the roads and the trucks were equipped with snow chains.

We continued to comb the mountains looking for Black Hills Beetles in the Ponderosa Pine Trees. We would form a line with about twenty feet between each man. We had to maintain visual contact with the man on each side of us. At times, someone would disappear, having dropped off into a snow drift. We would yell to halt the line and stop long enough to retrieve the man from the snowdrift. The heat from our body would cause the snow to melt on our outer clothing, then ice would form. When we returned to the barracks at the end of the day, our clothing contained so much ice the trousers would stand alone when you leaned them against the barracks wall. Our feet were always cold. Some of us suffered from frostbite. To this day, I have difficulty understanding why people will pay good money to go to a Ski Resort to wallow around in the snow.

By the middle of January 1938 my enlistment expired and I decided I had wallowed around in enough snow to do me a lifetime and I would not reenlist.

RETURN TO TEXAS

I was taken by truck to Alamosa to catch the train for Texas. When we stopped in Walsenburg, I was happy to see my friend Mervin Cagle come aboard the train. He had also had enough snow to do him for the rest of his life. We traveled by train to Dallas, then by bus to Sherman and on to Honey Grove. Granddad met me at the Bus Station in Honey Grove then back home to the farm. Even the mules seemed happy to see me.

The farm routine had not changed since I left home. Pretty soon it was time to plow the land and get ready for Spring planting. The mules were as difficult as ever, however I had something to look forward to on Saturday night. I had discovered girls! Mervin Cable lived nearby and he had purchased a Model A Ford. There were many local girls and some in Honey Grove we dated on Saturday night. We had little money, however gasoline was 10 cents per gallon and the movie was also 10 cents. Soft drinks were 5 cents. If you could put together 50 cents, you could look like a big spender on Saturday night!

My good friend Lloyd Vessels lived on the adjoining farm. If Mervin Cable was otherwise occupied Lloyd was usually able to borrow his Father's car on Saturday night. During the Summer, the "Holy Rollers" (now called Church of God, Nazarene, Pentecostal or Assembly of God), would build a "Brush Arbor" on the sheet limestone at Brawley Pool Creek and conduct their services. Instead of going to the movie, we would go down and watch them hold services. This was a lot more fun than going to the movies. Their services were not like those held today. These were great emotional affairs. The congregation would become emotionally involved and at the height of the emotional outlets someone would get the "Holy Ghost". They would jump up and yell "I've got it". In extreme cases, the person would act like they were having an Epileptic Seizure. They would roll on the ground and froth at the mouth all the while the congregation would be praying for them and urging them on to greater heights of glory. For those of us who were used to a more sedate Religious Service, this was entertainment at its best.

Spring planting was soon completed and in short order it was time to "chop cotton" and plow the cotton and corn. When the crop was "Laid By" in July (no further hoeing or plowing required), I discovered that since I had been out of the CCC for 6 months, I could reenroll. I was not thrilled about looking forward to picking cotton starting in August, so in late July 1938, I again enlisted in the Civilian Conservation Corp.

WOLFE CITY

Much to my surprise, upon again taking the oath of enlistment in the CCC at Wolfe City, Texas, I was told that I would remain at the Camp in Wolfe City. This was only 20 miles from home and I would be able to go home almost every weekend. The camp at Wolfe City was assigned the mission of Soil Conservation. The other camps I had served in were all under the Forest Service.

The mission of the Soil Conservation Service was to try to salvage and reclaim the depleted farms in Hunt, Fannin and Delta Counties. The camp, like the others, was commanded by an Army Officer for the day to day operation. The work assignment was under the direction of relatively young College Graduates from Texas A. & M. College. One team would contact farmers in the area served by the camp and try to persuade the farmer to join the program. If the farmer agreed, his only expense was for the cost of wire and post to fence any area that should be returned to pasture, plus $100.00 per mile for the construction of any terraces that might be required to stop the soil erosion. All other work would be accomplished by the CCC enrollees.

My work assignment was to the Survey Crew. Once the farmer agreed to an enlistment in a 5 year program to improve his farm, the Survey Crew would be sent out to survey the farm, prepare a soil map and a topographic map. This information would then be sent to A&M and a plan would be drawn up for the individual farm. The areas of severe erosion would usually be fenced, the gullies sloped and then sodded with Bermuda Grass Sod. Areas of moderate erosion would be terraced, using the newly designed 30 foot wide terrace. Most farmers hated terraces since they were usually about 5 feet wide and could not be farmed. They were a good source for the spread of Johnson Grass. The new 30 ft. terraces on the other hand could be farmed and required very little maintenance.

My initial job was to carry stakes and to drive one into the ground when told to do so. When the weather was too bad to work or too muddy to get into the field, the young Engineer in charge of the Survey Crew would conduct formal classes for the members of the Survey Crew. The turnover in the Survey Crew was almost constant. If a person could find a job, he could request an immediate discharge. Also the maximum time a person could remain in the CCC was two years. As a result of the turnover, I soon found myself assigned to a more responsible position. First running the chain and the Surveying Rod and by the end of 1938 I was running the Surveying Instruments, known as a Surveyors Level and another instrument called a Telescopic Alidade used in making Maps. The work was very interesting and time passed quickly. In the Spring of 1939 I was placed in charge of the

Survey Crew. I feel this was a direct result of the training provided by the young Engineer who took the time to provide the training needed to accomplish the job.

The time spent at Wolfe City was a period of great fun. I enjoyed the work and even though we were not supposed to own an automobile, I purchased a Model A Ford and later a 1934 Ford V8. I kept the car at the home of my Uncle Dewey. He could use the car during the week, but he was to pick me up every Friday about 6:00 p.m. This arrangement worked out just fine. I had the car all weekend and he would return me to camp Sunday night. This was also a great time for dating. I had several steady girlfriends and enough money to entertain them.

In the late Summer of 1939 my good friend John Wade and I both discovered we would have served our two years in the CCC in January and we had better start looking for something else to do. War had broken out in Europe and in September 1939, Hitler invaded Poland. John Wade and I decided that since there were no jobs to be had we would join the U.S. Marine Corps and get some training, since the United States would probably be in a war before long. I am not sure why we chose to join the Marines. We did not know anything about the Marine Corps, except we had heard they were tough and that was good enough for us.

John Wade and I found the Marine Corps Recruiting Office in Dallas. The Sergeant in the office was not very friendly. He wanted to know why we were in his office. We told him we wanted to be Marines. He said "What makes you think you can get into the Marines in the first place?" We assured him we were eager to serve. (We didn't mention we would have to leave the CCC in January and the prospect of going hungry did not appeal to us). We completed the necessary applications and were told we would be notified by mail if we were considered to be suitable material for the U. S. Marine Corps.

THE U.S. MARINE CORPS

Around the middle of November, 1939 both John Wade and I received a letter from the Marine Corps saying that our applications had been carefully considered and we were after all considered to be suitable material for enlistment in the U. S. Marine Corps. We were told to report to the Recruiting office in Dallas on November 24, 1939 to be sworn in and we should be prepared to leave for Recruit Training at San Diego, California immediately after taking the oath of enlistment.

We presented our letter of acceptance to the Commanding Officer of the CCC Camp at Wolfe City and were assured we would be discharged effective November 24, 1939.

The Lamar Creamery in Paris, Texas ran a Milk Truck to Dallas every day. They dropped off the daily milk supply at the Camp at 4:40 a.m. daily. The driver of the truck was not allowed to carry passengers, however John Wade and I conned him into giving us a ride to Dallas. He was afraid he would be fired if he were caught with passengers in his truck, so he dropped us off near Fair Park. At that time, Fair Park was on the East edge of Dallas. We walked the rest of the way to the Recruiting Station. We were treated much better by the Recruiting Sergeant and were sworn into the Marine Corps by an ancient major, an obvious World War I Veteran since he had a chest full of Campaign Ribbons. We were told that other Recruits would arrive from San Antonio the next day and we would be put up in a Hotel overnight and all of us would leave for San Diego together.

We spent the night of the 24th in a small hotel in Dallas. Across the street, workmen were busy digging a huge hole in the ground. We had no idea what was going on, but the hole was at least 30 feet deep and they were still digging. After World War II, I found out the hole in the ground was the basement for the Mercantile National Bank.

We departed by Train for San Diego on the morning of November 25. In addition to John Wade and me, there were two Sanford brothers from San Antonio. We arrived at the Marine Corps Base in San Diego two days later, about 2:00 a.m. It seemed like we had just gotten into bed when we were awakened at 5:00 am by a Corporal with a loud whistle. He reminded us we were Marine Recruits the lowest form of humanity, and we would be seeing a lot of him until there were enough of us to form a Platoon so we could start our training.

Our salary would be $21.00 per month but we would not see much of it for some time, since we were to be issued a bucket containing toilet articles, razor, shoe polish and a bundle of little strings called tie-ties that were to be used to tie our laundry to the clothes line. These items were to be charged against our salary and we would receive $5.00 per month until payment had been made in full. We performed routine housekeeping duties until there were enough recruits to form a Platoon. John Wade and I had no difficulty adjusting to the routine since it was essentially the same as the CCC routine. Some of the less cooperative recruits found themselves scrubbing the commodes and floor (henceforth to be called a deck) with a toothbrush and running extra laps around the Parade Ground.

In a few days, there were enough Recruits to form a Platoon. We learned there were only 18,000 men in the entire Marine Corps (less than the New York City Police Deportment) and the Marine Corps had been authorized to expand to 20,000 men. This was the first expansion of the Marine Corps since World War I.

The Marine Corps was caught short of uniforms, and as I was to learn many times during the next 21 years, the Marine Corps always makes do with what is available. Our first uniform was the cheapest shirt and blue bib overalls I have ever seen. Once outfitted in our bib overalls, the Drill Instructor lined us up for our first attempt at close order drill. He was the picture postcard of what a Marine should look like. I thought he was going to cry when he first looked at us. He said "You people are the sorriest looking bunch of Recruits I have ever laid eyes on. You are a disgrace to the uniform you are wearing". I thought to myself how could anyone disgrace an ill-fitting blue shirt and cheap bib overalls. No one ever accused me of being too bright, but I was smart enough to keep my thoughts to myself.

There were three Drill instructors assigned to each Platoon. An old time Sergeant and two young Corporals. Each drill Instructor carried a stick 40 inches long. We thought the stick was to whack us with, but were informed it was used to measure the distance between ranks. That may have been the official reason for the stick but many of the uncooperative Recruits felt the stick on their rear end plenty of times. After a full day on the Parade Ground trying to perform close order drill, about 9:00 p.m. we learned what the bucket was for. The last chore of the day was to wash the clothes we had worn during the day in the bucket and then tie them on the clothes line with the little strings. After a few days this became routine and presented no problem. We also had to shine our shoes in order to look sharp the next morning.

After a few days, we were issued regular Marine Corps uniforms. We were learning how to march and were beginning to look like Marines. We were soon issued World War I Springfield Rifles. After many hours of cleaning, we then marched with Rifles and learned to perform the usual drills using the Rifles. (We retained the Rifles as personal gear until they were replaced by the M-1 Rifle in the Summer of 1942). The 1903 Springfield Rifle was more accurate than the M-1, but could not be fired as rapidly as the Semi-automatic M-1. Some of the better Springfields were equipped with a

Telescopic Sight and used throughout World War II and Korea by the Scout Sniper Teams.

After a few weeks at San Diego, we were sent to the Rifle Range at Camp Matthews (this area is now occupied by the University of California at San Diego). We not only fired the rifle, but the pistol, Browning Automatic Rifle and Machine Gun. On the last day of firing for record, the bolt holding the Rifle to the Stock broke on my Rifle. Since they were unable to repair the Rifle, they issued me another Rifle and moved me to another Platoon that was a week behind us schedule wise. I performed quite well on all of the weapons, especially the Machine Gun. Some of the guys gave me the nickname "Gunner". That stuck with me for many years. In fact 50 years later at our reunion in San Diego some of them still called me "Gunner".

Upon completion of the weapons training at Camp Matthews, we returned to San Diego for final training. Upon graduation, we were to be assigned to the 6th Marine Regiment, Fleet Marine Force or to Sea Duty upon completion of additional training at Sea School at the San Diego Base. My view of Boot Camp was that it was a "Piece of Cake". I was only two months beyond my 17th birthday and had spent almost two years in the CCC. Some of the people had a tough time. I recall seeing one 26 year old Recruit cry like a baby. He had never been away from home and thought the Drill instructors were abusing him. I thought they were getting us in shape for things to come in the future. In fact as it turned out that is exactly what they were doing. I want to make one final comment about the CCC. During the past 50 years, I have run across many men that served in the CCC. I have never heard one "bad mouth" the organization. They all say it was the best thing that ever happened to them. They performed many useful things for the country. Most of the various State Parks and many of the National Park facilities were built by the CCC. If you travel over Fannin, Hunt and Delta Counties today you can see the result of the conservation practices introduced by the CCC. The more well preserved less eroded farms were participants in the conservation program. In addition, the CCC provided a pool of semi- trained personnel for World War II that was fast approaching.

One funny incident happened to me on our Graduation Day. Two very senior Sergeants came to our Platoon and asked for volunteers to go to Field Music School. I did not have the foggiest notion what Field Music School was, but was eager to volunteer for anything and raised my hand. My Drill Instructor was standing behind me. He yanked my hand down and said "Graves, get your damned hand down, you don't want to be a damned Field Music". I later learned a Field Music was a "Bugler" and was considered the lowest form of humanity.

It seems the Drill Instructor was looking out for me. I ran into him many years later when I was a Captain, and he was a Lt. Colonel. I reminded him of the incident and we both had a good laugh.

The Marine Corps had a unique classification system in 1939. We were always in formation according to height. On graduation day, everyone over 5'11" was assigned to Sea School for further training and assignment to the Fleet. The smaller guys were assigned to the 6th Marine Regiment to carry the Mortars and Machine Guns.

Those of us assigned to Sea School were issued Dress Blue Uniforms and given extensive training on the large Naval Guns we would be assigned to man aboard ship. We spent many hours at close order drill on the Parade Ground and turned out to be a sharp looking outfit. We had come a long way from the stragglers in our initial uniform of blue denim overalls. We spent many hours learning what Marines were supposed to do on Battleships and Cruisers. I cannot recall receiving any training concerning an Aircraft Carrier. There were only 5 Aircraft Carriers in the entire U. S. Navy at the time and I suppose they felt the likelihood of any of us being assigned to an aircraft carrier was rather remote.

THE U.S.S. ENTERPRISE (CV-6)

In early February, 1940 we had finished our Sea School Training and were available for assignment to Sea Duty. We were told we were being assigned to the U.S.S. ENTERPRISE, however no one seemed to know what kind of ship it was. We were transported to the Dock at the nearby Naval Training Station for transportation to North Island, where the ENTERPRISE was tied up. There were 20 of us, and with our Sea Bags, Rifles and miscellaneous equipment we just about filled the small boat assigned to transport us to North Island. Upon arrival at North Island, we were greeted on the Dock by First Sergeant Benjamin Franklin Hearn. He had us fall in and stand at attention for inspection. He stated we were the "crummiest" looking bunch of Recruits he had ever had the misfortune to encounter. We decided he was putting on an act because we were a pretty sharp looking group. First Sergeant Hearn looked pretty sloppy to us. He had a big belly that spilled over his belt like he had been drinking too much beer. We soon met Gunnery Sergeant Fred Smith who was to be our mentor and butt kicker during our tour aboard the ENTERPRISE. Fred Smith looked like he should be the one to pose for the Recruiting Poster. He was about 6'2" tall, very muscular and not an ounce of fat on him. His face was wrinkled and looked more like leather than skin. He looked a lot like the old Movie Actor, Victor McLaughlin, except he was lean and muscular. We later learned that in spite of his obvious toughness he had a heart as big as he was.

Alter what seemed to be hours of waiting, we were allowed to go aboard the ENTERPRISE for our assignment to what was to be our living quarters for a long time. As we stepped into the Hangar Deck, a farm boy from South Dakota observed "boy you could put a lot of hay in here". The ENTERPRISE carried 4 squadrons of 18 planes for a total of 72 Airplanes. All of them could be stored in the Hangar Deck or on the Flight Deck. There were three large Elevators to move the Airplanes from the Flight Deck to the Hangar Deck and back again. The Marine Compartment was located on the first deck below the Hangar Deck. We were assigned a bunk which were stacked 4 deep with about two feet between each bunk. We were also assigned a Locker about the size of a 19" TV Set. Our Blue Uniforms and Overcoat would be stored in a separate community locker. All other items, underwear, socks and personal articles, had to be stored in our locker.

We soon learned to take advantage of every inch of space since any item not stored away would end up in the "Lucky Bag" and you would have to perform extra work to get them back and were assigned various guard duties: Gangway Sentry, Brig Guard, Captain and Admirals Orderly (messenger).

At one time I served as Orderly for Admiral William F. Halsey whose Flagship was the ENTERPRISE. Our Battle Station assignments were four 5" guns located on the after part of the ship. There were also four 5" guns located on the forward part of the ship that were manned by Navy Personnel. The Commander of the Marine Detachment was Captain Presley M. Rixey. The Platoon Commanders were First Lieutenant Frank Shine and Second Lieutenant Jessie P. Ferrill. Captain Rixey was stern but fair. He insisted we perform all duties to the best of our ability. Any spare time was spent training on the 5" antiaircraft Guns under the strict supervision of Gunnery Sergeant Fred Smith. The extra training was most effective and in later Gunnery Practice, the Marines consistently outperformed the Navy Personnel assigned to the forward 5" Guns.

After a few days in Port in San Diego, the ENTERPRISE put to sea for Flight Operations. The Air Group that had been stationed at the Naval Air Station North Island while the ENTERPRISE was in Port, came aboard shortly after we were at sea. I was fascinated by the Air Operations. The Air Group passed over the ship and the Fighter Squadron peeled off and dropped down into the landing pattern while the ENTERPRISE swung around into the wind. I found out they always wanted to have 25 knots of wind across the Bow for Air Operations. If the wind was light, the ship would speed up to provide the 25 knots of wind. The Fighters landed in short order and after catching the arresting wire with the tail hook, they would taxi forward to make room for the next plane. The Fighters were followed by the Scouting Squadron, next the Dive Bombing Squadron and last, the Torpedo Squadron.

The Fighters were built by Grumman Aircraft Corporation and were called F3F's. They looked almost like a Bumble Bee with a Large Engine, fat Fuselage and two canvas covered wings. The tail was also canvas covered. They were highly maneuverable and seemed to almost leap into the air.

The Scouting Planes were also metal fuselage, two place, pilot in front and the radio man/gunner in the rear seat. They had two wings, fabric covered and a fabric covered tail. They were an ungainly looking lot and could just barely fly. They were seriously underpowered and on takeoff they didn't fly off the end of the deck, but appeared to roll off of the end of the flight deck and become airborne between the flight deck and the water. The Planes were built by the Curtiss Wright Corporation and were designated SBC'S.

The Dive Bombers were fine looking aircraft, but they also suffered from being underpowered. They were of all metal construction with a single, all metal wing. The landing gear did not fully retract and when airborne did not present a clean appearance. They were built by the Northrop Corporation and were designated BT-1. They did have enough power to fly off the flight deck.

The Torpedo Bombers were larger than the other planes and were the Navy's first all metal, single wing Airplane. They entered Squadron Service in 1934 and by 1940 they were getting a little tired, as were all of the Navy Planes at that time. The Torpedo Planes were built by the Douglas Aircraft Corporation and were designated TBD'S. They had a three man crew, Pilot, Bombardier and Radio Man/gunner all sitting one behind the other. When used as a Torpedo Plane, the Bombardier stayed on the Carrier. He only went along on Bombing Missions. The TBD could carry a single torpedo. About half of the torpedo was internal in the bomb bay and about half of it sticking out under the plane, a really funny looking arrangement. The top speed when carrying a torpedo was 90 knots. When used as a high level bomber, the TBD could carry a 1,000 pound bomb in the bomb bay and a 100 pound bomb under each wing. Still a slow inefficient aircraft.

The ENTERPRISE was designed to permit planes to fly off of the 808 foot long flight deck and to also launch planes by Catapult from the hangar Deck. This was a "Rube Goldberg" arrangement if I ever saw one. I was an uneducated farm boy and did not think the Hangar Deck Catapult would work. Logic would dictate that if you needed 25 knots of wind across the Bow to fly planes off of the Flight Deck, you also needed 25 knots of wind on the Starboard Beam to Catapult Planes from the Hangar Deck at the same time they were being flown off of the Flight Deck. When the time came to test the Hangar Deck Catapult, I found a good position to watch the show. (The ENTERPRISE was commissioned in 1938 and they had never tried the Hangar Deck Catapult before).

The Hangar Deck Catapult was operated by a large Hydraulic Pump. There was a metal ring attached to the thing that was to fling the airplane into the air. The Hydraulic Pressure would be increased as the pilot increased the power to maximum output. Soon the metal ring on the Catapult broke from the pressure from the pump and the power of the aircraft. Swoosh, the plane was sent hurtling straight into the water. In those days, all airplanes operating from all Aircraft Carriers were equipped with a flotation device that popped out of the wings when a plane hit the water. The plane remained afloat and the half dead pilot struggled out of the cockpit looking like a drowned rat as he was hoisted aboard the ship. The ship's crane was extended, a sailor attached the hook to the airplane and it was hoisted onto the deck. The force of the propeller hitting the water pulled the engine from its mounts and it was hanging limp by the broken engine mounts.

The Navy did not learn very rapidly. They tried the Hangar Deck Catapult two more times with identical results. The only different part was they did not hoist the wrecked airplane aboard ship. After retrieving the half drowned pilot, they dropped a sailor over the side with a knife to puncture the flotation device and let the wrecked airplane sink. Thank God they only had a pilot aboard the SBC's. If they had included the Radioman/ Gunner, someone might have been lost. It struck me as being a near miracle they did not lose a pilot. I never did find out whether they decided they had lost enough airplanes or if the pilots refused to participate in the debacle! In any event, when we went to the Navy Yard at Bremerton, Washington for overhaul soon after this experiment, the Navy Yard Workers came aboard with cutting torches and removed the Hydraulic Catapult and all of the associated parts.

We continued Air Operations for several more days, then the Air Group returned to North Island. We tied up to the Dock and the word was passed we would be going to the Navy Yard in Bremerton, Washington for extensive overhaul. The ship was now two years old and the bottom needed to be scraped and painted as well as other repairs. It was also announced that any Officer or Member of the crew who wanted to transport his Automobile to Bremerton could do so. We spent the next few days hoisting Automobiles aboard the ship. When finished, there must have been at least 300 cars on the Flight Deck and Hangar Deck. Upon arrival in Bremerton, the automobiles were unloaded and preparations were made to move the ship into Dry Dock.

A Dry Dock is similar to a huge swimming pool with a waterproof gate at one end. The ship is gently moved into the Dry Dock, the waterproof gate is moved into position and then the water is pumped out of the Dry Dock, permitting the ship to settle onto large wooden blocks called Keel Blocks. The crew was warned to put on work clothes and prepare to go over the side to scrape and paint the ship. The Navy Personnel rigged large boards suspended by ropes all around the ship. Each person was assigned an area about four feet wide to scrape all the way down the side and under the ship all the way to the keel. As the water was pumped out, the scraping was begun. This lasted two or three days. Painting took another three days and was much more dangerous than the scraping. When scraping, if you should fall you would land in the water. Since all of the water had been pumped out the only thing to land on if you should fall would be the concrete at the bottom of the Dry Dock. We painted with one hand and held onto the rope holding the stage with the other.

After the ship had been scraped and painted, the Dry Dock was flooded, the gate removed and the ship was moved to another area in the Navy Yard where the civilian Navy Yard Workers repaired other parts of the ship and made a number of modifications to improve the operation of the ship. We were permitted to go on Liberty when not on duty. Most of the Marines caught the ferry which ran from Bremerton to Seattle about every two hours. It was about 17 miles from Bremerton to Seattle by Ferry. Seattle was known as a good liberty town since there were many friendly young (and not so young) girls available. We remained in Bremerton about three months. The only thing I did not like about the place was that it was always raining.

The rain in the Seattle area was never heavy, but a slow drizzle, just enough to get you wet. The Marine Corps did not have a raincoat in those days, instead, we were issued a heavy wool overcoat. The overcoat was heavy to begin with, but after being out in the rain for two or three hours it must have weighed 40 pounds and did not smell all too good. As I recall, I saw the sun two times during our three month stay in Bremerton.

After completing the Yard Overhaul, we put to sea and appeared to go in circles for about a week. The explanation was they were calibrating the new equipment. Finally we sailed back to San Diego. I was happy to be back in the warm sunshine of Southern California.

After a few weeks in San Diego, we put to sea. The Air Group came aboard and we were told we were going to Pearl Harbor. The trip to Pearl Harbor took about a week, so air operations were conducted on the way. When we arrived off of the Island of Oahu, all of the Air Group was launched and sent to the Air Station at Ford Island. Ford Island is located in the middle of Pearl Harbor. As we arrived off Diamond Head, I was struck by the beauty of the place. I had never before seen water so blue as the water around the Islands.

I could not believe all of the Ships that were in Pearl Harbor. There were at least 10 Battleships, many Cruisers and Destroyers as well as supply and repair ships. There were two squadrons of PBY Flying Boats (Sea Planes) based on Ford Island. These planes would take off at daylight and fan out in all directions and search an area about 600 miles out every day (This was in 1940). They continued to do this until about one week prior to December 7, 1941! In May 1940, I was promoted to Private First Class. This increased my pay to $30.00 per month. On the recommendation of Gunny Fred Smith, my best friend Art Vangsness and I were assigned duties taking care of the 5" Guns on the after Starboard Side. My gun was #5 and Art was assigned #7. They were only about 10 feet apart and on the heavy jobs we would assist each other. Our job was to keep the guns clean and well oiled. After each firing exercise, we had to take the breech mechanism apart (under the supervision of a Navy Gunners Mate), polish the burrs off the moving parts with a fine emery cloth and then reassemble the entire mechanism. This was a choice assignment and was soon pretty much of a routine. It also led to our early promotion to Corporal.

Liberty in Honolulu left a lot to be desired. Everything was very expensive and there were so many Sailors, Marines and Soldiers on the streets it was difficult to walk down them. The small village of Pearl City was also located at Pearl Harbor. The village consisted of a few small stores and beer joints. It was also the Base for the China Clipper. This was a large, 4 engine Flying Boat that operated out of Treasure Island in San Francisco Bay. It took 17 hours to fly from San Francisco to Pearl Harbor. It left Pearl Harbor and went to Midway, Wake Island, Guam, Manila and Shanghai. It then came back the same way, taking a full week to make the trip. There was a second one that went from Pearl Harbor to Samoa, Fiji, Auckland, New Zealand, Sydney, Australia and then back. It also took a week for the trip. These were marvelous machines for their day, but extremely inefficient by today's standards.

Fleet Exercises were a sight to behold and will never be seen again. The large Battleships were surrounded by many Cruisers and Destroyers and followed by Aircraft Carriers.

The Battle Plan called for the Destroyers and Cruisers to be strung out on a wide front, followed by the main battle line, the Battleships. The Aircraft Carriers were assigned a secondary role providing scouting and air support for the main battle force, the Battleships. The Japanese probably did us a favor by sinking most of the Battleships in Pearl Harbor. At least they were later raised, repaired and saw extensive service in the Philippines and other Island operations. If the Japanese had declared war, the Battleships would probably have steamed out to meet the Japanese Fleet and been sunk in deep water. This is exactly what happened to the British Battleships later off the coast of Malaya.

In the Fall of 1940, we returned to San Diego. The old Biplane Grumman Fighters were replaced by a beautiful new all metal, single wing Fighter called the Brewster Buffalo. It turned out to be all show and not much go.

In the 30's and early 40's, both the Navy and Marine Corps had many enlisted pilots. One of the enlisted Fighter Pilots told me the new Brewster Buffalo was the sorriest plane he had ever flown. He said it was a full-time job just keeping it in the air and if war came, there was no way to fight with it. When the new planes landed aboard ship, the landing gear collapsed on one of them. Within a week of flight operations, most of the squadron suffered the same fate. The landing gear could not take the stress of carrier landings. After much head scratching, it was decided the Brewster Buffalo was not suitable for carrier operations. What to do with them? Give them to the Marines! Marine Pilots were also required to be Carrier Qualified! The Marines could use them for island defense. Some of them were assigned to Midway Island. All were shot down at the Battle of Midway! It seemed as though the Navy enlisted Pilot was correct about the qualities of the airplane.

I can't imagine how the Navy bought so many of the Brewster Buffalo Fighters without giving them extensive Carrier Testing. There must have been a lot of politics involved. The Navy eventually gave some of the Brewster Buffalo Fighters to the Dutch to be used in Java and Sumatra. I understand they were all destroyed by Japanese Fighters. Others were sent to England under the Lend Lease Act. The story was the British took one look at the airplane and did not bother to uncrate the rest of them.

After the fiasco with the Brewster Buffalo Fighters, the Enterprise Fighter Squadron was equipped with a new Grumman Fighter called the F4F. This was an all metal single wing plane that looked a lot like the old Biplane, except for the single wing. It was faster and just as rugged as the old Grumman Fighter. This plane proved to be a real "workhorse" in the Pacific War.

Shortly after the new Fighters arrived, both the BT-1 Dive Bombers and the SBC Scout Planes were replaced by the new Douglas SBD'S. This was a tough, clean, well designed plane with a fully retractable landing gear. It was used extensively during World War II in all areas of the Pacific against the Japanese.

We returned to Hawaii and performed extensive training with the Pacing Fleet. We would frequently drop anchor at Lahina, Maui. I never was able to get ashore at Maui. It seemed I always had the duty when liberty was available on the Island of Maui. It was a marvelous sight to see the entire Pacific Fleet anchored in those beautiful blue waters surrounded by the Islands of Maui and Lanai.

In the Summer of 1941 Captain Rixey was promoted to Major and was replaced by a young Captain, Carey A. Randall. Captain Randall took one look at our battle stations on the 5" Guns and immediately started lobbying the Gunnery Officer (Commander V. R. Roan) and the Captain of the Ship (George Murray) to move the Marines from the 5" Antiaircraft guns and place them on the .50 Caliber machine guns that were placed on the Catwalk around the Flight Deck. His argument was if we went to war, there was the possibility the ENTERPRISE would suffer damage to the 5" Gun Galleries. He stated he did not want to lose half of the Marine Detachment to a single bomb hit. He no doubt made a strong case for his reasoning because the Gunnery Officer and the Captain of the Ship approved his recommendation. The Marines were transferred to the .50 Caliber Machine Guns and we were assigned the job of training Navy Personnel to replace us on the 5" Guns.

Shortly after we were transferred to the .50 Caliber Machine Guns we had a prominent visitor come aboard ship. He was Captain Louis Mountbatten, Royal Navy. (He later became Admiral Lord Louis Mountbatten, Chief of the Royal Navy and later the last Viceroy of India. He was killed by the Irish while fishing in Ireland many years later). His ship the H.M.S. EAGLE had been sunk in the Mediterranean by German Dive Bombers. He inspected our operations and stated we needed many more Antiaircraft Guns. At that time, the ship had Eight 5" Guns, Two Batteries of 1.1" 4 barrel Guns (these were almost useless because they would not work about half the time), and 16 .50 Caliber Machine Guns.

I had been promoted to Sergeant in October and because of my proficiency with the Machine Gun, myself, PFC Philip McCully, and a Navy Gunners Mate were assigned to the Fleet Machine Gun School located near the entrance to Pearl Harbor. We were to complete training on the .50 Caliber Machine Gun and the new 20 MM Machine Gun and then return to the Ship to instruct the other Marines and Navy Personnel in the use of these weapons.

The ENTERPRISE put to Sea soon after we were assigned to the Machine Gun School. We assumed they were going out for more routine Flight Operations. It turned out their mission was anything but routine. They took a Marine Corps Fighter Squadron aboard and slipped out unseen to Wake Island where they left the Marine Fighter Squadron. When I say slipped out unseen, I mean that literally. The Naval Treaty of 1921 prohibited the United States from sending a ship larger than a Cruiser beyond the 180th Meridian. Similar restrictions were placed upon Japan. Around the 1st of December, Phil McCully and I noticed some strange things taking place. For almost two years, we had watched the PBY Flying Boats take off every day (seven days a week) on their search missions around the Islands for up to 600 miles in all directions. The Coast Guard had several fast Cutters stationed in the Islands. Any time a Japanese Ship appeared on the horizon, in just a few minutes the Coast Guard Cutter would be after him. They would check them out thoroughly before permitting them to proceed. You could almost set your watch by how quickly the Coast Guard would respond.

The strange things that were taking place was that the PBY'S were not conducting their search operations. They were sitting on the ramp (out of the water) at Ford Island. The Coast Guard Cutters were no longer challenging the Japanese Ships that came and went. Phil McCully, the Gunners Mate and myself had completed our training at the Fleet Machine Gun School and were waiting for the ENTERPRISE to return to port so we could return to the ship. Across the fence from the Fleet Machine Gun School was an Army Base, Fort Weaver. Starting in 1940, the Army started drafting men for one (1) year of active duty. For reasons known only to the Army, they shipped a large number of draftees to Fort Weaver for training. They were trying to teach them to march and do close order drill. We were amused at their efforts. They all appeared to be singing. "I'll be back in a year little darling". As things turned out, I doubt any of them made it back in a year.

The ENTERPRISE had been in Hawaii for almost two years and was due for another Navy Yard Overhaul. We were scheduled to return to the United States on December 13, 1941. On Saturday, December 6, Phil McCully and I decided we would get some beer from the Exchange and go down to the Beach and celebrate our returning to the United States on December 13th.

While on the Beach, we discussed the fact that the PBY'S were still sitting on the ramp at Ford Island. As we were speculating about the reasons for such inability, a Jap ship appeared on the horizon. We both speculated about how long it would take for the Coast Guard Cutter to be on him. To our surprise, the Coast Guard Cutter did not appear! The Jap ship steamed toward the entrance to Honolulu Harbor, turned and sailed straight to the entrance to Pearl Harbor. He stopped at the entrance to Pearl Harbor for a short time, turned about and steamed over the horizon. He was not challenged by the Coast Guard or anyone else. Phil McCully and I were both amazed at the inactivity on the part of our people.

We finished our beer and decided that since we were returning to the United States in a few days we would return to our tents and make sure our gear was packed, since the ENTERPRISE would no doubt soon return to Pearl Harbor.

I was blessed with good eyes and ears and after many hours of training aboard the ENTERPRISE, I could identify an airplane by types about as far as I could see. At night I could identify the type airplane by the sound of the engine about 98% of the time. On Sunday morning, December 7, 1941, I heard a strange airplane engine. I immediately stepped outside my tent and to my surprise, about 100 feet over my head was a formation of Japanese Torpedo Planes. There was no mistake. I started yelling "Japs" and the other people started coming out of their tents staring in disbelief. About that time, a Jap Gunner in the rear seat of one of the Torpedo Planes started shooting at us. Fortunately his aim was not too good. The only casualty was one guy that lost a toe. Our 20mm and .50 Caliber Machine Guns were under lock and key in the gun shed. Phil McCully and I decided we would break the lock on the gun shed and set up our 20mm Guns. An "Old time" Gunnery Sergeant yelled "hey you guys can't do that, you don't have the authority". We said "To hell with the authority" and proceeded to tear the lock off of the door.

We managed to get one 20mm Machine gun in operation in short order. About that time, it was obvious Pearl Harbor was taking a pounding. In addition to the Torpedo Planes that passed right over us, we could see Dive Bombers making their runs on the ships in the harbor. We could not understand why there was no Antiaircraft fire coming from Pearl Harbor. About this time, there were several new type B-17's attempting to land at Hickam Field. This was a type B-17 not seen in Hawaii before and some of the people thought they were Japs. Phil McCully and I knew they were the new type B-17's we had been taught to recognize. Their final approach to Hickam Field was directly in front of the Machine Gun School. As the Jap Fighters would get on their tail, we would "dust them off" with our 20MM Gun.

The "Old time" Major in Command of the Machine Gun School eventually arrived on the scene and got things organized. The remaining guns were set up and crews were assigned to each gun. Anytime a Jap plane came within range, we would open fire on him. After a while, they did not venture over our area.

There appeared to be absolute chaos across the fence from us at Fort Weaver. The new draftees in training had never fired a weapon. The Army issued them Rifles, Machine Guns, Pistols and Browning Automatic Rifles. As darkness settled in, they shot at any movement or noise. All night long, there were bullets whizzing through our area from Fort Weaver. At that moment I was more concerned about being shot by an Army Draftee than by a Jap. Chaos reigned supreme! All night long, we kept hearing radio reports that the Japs were landing first on the North Beach, then near Diamond Head, next by landings at Kaneohe. The truth of the matter was the Japanese could have no doubt taken the Island had they brought landing troops with them.

Early in the evening, after dark, a group of planes approached the Island from the Southwest. As they passed over the Machine Gun School, we could tell by the sound of the engines, they were our planes. It turned out they were from the ENTERPRISE. The ENTERPRISE was returning from Wake island and launched the planes to land at Ford Island. Instead of going straight into Ford Island, the planes circled Pearl Harbor. The large number of fires in the area may have confused the pilots or they may have been just sightseeing. In any event, as they passed over West Loch Naval Ammunition Depot, someone started shooting at them. At that time every gun on the island opened fire. As the planes passed over the Fleet Machine Gun School, we also opened fire. We thought they were our planes but since everyone else was firing at them, we thought they must know something we did not know, so we opened fire. The next morning, there was a sad sight in the mud flats in front of us. We had shot down one of the SBD Dive Bombers from the ENTERPRISE. Some of the planes from the ENTERPRISE landed at other airfields and some of them were never found. It was presumed they were shot down by our own people.

Late the next day, December 8th, the ENTERPRISE returned to Pearl Harbor. The Major in Command at the Machine Gun School told us he was going to get us back to the ship if we had to hike some 15 miles back around the Harbor. He finally scrounged up a small Motorboat. To get to the boat, we had to cross Fort Weaver. We were challenged by Draftees several times and thought we would be shot as Japs at any time. We finally got to the small boat and were fired upon while going down the channel. Some of the trigger happy people thought we were a submarine! We finally made our way back to the ENTERPRISE. They were busy taking on fuel and supplies. After our ordeal, Phil McCully and I were relieved to be back aboard ship. Pearl Harbor was a mess. The Battleship Oklahoma had capsized. The Arizona appeared to be turned wrong side out. Several other Battleships were sunk in the harbor with their decks awash. The PBY Squadrons, sitting on the ramp at Ford Island were destroyed. Two Destroyers in Dry Dock were in bad shape, one had its Bow blown off, the other one was laying on its side. There were many other ships sunk and damaged. One strange thing however, the nearby Submarine Base was undamaged as well as the Fleet Fuel Depot! Soon after our arrival back aboard ship, the word was passed over the loud speaker that the ship would get under way at 2:00 a.m. This was unheard of! Ships did not depart Pearl Harbor at night and there was always a Pilot aboard any time a ship came into harbor or departed. At 0200 (2:00 a.m.) the ship swung clear of the Dock, no Pilot aboard. Captain George Murray took the ENTERPRISE down the channel and by the time we had cleared the channel into open water, we were doing 20 knots.

During the attack on Pearl Harbor a number of ships attempted to clear the harbor for the open sea. The U.S.S. Battleship Nevada was torpedoed in mid channel. Rather than block the channel, the Captain beached the Nevada near the part of the channel that went around Ford Island. A few Destroyers did manage to get to sea. Shortly after daylight on December 9th, a Destroyer appeared on the horizon. The Destroyer signaled by blinker light "requesting permission to join your task force". Admiral Halsey and Captain Murray thought this was rather unusual and signaled back, "What is the name of your Commanding officer?" The signal came back "Chief Boatswains Mate" (I do not remember his name). It seems all of the Officers were ashore and the Chief and the remainder of the crew took the Destroyer to sea. After a few days, the Admiral sent the Destroyer back to Pearl Harbor to turn the ship back to the proper Commanding Officer. The Admiral was impressed with the initiative shown by the Chief Boatswains Mate and the rest of the crew.

We spent about two weeks supposedly clearing the shipping lanes of Jap Submarines. I think we bombed a number of whales and one Periscope we wasted a lot of ammunition on what turned out to be a swab (mop) someone had lost overboard. The floating mop handle did look a little like a Periscope.

Phil McCully and I were assigned to different 20 MM Batteries. Because we were at General Quarters (all stations fully manned) or Condition II (4 hours on duty and 4 hours off) most of the time, we did not see each other very often. After I left the ENTERPRISE I never ran into Phil McCully and did not know if he had survived the war. Forty five years later, at a Reunion of ENTERPRISE Marines, Phil McCully showed up. In discussing the Pearl Harbor Attack we were surprised that both of us had arrived at the same conclusion concerning the stand down of the PBY Flying Boats and the inactivity of the Coast Guard about a week prior to the attack.

We had both decided someone high up in the Administration had ordered the Flying Boats to stand down and the Coast Guard into inactivity because they knew an attack on Pearl Harbor was imminent. They wanted an incident to get the American People stirred up. We had always had an incident to get us into war. The Spanish American war, "Remember the Maine" or the Lusitania incident for World War I. "No taxation without representation" for the American Revolution.

We also believed the Jap ship that went unchallenged at the entrance to Pearl Harbor on December 6, 1941 was somehow involved with the midget Jap Submarines that penetrated Pearl Harbor on December 7. One of these ran aground in the Harbor and was captured.

In typical American fashion, after the debacle of Pearl Harbor everyone started looking for a "Goat" to pin the blame on for the disaster at Pearl Harbor. The politicians in Washington found two "Goats": General Short, the Army Commander in Hawaii and Admiral Kimmel, the Commander of the Pacific Fleet. They wasted no time in pinning all the blame on these two men. I have always believed they were following orders from Washington and the blame rested in Washington and not in Hawaii.

After spending two weeks cleaning the shipping lanes (mostly of whales) we returned to Pearl Harbor. We spent several days loading fuel and supplies for what appeared to be a long stay at sea.

We departed Pearl Harbor with two Cruisers and several Destroyers. After a few days at sea we were joined by two Troop Ships and assorted escort vessels. We provided Air Cover for the Troop Ships, (as it turned out, they were loaded with a Marine Corps Defense Battalion), and escorted them to Samoa where they were assigned to protect the Island.

After leaving the Marines at Samoa we joined up with the U.S.S. YORKTOWN (The sister ship to the ENTERPRISE) and several escort vessels, including more Cruisers and Destroyers. We sailed to the Northwest for several days and in early February, launched an Air and Naval Gunfire attack on the Japanese held Marshall and Gilbert Islands.

Commander V. R. Roan who had been the Gunnery Officer on the ENTERPRISE had been transferred to a Destroyer as Commanding Officer. We on the ENTERPRISE had always thought he was somewhat unusual, however in the Marshall Island raid, all doubt was removed. He took his Destroyer inside the Lagoon to shoot up Japanese small craft and installations. He got away with it and later rejoined the Task Force without receiving any hits from the Japanese shore batteries.

The pilots made several attacks on the Islands and returned from the last attack around 2:00 p.m. They convinced the Admiral and Captain Murray there was not a Jap plane in the Islands that would fly. They also said all facilities on the Islands were destroyed. The Captain decided the crew of the ship was exhausted from the long period at General Quarters and since the Japs had been clobbered we would secure from General Quarters and give the crew a rest and some hot food.

Around 3:30 p.m. all hell broke loose. I was below deck in the Marine Compartment. There were several loud explosions, paint flew off of the bulkhead (wall) and the lights went out momentarily. The ship bounced around and I headed for my battle station. As I ran across the Hangar Deck, there was a lot of gunfire and another loud explosion. By the time I arrived at my battle station, the excitement was over for the time being. It seemed that several large twin engine Japanese Bombers had slipped in on us and the loud explosions were from near misses. One of the Bombers was damaged severely. The pilot pulled out of the formation and tried to crash into the Flight Deck. He almost made it but a sailor in the rear seat of a Dive Bomber that was sitting on Deck opened up with his twin .30 Caliber Machine Gun and hit the pilot. The Jap plane hit the Flight Deck with his right wing, destroyed one parked Dive Bomber and started a fire. The fire was quickly brought under control and other than some damage to the catwalk and the loss of one Dive Bomber, we were in good shape. About two hours later, we were again attacked by nine (9) twin engine Japanese Bombers. They were at about 15,000 feet. Captain Murray had the ENTERPRISE wound up to flank speed (maximum) and was watching the bombers with his Binoculars from the Open Bridge. When he saw the bombs leave the Bombers, he gave the command "Hard Left Rudder". I thought the ENTERPRISE was going to capsize. He made a 90 degree turn to the left and all of the Japanese Bombs landed where we would have been except for the hard left turn. I don't think Captain Murray ever again took the pilot's word concerning damage to Jap installations. The last I heard of him, he was a Vice Admiral.

As soon as all planes had been recovered, the Task Force "turned tail" and headed back toward Pearl Harbor. Our first attack against the Japs had been a success. However compared to events yet to come, it was a minor skirmish. The pilots were somewhat sloppy and we in the gun crews could use a lot more practice.

A few days later, we arrived in Pearl Harbor. The news of our strike against the Marshall Islands had been received before our arrival. As the ENTERPRISE entered the Harbor, the crews of the many ships that had been damaged on December 7, 1941 stopped work and cheered at the top of their lungs. One would have thought we had won the war. We were to tie up at 1010 Dock rather than as usual at the Quay at Ford Island. In order to do so, it was necessary to go around Ford Island (Ford Island is in the center of Pearl Harbor). The cheering continued as we circled Ford Island and did not stop until we were tied up at 1010 Dock.

It soon became obvious why we tied up at 1010 Dock. Trucks could come directly to the ship from the Navy Yard. Soon there was a steady stream of trucks bringing food, bombs, ammunition and various spare parts. You did not have to be a genius to figure out our stay in Pearl Harbor would be short and we would be pulling out soon.

On February 14, 1942 we departed Pearl Harbor. After we had been at sea for several hours, Captain Murray came on the loud speakers and announced we were going to attack Wake Island! The crew was happy to hear this news, especially the ENTERPRISE Marines since the Marine defenders of Wake Island had put up a good fight against overwhelming odds and were forced to surrender just before Christmas 1941.

The Raid on Wake Island on February 24, 1942 got off to a bad start. There was an overcast sky and the humidity was extremely high. Aircraft were usually launched before dawn and the Fighters managed to get off with difficulty. The humidity was so high that when the planes powered up for takeoff (In those days, all planes were flown off the deck rather than catapulted) there was a sheet of vapor surrounding the plane. The Dive Bombers were always launched after the Fighters and they were followed by the slow lumbering Torpedo Planes. The Dive Bombers had an exhaust stack that extended from the cowling several inches back on the lower fuselage of the plane. During takeoff the fuel mixture was set on rich. This created a yellow-blue flame about two feet long on each side of the plane. The bright flame from the engine created a reflection from the sheen of vapor surrounding the plane. As a result, the pilots could not see. The first Dive Bomber to take off crashed into the sea. A Destroyer escort rescued the injured pilot, however the Radio-Gunner was lost. Flight operations were delayed until daylight so the pilots could see. This delay removed the element of surprise and gave the Japs time to organize their Anti-Aircraft defense. The pilots reported extensive damage to the facilities on Wake Island.

After the raid on Wake Island, we did not turn toward Pearl Harbor as expected. Instead, we headed northwest and were met by a tanker the next day. We soon learned we were to strike Marcus Island, a Japanese Island about 650 miles northwest of Wake Island and about 1000 miles southeast of Tokyo. We also heard the unsettling news that we would leave the Destroyers behind and have only the two (2) cruisers as escorts. This was because the Destroyers did not have enough fuel for the sustained high speed run that was anticipated.

The raid on Marcus Island was a little different from the raid on Wake and the Marshall Islands since the ship's Radar was used to guide the pilots to the target. As a result, the pilots did not spend a lot of time milling around in the dark trying to find the target. They went straight from the ship to Marcus Island and arrived over the target while it was still dark. They made their attack, saw several fires but did not know the extent of damage inflicted. We lost one Dive Bomber. The pilot made a successful water landing and the pilot and radio-gunner were seen in their rubber life raft paddling away from Marcus Island. They were taken prisoner by a Jap Destroyer and it was learned after the war they were beheaded and thrown overboard.

The raids on Wake and Marcus Island were notable in another respect. The ENTERPRISE would stay out of range of Jap land based bombers during the day before the raid. As soon as it was dark, the ship would go to top speed for the "run in" to the target, arriving within striking distance before daylight. This was a procedure used by the Navy throughout the war. Another lesson was the value of the Weather Officer. We were fortunate on the ENTERPRISE. If there was a weather front anywhere in the vicinity of the target area our weather guy would find it. In the Marshall Island raid, we would launch aircraft, duck into a rain squall until time to recover planes, launch again and then back into the rain squall. After the raid on Marcus Island, Tokyo Rose announced that we were surrounded by a ring of steel and we would never make it back to Pearl Harbor. Normally, Tokyo Rose was always good for a few good laughs. In this case, however we were not doing a lot of laughing since we had no Destroyer escort and the two Cruisers had no way of detecting a Submarine.

Our Weather Officer outdid himself this time! We altered course to the north instead of east toward Pearl Harbor. Soon we encountered the worst storm I had ever seen. It was no doubt the tail end of a huge Typhoon. At least the weather was so bad land based bombers could not find us and Jap

Submarines would have a tough time hitting us if they should find us. There were waves 30 - 40 feet high. We reduced speed and our course was parallel to the waves. The Ship rolled from side to side and anything not tied down went sailing across the ship. My Condition II Battle Station was Control Officer of Group III 5 inch Anti-Aircraft Battery, located on the Starboard Quarter of the Ship. The Battery consisted of two 5 inch guns. During Condition II, one half of the crew is on duty and the other is off duty for 4 hours. There were 20 of us on the Gun Battery rather than the usual 40 when we were at General Quarters. We had the 5 inch guns elevated to 35' and when we would roll to Starboard the guns would be pointed into the Water. At one point instead of starting to roll back to Port, the ship continued to roll to Starboard. We thought the ship was going to roll-over. I was not apprehensive, I was scared! That last roll apparently got Captain Murray's attention also for we immediately changed course so we were headed into the waves. The Flight Deck was 60 feet above the water and with every wave, a lot of water came over the Flight Deck. The ship groaned and shook like it was going to come apart. The ship held together and after about a day and a half in the storm we broke out into the calm clear Pacific, joined up with our Destroyer escort and the tanker. We refueled and then headed back to Pearl Harbor. Everyone I knew gave a big sigh of relief.

We returned to Pearl Harbor, arriving about the 10th of March, 1942. The usual bombs, ammunition, food, fuel and spare parts were brought aboard. In addition, civilian employees from the Navy Yard swarmed aboard and removed the .50 Caliber Machine Guns. These were replaced by the 20MM Guns that Phil McCully, Hawkins, Burns and myself had been trained to operate at the Fleet Machine Gun School. This was the reason we were at Pearl Harbor on December 7, 1941.

Of even greater importance to the members of the Marine Detachment, Captain Cary Randall the Commanding Officer of the Marines had finally convinced the Gunnery Officer and the Captain of the Ship to move the Marines from the two 5 inch Gun Batteries and assign us to the 20 MM Batteries. His main argument was Marines were by training more proficient when assigned to smaller caliber weapons and with the entire Marine Detachment concentrated on the after part of the ship if we should sustain a bomb hit on that part of the ship, all or most of the Marines would be killed. With the 20 MM Batteries scattered completely around the Flight Deck the possibility of all of the Marines being killed or wounded was remote. As soon as the 20MM Guns had been installed, we started an intensive training program. Those of us who had attended the Fleet Machine Gun School were assigned the responsibility to train the other Marines. In addition, we trained Navy Personnel that were to replace us on the 5 inch Guns. The transition went smoothly in spite of grumbling by some of the Marines who thought we should remain on the 5 inch Guns. An event was to occur in August 1942 in the Eastern Solomons that would silence the grumbling about moving us from the 5 inch Guns and make Captain Randall our Hero.

In early April, 1942 the Enterprise again sailed from Pearl Harbor with our usual escort of two Cruisers and four Destroyers. In addition something different was added. There was a large Tanker with our group. We cleared the Channel at Pearl Harbor and took a course to the Northwest after the Air Group came aboard. We did not know where we were going, but a farm boy from Fannin County, Texas could figure out that with our own Tanker along we were in for a long cruise!

We continued on a Northwesterly course for several days. There were repeater compasses at various places on the ship which we could see. However by this time I had developed an ability to determine our course within a few degrees by looking at the stars at night and by using my watch and the sun during the day. If there was an overcast I had to check the compass.

After cruising in a Northwesterly course for several days, we did not know our exact position, however each day it grew colder which told us we were in the northern latitudes rather than the sub-tropics. Around the middle of April on a cold, damp morning we spotted a group of ships on the Starboard Side in the mist and there appeared to be an Aircraft Carrier in the group. We had heard rumors about a new Aircraft Carrier HORNET that was to come to the Pacific to give us a hand. The rumor soon spread that the ship was indeed the HORNET. As we came closer, we could see what appeared to be large planes on the Flight Deck of the HORNET rather than the usual navy planes. It soon became obvious they were Army B-25 Bombers. The next question on everyone's mind was, how do you operate B-25 Bombers from an Aircraft Carrier? The answer was obvious, you can't. You might be able to launch them, but there was no way they could land. In fact, with the Army Bombers on deck, the HORNET could not operate their own navy planes. They were all stored below in the Hangar Deck. Our curiosity was soon answered by Admiral Halsey when he announced our present position was about half-way between Midway Island and the Kamchatka Peninsula of Siberia (small wonder we were about to freeze in our tropical clothing). Our mission was to approach to within 500 miles of Japan and launch the Army Bombers. They were going to bomb Tokyo! There was a loud cheer throughout the ship. The crew thought this would be a partial revenge for the bombing of Pearl Harbor. The Task Force took up a course to the West for several days. I was impressed by the size of the Task Force. We had not seen this many ships in one force since before the war when we held Fleet Exercises off the Island of Maui. Most of the Battleships that made up the great Pacific Fleet were now destroyed or damaged with their main decks awash in the dirty water of Pearl Harbor. After steaming due west for three or four days, all ships topped off their fuel tanks and then left the Tanker and Destroyers behind, for the "run in", the same routine as at Marcus Island.

Also, the same as at Marcus Island, the crew, including myself was nervous because without the Destroyers, we had no effective defense against Submarines. By this time, the Aircraft Carrier SARATOGA had been torpedoed by a Jap Submarine near Hawaii. The SARATOGA was a sister ship of the LEXINGTON. Both ships were larger than the ENTERPRISE. They were originally designed as Battlecruisers but because of the Naval Treaty with Japan in 1923, they were converted to Aircraft Carriers. Both ships had a unique propulsion system instead of the usual Steam Turbine to drive the propeller shaft, they generated electricity and the propeller was driven by an Electric Motor. They were the fastest large ships in the Navy. The Lexington set a speed record from San Francisco to Hawaii in the 1930's that as far as I know may still stand.

The "run in" was a rough ride because of heavy seas. The plan was to continue the high speed run toward Japan until late in the afternoon and then launch the Army Bombers so they would arrive over Tokyo at night. After bombing Japan they were to proceed to China and land at Chinese Air fields in the inland area of China, since the Japanese had occupied the coastal areas in China.

In war as in life, things do not always go as planned. Early on the morning of April 18, 1942 we ran into a group of small Jap ships. Our Fighters, Dive Bombers and one of our Cruisers soon took care of the Jap ships, however the Admiral was sure the ships had alerted the Japanese of our presence. Not in any mood to risk his carriers to enemy land based bombers, Admiral Halsey ordered the Army Bombers launched about seven hours earlier than planned. This would put the Army Bombers over Japan during daylight hours. He also knew they would not have enough fuel to reach the designated Chinese Air fields. The situation was desperate but he had no other choice under the circumstances. Shortly before 9:00 a.m., we swung into the wind and the Army Bombers were launched. I watched every move on the Hornet from my gun position on the ENTERPRISE. Both carriers were pitching violently from the heavy seas. The first Army Bomber started its roll down the deck of the Hornet and just barely became airborne as it left the end of the Flight Deck. He arrived at the end of the Flight Deck just as the ship's bow was pitched in the down position. All observers on the ENTERPRISE held their breath for fear he would crash into the large waves. For the second and remaining planes, the launch officer on the Hornet was able to coordinate the roll of the plane down the deck in such a manner that the Army Bomber arrived at the end of the Flight Deck while the bow of the ship was pitched in the up position. This gave the plane an additional 50 to 60 feet of altitude the first plane did not have.

As soon as the last Army Bomber had cleared the Flight Deck of the Hornet, the Task Force "turned tail" and headed due East away from Japan as fast as the heavy seas would permit. The following day, we rejoined our Destroyers and the Tanker and heaved a sigh of relief that now we at least had some protection from enemy Submarines. We were still within range of Jap land based bombers and still could not relax.

We arrived back at Pearl Harbor the last week in April and all hands were permitted to go on liberty in Honolulu. We all looked forward to a few hours of relaxation after some tense and trying weeks.

By this time, the Japanese had conquered the coastal areas of China, the Philippine Islands, Borneo, the Dutch East Indies, part of New Guinea, New Britain and they were now moving into the Solomon Islands. It was obvious their expansion to the Southeast would cut the sea lanes to Australia and then Australia would be theirs for the taking.

Our stay in Pearl Harbor was short lived. On April 30 we again headed down the channel into the open sea with the Carrier HORNET, four Cruisers and eight Destroyers. This time we were headed to the Southwest. Unlike our last cruise to the Northwest when the weather tamed cool, then cold after a few days, this time it became hotter each day. For reasons known only to themselves, the U.S. Navy had a habit of serving "Hot tea and green liver" in the mess hall when we were in the tropics. I am unable to eat liver to this day! I could manage the beans and combread for breakfast, but when they served liver I ate bread and butter.

After several days, we crossed the Equator and continued our course to the Southwest. I was amazed at the difference in the sea in the South Pacific from our recent experience in the North Pacific. Instead of the large swells that caused the ship to roll and pitch, the South Pacific was glassy smooth. We often encountered schools of Porpoise and Flying Fish. Actually they should be called sailing fish. They would zoom out of the water and extend their wings and sail to the next destination, usually about 100 feet or less. At least the Porpoise and Flying Fish provided a form of entertainment. Another strange thing was the high phosphorus content of the water. At night, there was a virtual light that swept back from the bow of each ship and the wake was bright for miles behind the ship. This light was like the luminous dial on a watch. We thought we would be a sitting duck for an enemy bomber. Fortunately there were none in this area.

As we proceeded to the Southwest, news came in that our sister ship, the YORKTOWN and the larger carrier LEXINGTON were engaged in battle with Jap Aircraft Carriers near the Solomon Islands in the Coral Sea. We then found out our mission was to give them a hand. By the time we arrived in the Coral Sea, the battle was over. The mighty LEXINGTON was sunk and our sister ship the YQRKTOWN was damaged but still afloat. We launched the Marine Fighter Squadron we had aboard and they headed for the French Island of New Caledonia. We hung around in the area a couple of days and were spotted by a four engine Jap patrol plane. The Admiral would not let the Combat Air Patrol shoot the Jap Patrol Plane down. We thought this was odd as Admiral Halsey was always eager to kill as many Japs as possible and this action was a complete mystery to the crew. After the

Admiral was sure the Jap Patrol Plane had reported our presence so the Japs would know all our Carriers were in the South Pacific, he ordered the Combat Air Patrol to shoot it down. This they did in short order. By this time, it was late in the afternoon. The Combat Air Patrol landed just before dark. As soon as all Fighters had landed, the Task Force turned tail and set a course to the Northeast toward Pearl Harbor at high speed. We continued toward Pearl Harbor at high speed. Everyone aboard knew that something was up, but we did not know what.

Our trip to the South Seas appeared to be of minor importance. We did carry a Marine Corps Fighter Squadron to New Caledonia and our Fighters shot down a Jap 4 Engine Flying Boat. For our part we lost two Dive Bombers to unknown reasons and a Fighter Crashed on takeoff. I personally saw the pilot struggling to free himself from the wreckage. By the time the Plane Guard Destroyer got to the scene of the crash, both plane and pilot had disappeared.

We arrived at Pearl Harbor the end of May and were greeted with a flurry of activity. The crew was not granted liberty and all hands turned to bringing food and supplies aboard. At the same time, fuel was being pumped into the fuel bunkers and aviation gasoline was being pumped into the gasoline tanks. The civilian Navy Yard workers were swarming over the damaged YORKTOWN making repairs; they reminded me of a bunch of ants. Word spread throughout the ship that Admiral Halsey was sick and that he would not be with us on our next mission. We departed Pearl Harbor after one day. We all knew that something big and important was coming up but we did not know what. We were uneasy without Admiral Halsey and we had a Cruiser Admiral, Rear Admiral Spence aboard commanding the Task Force. It is just as well that we did not know that we were headed into a battle that would change the course of history.

After clearing the Pearl Harbor Channel we set a course to the Northwest toward Midway Island. In the afternoon our Air Group came aboard. Our Fighter Squadron had been equipped with an updated version of the Wildcat, the F4F-4. These planes had folding wings which meant that they took up less space on the Flight Deck. The Squadron now had 27 Fighters rather than the usual 18. We all thought this was a good omen. We could use a good omen because the word was passed that our Intelligence people had discovered that the Japs were going to invade Midway Island on June 4, 1942. This was only 3 days away. Our job was to stop them! We took up station Northeast of Midway Island and waited. Our Task Force consisted of the ENTERPRISE, HORNET, several Cruisers and Destroyers and any auxiliary vessels that could be scraped up. We were a puny force to take on the greater part of the Japanese Fleet! The Carrier SARATOGA was still being repaired, the LEXINGTON sunk, the YORKTOWN damaged and our Battleships sitting in the mud at Pearl Harbor. To say that we were apprehensive would be an understatement. Most of us were just plain scared.

Up to this point, the Japanese had appeared to be invulnerable. They had conquered all of Southeast Asia, the Philippine Islands, Wake Island, Guam, the greater part of the Solomon Islands and were knocking on the door of Australia. It was believed that they planned to take Midway Island and use that as a jumping off place to invade the Hawaiian Islands. The Marines on Midway were being strengthened with what forces were available. Their Air Group consisted of a Squadron of old obsolete Dive Bombers, a reinforced Squadron of Brewster Buffalo Fighters. These were the type that we tried out on the ENTERPRISE before the advent of the Wildcat. Of the 18 planes in the squadron, most of them crashed on deck while landing. The Landing Gear would collapse. As frequently happened in those days anything that the Navy had that would not work, they gave it to the Marines. They also tried to give them to the British, but the British would not use them. They sent some of them to the Dutch in the East Indies, but when the Japs invaded, their Fighters chewed them up in a hurry.

We continued to wait and sweat. On June 3rd it was announced that the Japs had invaded the Aleutian Islands in Alaska. We were informed that this was believed to be a diversion and the main Jap Force was headed for Midway Island. One of our Submarines reported a large number of Jap Troop Ships and other Supply type ships to the Southwest of Midway. Due to bad weather the search planes from Midway had not spotted the main Japanese Battle Force.

On June 4th the weather was still messy. Everyone was jumpy and on edge. Still no Word on the location of the Jap Fleet. We had a bit of excitement when several B-17's from Midway started to make a bombing run on us. From 20,000 feet one ship looked like another to the Army. Ship identification was not their long suit. In those days, the Navy could not communicate with the Army and vice-versa because of different Radio Frequencies. I do not remember whether our Combat Air Patrol intercepted them or what, but I do remember that the sailors painted a large white cross down the length of our Flight Deck and across the Flight Deck in a hurry. It was thought that this might prevent the Army from bombing us since the Japs had a large red circle painted on the Flight Deck of their carriers.

We had been at battle stations since long before daylight, prepared for anything that might come our way. My battle station was the 20 MM Battery along the Flight Deck located about halfway from the Island Structure to the forward 5 inch Gun Battery. We had a good view of the Radar Antenna and would watch to see if it continued to make its regular tums. When it stopped turning and backed up slightly we knew that it had spotted an enemy aircraft or surface ship. Our own airplanes carried a device that gave off a signal to the Radar to indicate that they were friendly planes.

About mid-morning word was passed that the Jap Fleet had been located and our planes were launched. In the meantime it was reported that Midway Island was under heavy attack from the Jap Aircraft Carriers. Our planes had a difficult time locating the Japanese Fleet. Because of the overcast sky, the planes became separated from the Fighter Aircraft. The Torpedo Planes made an attack on the Jap Carriers. As I recall, all of our Torpedo Planes were shot down except three. The Dive Bombers finally located the Jap Carriers just as they were shooting down the last of the Torpedo Planes. They sunk three of the Jap Carriers and damaged other ships. In addition to the Torpedo Planes, we lost a number of Dive Bombers and many returned to the ship with huge holes in them, many wounded aircrews, and one Dive Bomber had most of its Rudder shot away. How the pilot managed to land it on the carrier was a mystery. The planes that could still fly were refueled, rearmed and launched for another strike since there was still an undamaged Jap Carrier to take care of.

The Carrier YORKTOWN had been patched-up and joined our group on June 3rd. We were happy to see her increase our force by one third.

Shortly after our planes were landed from the attack on the Jap Carriers on June 4th the Radar Antenna stopped turning. It was announced that a group of enemy planes were headed our Way. Everyone braced themselves for the coming attack. It so happened that the YORKTOWN was the nearest Carrier to the incoming enemy planes. They concentrated their attack on the YORKTOWN. Several hits were made and the YORKTOWN was badly damaged. We never fired a shot, since the enemy planes were out of range of our guns.

Late in the afternoon, our planes located the 4th Jap Carrier and sent it to the bottom of the Pacific. Some of the planes landed after dark and others ran out of fuel and crash landed in the Water. Many were lost, but some were recovered by our Destroyers the next day. The damaged YORKTOWN was finally sunk by a Japanese Submarine on the 7th of June. We also lost the Destroyer HAMMANN that was alongside the YORKTOWN at the time of the Submarine attack.

It seems somewhat ironic, that I participated in the Battle of Midway, the battle that was to change the course of history, as a spectator since I never fired a shot!

The Battle of Midway was unique as Naval Battles go. There was no contact by surface ships. All combat was by airplanes. There was a terrible toll of Navy and Marine Corps pilots and air crews.

We learned that all of the Marine Corps Brewster Fighters from Midway were shot down and most of the obsolete Dive Bombers. We learned that the four Japanese Aircraft Carriers sunk at Midway were part of the force that attacked Pearl Harbor on December 7, 1941. It was also learned that the other two Jap Carriers that struck Pearl Harbor, were damaged in the Battle of the Coral Sea by planes from the YORKTOWN and LEXINGTON. They were in Japan undergoing repairs at the time of the Battle of Midway. In addition to the four Aircraft Carriers lost at Midway the Japanese lost almost 300 of their best pilots.

After the Battle of Midway, the war seemed somewhat different. Prior to Midway our offensive actions were of a "hit and run" nature. We never did any really serious damage to them. They controlled the seas and we were pushed around. Historians say that the Battle of Midway dealt the Japanese a serious blow from which they never recovered.

Shortly after the Battle of Midway was over, the Carrier SARATOGA arrived on the scene. This was the sister ship of the LEXINGTON and had just returned from several months in the states undergoing repairs of the torpedo damage received near Pearl Harbor. The ENTERPRISE had been a part of every action since the war started except for the Battle of the Coral Sea. This action was over before we arrived on the scene. The resentment of the ENTERPRISE crew against the crew of the SARATOGA was intense. On the rare occasion when the ENTERPRISE and SARATOGA crew had liberty at the same time in Honolulu, the ENTERPRISE sailors would deliberately provoke the SARATOGA sailors into a fist fight.

We arrived back in Pearl Harbor around the middle of June. There were many changes to be made! Captain Murray was replaced by Captain Arthur C. Davis as skipper of the ENTERPRISE. All of the surviving pilots and crews of the Air Group were transferred back to the United States. We spent two weeks in the Navy Yard at Pearl Harbor on maintenance and repairs to the ship. It seemed that the many high speed runs had taken its toll on various parts of the ship. We also enjoyed liberty in Honolulu every other day, since only one-half of the Marine Detachment could be absent at any particular time. Captain Randall was promoted to Major and transferred to the United States.

The middle of July 1942, the ENTERPRISE again steamed down the Pearl Harbor Channel for the open sea. This time, things were different. In addition to our usual two Cruisers and four Destroyers, we had plenty of company. The new Battleship NORTH CAROLINA and the new Anti-Aircraft Cruiser ATLANTA. We were impressed with these new ships. The NORTH CAROLINA did not look like the old Battleships that were slowly emerging from the mud bottom of Pearl Harbor. It was trim and modern looking and could keep up with the ENTERPRISE when it became necessary to make a high speed run. The new Cruiser ATLANTA was a sight to behold. It was smaller than a regular Cruiser but larger than a Destroyer. It had the clean lines of a Destroyer, but was covered with Anti-Aircraft Guns. The main purpose of the ATLANTA was to provide Anti-Aircraft protection for the Task Force. We had an additional surprise when the new Air Group came aboard. The Fighters and Dive Bombers were the same type, but new and updated. The big surprise was the new Torpedo Planes. They were a new design, looking a little like the Fighters, since they were also designed and built by the Grumman Corporation, but much larger. They were much faster than the old TBD's that were lost at Midway. They carried a four man crew, including an electrical powered Ball Turret with .50 caliber guns rather than the old free .30 caliber guns in the TBD'S. There was also a large internal bomb or torpedo bay that gave the plane a neat clean appearance. The additional new ships and the new Air Group with their new planes gave the crew a boost and increased our morale greatly.

Once the new Air Group was aboard, the ship swung around and set a course to the South. Each day, the temperature and humidity increased and we knew we were again headed for the Equator and the South Seas. There were no good rumors floating around. We were into our usual routine of 4 hours on our battle stations and 4 hours off. The 4 hours off was a misnomer. During this time we had to eat, bathe and sleep if we could. This had been the routine since the war started and was to be expected when we were at sea, unless we were at General Quarters, in which case all hands were on constant duty. To my disgust, the Navy started the old routine of Hot Tea and Green Liver (when liver is old it takes on a green appearance) for the evening meal. I resorted to my bread and butter routine. I knew that I had lost weight, but did not know how much. All of the others had lost weight also. One tough looking, muscular new man from a farm in South Dakota lost so much weight that the other Marines started calling him "Bones".

We continued South after crossing the Equator for several more days. Finally one morning we arrived at a low Palm Tree covered Island. We were told that it was the Tonga Islands (British) about 600 miles north of New Zealand. To our surprise, as we were pulling into the Harbor, there were several Transport Ships loaded with Marines! They were equipped with small landing craft. We soon figured out that this was no "hit and run" operation but that we were going to provide air support for a Marine Landing. The next question was where? There was a small town called Nukualofa on the Island and the crew was granted a few hours liberty. The crew of the ENTERPRISE was disgusted when they discovered that the strongest thing on the Island to drink was warm tea! The most exciting thing that happened to us in the Tonga Islands was that two Marines from the Units that had just departed, deliberately missed their ship and surrendered to us. Instead of throwing the wayward Marines into the Brig, as would be expected in this situation, Captain Ford had them assigned to the same duties as the rest of the Marine Detachment. Cleaning, Gunnery Drills, and 4 on and 4 off duty assignments. They had some difficulty adjusting to our routine. When General Quarters is sounded on a warship all hands literally run to their assigned battle station, whether it be in the Engine Room, in Sky Control high in the air above the superstructure, or one of the Anti-Aircraft Guns. When the General Quarters alarm is sounded it is like poking 3,000 men in the rear with a cattle prod at the same time. They start to move in a hurry like their very life was at stake, as it might very well be.

We caught up with the Marines on the Troop Transports in the Fiji Islands. They were to conduct a rehearsal landing and our aircraft were to supply air support and our escort vessels would provide Naval Gun fire

Support. The wayward Marines decided that they did not care for our rigid lifestyle and they wanted to rejoin their old units from which they had deserted. Captain Ford arranged for a small boat to transport them ashore and that was the last we heard of them.

We spent several days milling around the Fiji Islands and then pulled out, heading west. We still did not know where we were headed, but we knew the Marines were going to make a landing somewhere and we were to provide Air and Naval Gunfire Support. We were finally told that we were headed for the Island of Guadalcanal in the Solomon Islands and the Marines were to land and occupy the island. The Solomon Islands are roughly 1,000 miles northeast of Australia. They had recently been occupied by the Japs and we were going to kick them out!

After leaving the Fiji Islands, we continued on a course to the Southwest. Our training routine intensified. Planes of the Airgroup would be launched before daylight and we would go to General Quarters before daylight and before sunset. At other times we would be training and following our condition II routine of 4 hours on watch and 4 hours off. The Airgroup would have an airplane tow a sleeve (looked like a large long sock open at both ends) attached to the plane by a long cable for us to shoot at. The ship would rig a wooden sled from the stern of the ship attached to a long cable. The planes would practice dive-bombing and strafing attacks on the sled. Some days the sled would be brought back aboard intact, at other times only the cable would be left. The bombs were made of light metal and filled with water so it took a direct hit to damage the sled. The .50 Caliber machine guns from the fighters would chew it up pretty badly.

During my tour on the Enterprise, I had witnessed many airplane crashes, both on deck and into the water. The ship had a crash warning siren that sounded like a police car or fire truck. When I heard this sound, I always stopped what I was doing (as did many others) and tried to see what was going on. One afternoon as a fighter plane was returning from Combat Air Patrol, the pilot (a Navy Warrant officer) ignored a "wave off" from the Landing Signal Officer. This is the guy on the Port edge of the flight deck that has two paddles (they look like ping pong paddles). By use of the paddles, he signals the pilot that he is too high or too low, too fast or too slow. If the pilot is in the correct position, the Landing Signal Officer signals a cut. If not correct he signals a wave off. To ignore a "wave off" is serious business and results in the offending pilot having an audience with the Air Group Commander (in this case Commander John Crommelin, an outstanding pilot himself and one who expected only top performance from his pilots).

Immediately following the wave off, Commander Crommelin knew what was about to happen. He sounded the warning signal from his perch in Air Control and many of us looked up to see what was going on. The fighter plane missed the arresting cable, bounced over the crash barrier and landed on top of planes that were being serviced forward of the crash barrier. The spinning propeller of the fighter plane struck two members of the flight deck crew. To say that they were killed would be an understatement. They were sliced to bits! Body parts were spread over the forward part of the flight deck and into the gun galleries on the starboard side of the ship. Our gun gallery! We were sick, some lost their lunch and none of us on the gun gallery responded to "chow call" that night. The pilot of the plane was not injured. We continued to find small pieces of flesh in crevices on the gun gallery and in the recoil springs of our 20mm guns for several days.

We did not know what Commander Crommelin said to the pilot of the plane, but he put him back into the air the next day on Combat Air Patrol. When his four hour patrol was almost over, he was flying at about 12,000 feet off the starboard quarter of the ship, suddenly he nosed his fighter into a vertical dive and gave it full throttle. The plane came down faster than I had ever seen a plane dive before. It appeared that the pilot never tried to pull out of the dive. He crashed off the starboard quarter of the ship, the plane guard Destroyer did not bother to search the area, they probably figured that he could not possibly have survived the crash. The death of the pilot in this case was listed as accidental. Those of us that watched concluded that it had to be a suicide on the part of the pilot due to remorse for killing the two flight deck crewmen because he ignored a wave off. After this tragic incident, any time I heard the crash warning signal, I would get under something, usually the area under the edge of the flight deck where our 20mm ammunition was stored. For several years after this incident the sound of a siren would cause me to dive for cover, or if asleep, to jump straight up.

We arrived at Guadalcanal on August 7, 1942. This was not to be our usual "hit and run" routine, this was a hit and occupy operation, the first of many of this kind in the war with Japan. Reveille came early, about 3:00 a.m. We ate a hurry up breakfast and immediately went to General Quarters. The Air Group was launched before dawn, in order to arrive over the target area at daylight. The new battleship NORTH CAROLNA and our escort cruisers were sent to the landing area to shell the beach area with their big guns prior to the landing of the Marines. The Destroyers and the new anti-aircraft cruiser ATLANTA stayed with the ENTERPRISE.

Things went well aboard the ENTERPRISE on August 7th. The Marines on Guadalcanal appeared to be making good progress, they had secured the beach area and were taking the new Jap built airfield. They named it Henderson Field in honor of Major Loftin Henderson who was recently killed in the Battle of Midway. We were at battle stations all day, with a combat air patrol overhead and dive bombers on anti-submarine patrol. The remaining ENTERPRISE planes kept up a continuous bombing and strafing attack on Guadalcanal and the surrounding Islands. Our Radar did not work very well because of the mountains on the nearby Islands and those on Guadalcanal. After dark, we resumed our 4 hours on and 4 hours off routine.

August 8th was very much like the 7th. General Quarters before daylight and at our battle stations all day. The cooks would send sandwiches and coffee up to us for lunch. The planes took off before daylight and continued their air strikes in support of the Marines all day. After dark on the 8th, the Admiral in overall command decided that we had been in one place long enough. We moved off to the east of Guadalcanal. We were close enough to Guadalcanal that our planes could still provide air support for the Marines ashore on Guadalcanal. Our Cruisers and Battleship escort also rejoined us.

Late at night on the 8th, the Japs sent a large surface fleet down the chain of Islands that make up the Solomon Island group. Our Cruisers and Destroyers that had been assigned to protect the Marines on Guadalcanal engaged the Jap force. Three of our Cruisers and the Australian Cruiser CANBERRA were sunk. Damage to the Jap force was not known. When this news reached us on August 9th, there was a great deal of apprehension that the worst was yet to come. The Admiral in overall command of the operation ordered the partially unloaded transport ships in the beach area of Guadalcanal to cease unloading and depart the area! The Marines on Guadalcanal and Tulagi were left to get by on their own the best they could. At night, they were pounded by Jap Cruisers and Battleships. Our planes provided air support during the day but night air operations had not been developed yet.

I should mention the Admiral in overall command. He and the press referred to him as "Fighting" Frank Jack Fletcher. The crew of the ENTERPRISE (both officer and enlisted) referred to him as "Sinkem Fletcher". This did not refer to the sinking of Jap ships, but rather to the sinking of our ships. He was in Command when the SARATOGA was torpedoed in January. He was in Command in the Battle of the Coral Sea when the LEXINGTON was sunk and the YORKTOWN damaged. He was in overall command at Midway when the YORKTOWN was sunk and here he was in overall command at Guadalcanal. Little wonder that we were apprehensive after the four cruisers were sunk! The crew of the ENTERPRISE had nothing but praise for our old commander Admiral Halsey and our Task Force Commander, Admiral Kincade, but the mention of the name Fletcher and they would use swear words that should not be repeated.

After moving off to the east of Guadalcanal, we joined another Task Force built around the carrier SARATOGA. The SARATOGA had spent several months back in the states undergoing repairs after being hit by a Jap torpedo in January. She showed up at Midway one day after the Battle of Midway was over. Here she was at Guadalcanal with Admiral "Sinkem" Fletcher aboard! A few days later, the carrier WASP and several escort ships arrived. They had been in the Atlantic Ocean but were moved to the Pacific after the YORKTOWN was lost at Midway.

We were happy to see the additional carrier Task Force. Our morale increased from the low point of August 9th. We believed that with three carrier air groups and the additional escort ships we could handle anything that the Japs could throw at us. We failed to think about what Admiral "Sinkem" Fletcher might do to us.

After about 10 days, we started picking up reports of increased Jap activity to the north. To the north of the Solomon Islands was the Jap held Island of Truk (actually several islands). Truk was to Japan what Pearl Harbor was to the United States, a major Naval and Air Base. This was about 1,000 miles from the Solomons Islands. Mention a raid on Truk to members of the ENTERPRISE crew and their eyes would glaze over.

On the 23rd of August, our planes shot down a 4 engine Jap Flying Boat and made strafing and bombing runs on two Japanese Submarines running on the surface at high speed in the direction of Guadalcanal. It was obvious that something was in the works. At least it was obvious to everyone except Admiral "Sinkem" Fletcher. Early in the morning of August 24th he ordered the Wasp Task Force to the south to refuel! This reduced our strength by 1/3. By noon on the 24th of August, our scouting planes were reporting contact with Jap planes and the sighting of a Jap carrier Task Force. Planes from the SARATOGA also reported the sighting of a Jap carrier Task Force but in a different location. Our Admiral Kincade requested permission to launch an air strike against the Jap force reported by our planes. Admiral Fletcher said no. The pilots must have made a mistake since the ENTERPRISE pilots reported a Jap force in one area and the SARATOGA pilots reported a Jap force in an entirely different location He said we will send out an additional search flight and wait until we have better information concerning their exact location. By the middle of the afternoon, the search planes reported by radio the sighting of not one Jap Task Force, but two, all headed in our direction! Admiral Fletcher finally consented to launch a strike against the Jap force, but to keep about 1/3 of our planes in reserve and to increase the combat air patrol over the Task Force.

Around 5:00 p.m. our Radar picked up a large group of unidentified aircraft headed in our direction. We went to General Quarters. As I was running across the Hangar Deck to my battle station, I saw a navy Warrant Officer miss the hatch opening and crash into the bulkhead. He was out cold (we were all punch-drunk from a lack of sleep and exhausted from the 4 on and 4 off routine).

Additional fighter planes were launched and sent out in the direction of the unidentified aircraft that were rapidly approaching. The crew of the ENTERPRISE used words that should not be repeated when they observed Admiral Fletcher aboard the SARATOGA disappear over the horizon with the escort ships assigned to the SARATOGA. This left the Enterprise along with the NORTH CAROLINA, the antiaircraft cruiser ATLANTA, two other cruisers and four Destroyers. We were between the approaching Jap aircraft and the SARATOGA Task Force! Admiral Kincade, at the urging of Commander Crommelin disregarded the orders of Admiral Fletcher and gave the order to launch "every plane that will fly". In short order, all planes were in the air and the ENTERPRISE was braced for what was to come. All bombs had been stored in their proper storage area and the gasoline lines around the Flight Deck and Hangar Deck were drained to prevent the spread of fire if we should be hit.

A few minutes after the last planes were launched, Platoon Sergeant Joe Schinka, on the 20mm gun gallery on the port side, directly across the flight deck from my gun position yelled, "there the SOBs are" and he started firing. They were obviously out of range of his 20mm guns, but it told everyone else where they were. The 5 inch guns on the ENTERPRISE and the escorting ships started firing. As soon as the Dive Bombers were in range we opened fire also. These were the same type Dive Bombers that were used at Pearl Harbor. They had the familiar fixed landing gear and under each wing you could see the dive brakes that looked like a ladder hanging by one side (our Dive Bombers used split flaps with a lot of round holes in them). The round object between the landing gear was obviously the bomb! When dropped it looked like a giant ball coming toward us. I was always amazed to realize how much information could be stored in one's mind in a split second. At least two of the Jap Dive Bombers exploded in midair directly over the ENTERPRISE. It was no doubt caused by someone hitting the bomb with a direct hit from one of the anti-aircraft guns before the pilot could release it. Small pieces of the plane landed all over the place. The ENTERPRISE was moving at flank (top) speed and making sharp turns. The noise from the guns firing and the bombs hitting nearby were deafening. The concussion from the near misses knocked us down several times and we were nearly drowned from the geysers of salt water thrown up by the near misses. We knew that the ship had been hit, but we did not know where or how badly. The ship shook and bounced when we were hit. The attack lasted about five minutes (it seemed to be longer), there were burning Jap planes in the water all over the place. We soon learned that the ENTERPRISE had taken three bomb hits.

The most severe damage had been on the starboard quarter (right rear) of the ship. The Japs were using delayed action fuses on their heavy bombs. They would penetrate three steel decks before exploding. This caused severe damage below decks and blew a large hole in the side of the ship below the waterline. One of the bombs went through the ready service powder storage area on the 5" Gun Gallery on the starboard quarter causing the powder to explode. The explosion caused a large bump about two feet high in the Flight Deck immediately above the 5" gun position. All of the 37 men on the 5" Gun Gallery were killed instantly. These were the men we trained to operate the two 5" guns when Captain Randall convinced the Gunnery Officer and the Captain of the ship to transfer the Marines from the 5" Guns to the .50 Caliber and 20 Millimeter machine guns that were installed all around the

Flight Deck of the ship. All total, there were 83 men killed and many wounded. Four of the Marines were wounded, none killed.

Immediately after the last of the Jap planes departed, the Damage Control people started to repair the damage to the ship. The Flight Deck crew placed several large steel plates over the hole in the Flight Deck so that our planes could be recovered. The entire Damage Control Party on the 3rd deck was killed and it was necessary to organize other Damage Control Parties to start repairs on the damage on the 3rd Deck and to try to stop the flooding caused by the hole that was blown in the side of the ship below the waterline.

As soon as the Flight Deck repairs were completed, the ship turned into the wind and started taking our planes aboard. It took longer than usual to bring them aboard because of the bulge in the Flight Deck above the destroyed 5" Gun Gallery.

About the time the last plane came aboard, the U.S.S. SARATOGA with her escort ships appeared on the horizon steaming toward us with her signal lights flashing. To the surprise of no one, in a short time there were many men, officer and enlisted standing on the Flight Deck, shaking their fist and swearing at Admiral Frank Jack Fletcher on the SARATOGA. There was no way that this activity could be seen or heard from the SARATOGA but it gave the people involved an opportunity to relieve their frustration and dislike of Admiral Fletcher.

Our own Admiral Kinkaid and Captain A.C. Davis were watching this demonstration from the bridge but made no effort to stop it. They no doubt agreed with the people involved but were too dignified to join in the activity.

The activity on the Flight Deck was brought to an abrupt halt when without warning, the ENTERPRISE started making a sharp turn to the right. It was beginning to get dark and visibility was poor. The Captain had the warning whistle sounded just in time to prevent the ENTERPRISE from running over one of our own Destroyers.

It was soon discovered that the ships rudder was jammed in the full starboard (right) position. The rudder would not respond to control from the Bridge or from secondary control located in the after (rear) part of the ship. The ENTERPRISE was out of control and started making tight 360' circles. The escort ships had to scatter to keep from being run over by the ENTERPRISE. We continued in a tight circle for more than an hour before the problem could be corrected.

It was reported that the bomb damage had caused one of the two large electric motors that control the rudder to burn out. The remaining motor continued to function and caused the rudder to go to a full starboard position.

As it turned out, the delay caused by the Enterprise running in a circle for more than an hour was a blessing. Due to violent bouncing and shaking caused by the bomb damage, the ENTERPRISE Radar did not work properly. Our escort ships reported a large group of unidentified planes 50 miles away headed in our direction. It was not necessary to tell anyone what this meant. It was another group of Jap planes coming to finish us off.

The Jap planes approached our formation to about 15 miles and continued on a course that took them to where we would have been had we not lost time running in a circle while the damaged rudder control mechanism was being repaired. The Jap planes milled around in the area where we should have been for several minutes and then no doubt decided that they were not going to find us in the darkness, changed course and headed back to their own carrier.

We took up a course to the south to put us out of range of further Jap attacks for we were in dire need of repairs. Those Jap pilots must have had some uneasy moments of their own navigating back to their carriers more than 200 miles over open water in total darkness and then making night landings on their carriers. Night carrier operations were not developed until 1944 and even then it was on a very limited basis.

We also had another piece of good luck! The Jap bombs that hit the ship created severe damage because their delayed fuses did not go off until they had penetrated at least three decks. One small bomb exploded on contact when it hit near #2 Elevator. All of the near misses that created the huge geysers of salt Water that knocked us around and nearly drowned us must have penetrated at least 100 feet into the water before they exploded. Otherwise those of us manning the Anti-Aircraft Guns would have been torn to bits by bomb fragments had they been armed with contact fuses.

By dawn of the 25th of August we were well out of range of any further Jap air attacks. This was to be a busy day. The Damage Control people had worked all night making repairs. They built a framework of wood timbers and placed it over the hole in the ship's hull. They built a second frame of solid wood, placed it against the first wood framework, stuffed the area between the two with mattresses and pillows, then braced all of it with heavy timbers. Some water could still leak in through the repairs but the portable pumps were able to stay ahead of the leaks. The Air Group was launched, except for a few fighters and torpedo planes that were to remain aboard for our own protection. A few of the planes were sent to the SARATOGA and HORNET to replace losses from those ships. The majority of the Air Group was sent to Guadalcanal to help the Marines.

As soon as the Air Group departed, we changed course to the East and the word was passed that we were going back to the Tonga Islands. That was the British Island where we stopped before we went to Guadalcanal. The Navy Doctors and Hospital Corpsmen were busy taking care of the wounded and the job of cleaning up our old 5" Gun Gallery was assigned to the Marines! This was a chore that I shall never forget. We had trained the 37 Sailors that were killed on the two 5" Guns. We not only knew them, but except for the foresight and determination of Captain Carey A. Randall someone would be cleaning up our remains. All of the intact bodies were burned to a crisp. Their clothing did not exist, most were in pieces, but some were still in their assigned positions. The man that relieved me was still in the #5 Gun Trainers seat with his hands still on the control wheels. Our job was to place the bodies in a mattress cover, add a shell to make the body sink immediately (the shell weighed 58 pounds), then move the body down two decks to the stern and toss it overboard. This was done 37 times.

Anyone who thinks that War is glamorous might change his mind if he had to place burned body parts into a canvas mattress cover and then throw them overboard from a damaged ship. While the Marines were working on the 5" Gun Gallery, others were assigned the same type job removing the bodies of the 35 men that were killed on the 3rd Deck. One of the more intact bodies was prepared for burial in the traditional Navy method. This body was taken to the Quarter-deck of the Ship for formal services. The Chaplain held Memorial Services for all that were killed, the Marines fired a volley of three rounds, the table on which the body had been placed was tilted upward and the body slid fiom under the flag that had been properly draped and the body splashed into the water. If there were any dry eyes in the people attending the service, I was unable to see them for the tears in my own eyes! I try not to think about this episode in my life for the reason that after almost 50 years, I become emotional when I do so. Most of the Marines were unable to eat for at least two days. When they did eat, they discovered that the menu was rice, twice each day! The bomb damage on the 3rd Deck had wiped out most of the food supply. Some rice was salvaged, even the usual beans were destroyed.

The trip back to the Tonga Islands took several days. Everyone was busy cleaning and making repairs to the ship. When we arrived in the Tonga Islands, we discovered that the Navy had moved a Construction Battalion (commonly called SEABEES) to the Island. All of the fuel, water and anything else that could be moved was moved to the Port Side of the ship. This caused the ship to list to the Port Side, causing the damaged Starboard Side to tilt upward to where the hole caused by the bomb damage was above the waterline. The SEABEES welded steel plates over the hole, replacing the wood and mattress repairs made by the ship's crew. These repairs were not the best in the world, but they would keep the sea water out. We also took on fuel and some food. We were still on short rations, mostly rice, but the word was passed that we would go to Pearl Harbor for repairs at the Navy Yard. Everyone was happy to learn that we were on our way to Pearl Harbor and everyone believed that we would be there and away from the war for at least six months.

While we were still in the Tonga Islands, we learned that the SARATOGA had been torpedoed again! The SARATOGA had been torpedoed near Pearl Harbor in early December 1941 and had spent the first six months of the war back in the states undergoing repairs. The SARATOGA showed up at Midway a day after the Battle of Midway. After ducking out on August 24th when we were pounded by two Jap carrier Air Groups she had again been torpedoed by another Jap Submarine! The ENTERPRISE crew was really upset to hear this news, for they knew that the SARATOGA would spend at least another six months back in the states undergoing repairs.

The trip back to Pearl Harbor took about two weeks. We were on short rations but no complaints were heard. We had our usual drills and training but the crew was happy and could relax for the first time in several months. We were surprised on our return to Pearl Harbor. It appeared that everyone was waiting for us to arrive. Little did we know, we were escorted straight into the Dry Dock and as soon as the gangway was put into place the Navy Yard workers swarmed all over the ship like ants. We did not know that a Jap Submarine had sunk the Aircraft Carrier WASP in the same location where we were hit on August 24th. This left only the HORNET to assist the marines on Guadalcanal. Admiral Nimitz knew this and issued orders to the commander of the Navy Yard to assign top priority to the repair of the ENTERPRISE.

There were huge box-like pieces of steel all over the dock near the Dry Dock, in fact they looked like parts of a ship. They were indeed! As soon as Word reached Admiral Nimitz of our damage, he had plans of the ENTERPRISE flown out to Pearl Harbor and directed the Navy Yard to fabricate identical sections of the ship to replace the damaged areas. As soon as the water had been pumped out of the Dry Dock, the workers from the Navy Yard started cutting huge chunks of the damaged areas away. The workers worked 24 hours a day, seven days a week cutting the damaged sections with their cutting torches. The large Navy Yard Crane was moved alongside and as soon as a section was cut away it would be hoisted out of the Dry Dock and moved away. The workers cut more than 100 feet of the ship away, from the Flight Deck all the way to the bottom of the ship. When they had removed the damaged portions, the Navy Yard Crane would pick up one of the pre-fabricated sections, hoist it into place and the workers would Weld it into place. In a few days, the ship was beginning to look whole again. It was necessary to install all of the pipes and electrical lines, paint and spruce up the new sections, but in less than one month, the ENTERPRISE would put to sea again to return to Guadalcanal to help the struggling Marines. So much for the anticipated six months in the Navy Yard!

My friend Sergeant Charles R. Livingston and I watched the ENTERPRISE put to sea. We were not sorry that we were not aboard. We had been aboard the ENTERPRISE for almost three years, and we were transferred to the Marine Barracks, Navy Yard Pearl Harbor awaiting transportation back to the United States. We were about as happy a pair of Marine Sergeants as one would ever see. Livingston was headed for the First Sergeant's School in San Diego, and I was to be assigned to the Fleet Marine Force at Camp Elliott California near San Diego.

After about a week at Pearl Harbor, we went aboard the U.S.S. MOUNT VERNON for transportation to San Francisco. The MOUNT VERNON was a large troop transport. It had been a luxury Cruise Ship before the war, complete with a swimming pool and fancy oak and mahogany paneling. Most of the former staterooms had been torn out and row upon row of bunks installed, 5 deep with only about 16 inches between each bunk. There was just enough room to turn over in the bunk. The swimming pool also contained bunks, except that these were seven bunks deep (one on top of the other). What had been nice paneling now contained the initials of former troops that had occupied the spaces. I had thought that the wartime strength of the ENTERPRISE was crowded but we had plenty of room compared to the MOUNT VERNON. There were a lot of people being sent back to the states for reassignment to new ships and in addition, there were a lot of women aboard being evacuated. I have no idea how many since they had guards posted all over the place to make sure that the men did not enter the areas occupied by the women.

The trip to San Francisco took about seven days. We spent most of our time standing in line. Stand in line to eat, to use the head (bathroom) to go up onto the main deck for fresh air. By then it was time to stand in line again for the next meal. We finally arrived at the entrance to San Francisco Harbor. We passed under the Golden Gate Bridge and I was surprised at the size and height of the bridge. There was not a cloud in the sky, and the ship made a wide circle to get into the dock. The sun was bright and shining upon the city of San Francisco. The city was spread out all over several hills. After looking at nothing but ocean and some Islands for two years, I thought that San Francisco was the most beautiful city I had ever seen. We were to report to the Marine Corps Pacific Headquarters at 100 Harrison for transportation to San Diego.

We did not have the foggiest notion how to find 100 Harrison Street so we took a Taxi Cab to find the place. They issued our orders and provided a train ticket to San Diego. This was a Thursday and we were to report for duty at our new assignment on Monday. We thought that we would be given a 30 day leave and report at the expiration of the 30 days. They told us that we could get leave when we reported to our new duty station. We were naive enough to believe them! We arrived in San Diego late Friday night and spent the week-end on liberty in San Diego. I ran into my old friend John Wade from C.C.C. days. He was now a Platoon Sergeant, one rank ahead of me. He was on his way to St. Mary's University (near San Francisco) for Pre-Flight Training prior to transfer to Pensacola, Florida for Flight Training. He became a Marine Aviator and was promoted to First Lieutenant. He was killed in a plane crash in 1944. I never did learn the details of his death. He had been my best friend for several years and was one of the finest men I have ever known.

My three years in the Marine Corps had been, in spite of the trauma of combat and seeing friends killed, a reasonably happy experience. I was not prepared for what was about to happen to me. In modern terms, you would say that I was "stressed out". After ten months of almost constant combat, lack of sleep, and poor food I weighed 142 pounds. My normal weight was 165. In addition, I was a bit nervous and jumpy. An Ambulance or Fire Truck siren would cause me to jump straight up from a sound sleep.

I reported to Camp Elliott, California on Monday morning and was assigned to the 3rd Tank Battalion. I checked into the 3rd Tank Battalion and found them loading everything into trucks. I was told to get into one of the trucks. When I inquired as to what was going on, I was told that we were going to a new base at Oceanside, California called Camp Santa Margarita (later changed to Camp Pendleton) for some additional training and then we were going overseas.

I darn near fell out of the truck! I had just returned from two years overseas, had fully expected a 30 day leave, had been given a whole week end off and was headed overseas again! We finally settled into the new camp and I immediately applied for a 30 day leave. I was greeted with "no leave will be granted from this outfit, don't you know that there is a war on". I was lucky that I did not end up in the Brig when I said "what in hell do you think I have been doing since December 7, 1941?, I was at Pearl Harbor, the Marshall Islands, Wake Island, Marcus Island, Midway, Guadalcanal and had the hell pounded out of me off Guadalcanal".

The fact that my Combat Citation from the ENTERPRISE came in a couple of days later probably kept me from making Private and going to the Brig, for I had developed what we used to call a "crappy attitude". After moping around for a few days and dragging my feet, feeling sorry for myself, one morning, I said "what the hell" I might as well try to make the best of a bad situation. I had always been considered a Gung-ho type Marine and here I was acting like a jerk. I went down to the Tank Park to try to learn what I could about those things before we went overseas.

I had never seen a Marine Corps Tank! I couldn't believe what I was looking at. This was the biggest piece of junk that I had ever seen. They were put together with rivets and the weapons consisted of one .30 caliber Machine Gun and a 37mm gun in the turret. I said to the Warrant Officer in charge, "the damned Japs will open these things up like a sardine can". He didn't jump on me, but assured me that he had just returned from Tank School in Kentucky and that much better tanks would be provided by and by, until then we had to make do with these. This Warrant Officer (named Swackhammer) was one of the few decent people that I had encountered since checking into the Fleet Marine Force. The tanks had a siren on them that sounded exactly like the crash warning on the ENTERPRISE. Every time some jerk would set the siren off, I would duck for cover. This was a reflex action from the crash warning on the ENTERPRISE because of the two Flight Deck crewmen that were scattered over my gun position when the Fighter jumped the barrier and chopped them up with his propeller.

The Warrant officer observed my reaction and wanted to know what the problem was. After I explained the situation and told him that I would probably get used to the noise in time, he said "Why don't you go see the Battalion Doctor, he might be able to give you something to settle your nerves". As it turned out, this was the best advice I ever had. When I checked into the Battalion Aid Station I was greeted by the Hospital Corpsman who had the bunk next to mine in the Barracks. He took me in to see the Doctor (no hassle). The Doctor was not busy and invited me into his makeshift office. He wanted to know what my problem was. I told him that I was nervous, mad as hell because they had screwed me out of my leave and did not like the Tank Battalion. He wanted to know why I was nervous. I started with December 7, 1941 and gave him the whole "nine yards" including why I was jumpy around the tanks. He said "hell, no wonder you are nervous, I would be too". He said "this is a new base, they do not have proper medical facilities, tell you what I am going to do. I am going to send you to the Naval Hospital in San Diego for Observation. By the time they figure out that the only thing wrong with you is stress, they will give you a 30 day leave and by the time they get through screwing around with the paper work, this outfit will be overseas". I could not believe what I was hearing. With the exception of Warrant Officer Swackhanrmer this was the first person that had shown me the slightest consideration since my arrival in the United States.

The Doctor told me that he had to go to the Naval Hospital in San Diego on other business and if I could pack my gear and be ready to go in an hour he would take me to the Hospital. He said he would call the acting First Sergeant to tell him that I would be leaving. If he had said 15 minutes, I would have said I would be ready!

On the way to San Diego, the Doctor said that he would have me admitted for Observation, Undetermined Diagnosis. This would keep me in the Hospital for some time. That suited me just fine.

When we arrived at the Hospital, we went straight to the admissions office. The Doctor told them that I was to be admitted for observation. They wanted to know the diagnosis, he said "undetermined". When the necessary paperwork had been completed, the Doctor said he had other business to attend to. I thanked him and told him how much I appreciated his interest on my behalf. I was assigned to a ward, given a bunk and locker and told that they would call me when they were ready. I caught up on my reading for a couple of days and then was given a series of tests and interviews. To my surprise they gave me a weekend pass to be back at 0800, Monday morning. The following week there were more tests and the Doctor from the Tank Battalion from Camp Margarita came by to see me. He wanted to know how I was doing and also wanted to know if they were treating me OK. I told him that things were great and they had given me a week-end pass. I again thanked him, he departed and I never saw him again. However to this day, I still have a soft spot in my heart for Navy Doctors.

The next day, I had a long session with what we called a "Talking Doctor", a Psychiatrist. I had heard rumors about these people, but had never seen one. He lived up to everything that I had always heard about them. He said that the Medical Doctors had determined that I was suffering from stress and malnutrition, otherwise I was in good shape. He then proceeded to ask some of the dumbest questions that I had ever heard. Very much like Andy Griffith in No Time for Sergeants. He wanted to know if I was scared in combat, I said "hell yes, anyone that said he wasn't is a damned liar". He wanted to know what I thought about in combat, I told him "not a damned thing, you do what you are trained to do because things are happening too fast to think, you do your thinking when it is over". He dismissed me and that was the last that I saw of him.

The next day, I was called in to see the Doctor who was handling my case. He told me that my problem was stress and slight malnutrition. He said that he would recommend a high calorie diet and rest. I told him that I thought that a 30 day leave would cure my problem. I then explained that I had not had leave in over two years, he said "I think you are right".

In order to obtain leave, it was necessary to go before the Navy Captain in command of the Hospital. The Doctor made an appointment and escorted me to see the Navy Captain. He recommended that I be granted a 30 day leave.

The Captain wanted to know the circumstances. I told him that I had recently been transferred from the U.S.S. ENTERPRISE and also told him what we had been doing since December 7, 1941. When I said that I had not had leave in over two years, he said "30 day leave granted". You will report back to this Hospital at the end of the 30 day leave. I thanked him, gave a snappy salute and departed.

I had learned that there are times when you quit while you are ahead and I thought that I was really ahead of the run around that I had been given at the Tank Battalion. It took a couple of days for the leave papers to come through, but that didn't matter, I was going home for 30 days!

I rode a Greyhound Bus to Dallas with a layover in El Paso. I arrived in Dallas late in the afternoon and would have to wait until the next day to catch the train to Ladonia. I obtained a room in the Jefferson Hotel and started to think about what I was going to do until the next afternoon when the train left for Ladonia. I remembered that my former best friends, Lloyd and Sarah Vessels lived in the east part of Dallas. I had the address but did not know how to find them. I caught a Taxi Cab and he dropped me off at their house. They were really surprised and glad to see me. Little did I realize that this visit was to change my life forever and be the greatest thing that ever happened to me!

I was eager to find out if any of the girls that I once knew were still around. Everyone that I mentioned was either married or had moved away. Finally Sarah said, "why don't we introduce him to Christene, she should be home from work soon". They lived in a Duplex and as soon as Sarah heard noise next door, she went over and told Christene that she wanted her to come over and meet their friend. Sarah soon returned with what I thought was the most beautiful creature that I had ever seen! Her name was Christene McDonald from Wills Point, Texas. She had been caught in the rain and her hair was wet. She was embarrassed because she thought that she would be meeting one of their girlfriends. After we had talked for a while, I got up enough nerve to ask her if she would like to go down town and perhaps see a Movie. She accepted and departed to fix her hair and get dressed.

About an hour later Christene returned, she looked even prettier than before. We rode a Trolley into town and since she looked so nice, I suggested that we go to the Jefferson Hotel so that I could change uniforms. My Green Uniform was beginning to look messy, since I had spent two days on a bus in the same clothes. Christene waited in the Lobby while I returned to my room and hurriedly changed to my Dress Blue Uniform. When I returned to the Lobby, she really looked me over, thinking that I was some guy trying to pick her up. I explained that I was the guy she came with. She had never seen a Marine in Dress Blues before.

We went to a movie and later walked down to the Baker Hotel. They had a live Band and we danced to the music of White Christmas. We decided that that was our song! I wanted to order dinner, but Christene swore that she was not hungry. I later learned that she thought being in the Marine Corps I didn't have any money. The truth of the matter was I had money in my pocket and another $500.00 waiting for me in the Bank in Ladonia. I had been sending $25.00 per month to my Uncle Namon and he had deposited it in the Bank for me. In those days, $500.00 was a lot of money.

We talked and danced until around midnight and then took a Taxi back to Christene's home. I returned to the Jefferson Hotel and we agreed to see each other the next day. The next day, we ate Hamburgers and toured Fair Park. We had a good time and agreed that Christene would take the Train to Ladonia the next weekend to meet my folks. I took the Train at Union Station and three hours later arrived in Ladonia. In those days, there was passenger train service on a daily basis through Ladonia and also through Windom as well.

All of my folks were happy to see me and I was glad to be back into familiar territory. Things were different. All of the kids that I had known were no longer around. The boys were in the Military Service and the girls were married or had moved away. We were sworn to secrecy as to what was going on in the South Pacific and I soon ran out of things to talk to my folks about.

Christene was unable to come up to Ladonia for the weekend and it was decided that I would return to Dallas for the weekend. I stayed with my friends Lloyd and Sarah Vessels, next door to where Christene lived. We went to the movies and ate out both Saturday and Sunday. Christene had to work the following week and I returned to Ladonia. The following weekend, Christene came up to Ladonia and met my family.

We spent the weekend with my aunt and uncle Jack and Pauline Chaney in Windom. (In those days, unmarried couples slept in separate bedrooms). We had a picnic at Bonham State Park and attended a Movie in Bonham. We decided that a little diamond ring on display in the window of Brannons Jewelry Store would look nice on Christene's finger. (She still has the ring after 50 years). I realized that I was moving a bit fast, but also knew that I had to be back in San Diego in 10 days and that I had to allow three days to get back by bus. I also knew what happened to Marines that went Absent Without Leave and I didn't want any part of that. Christene returned to Dallas and informed her parents who were working in West Texas that she was engaged.

The following week, I said good bye to my folks and returned to Dallas. Christene's mother had returned to Dallas to get a look at the Marine who wanted to marry her daughter. She protested that we had not known each other long enough, but reluctantly gave us her blessing. We agreed to be married as soon as arrangements could be made. I did not know what awaited me in San Diego upon my return but considering my recent experience in the 3rd Tank Battalion, I was not looking forward to my return with a great deal of enthusiasm.

I returned to San Diego and checked back into the U.S. Naval Hospital for further assignment. They gave me another physical examination and pronounced me fit for duty. My orders stated that I would return to the 3rd Marine Division but I would not be reassigned to combat duty for at least six months. This suited me just fine and since the 3rd Marine Division was in the process of moving overseas, I was transferred to the Training Command at Camp Pendleton.

TRAINING COMMAND

The Training Command at Camp Pendleton, California was located 12 miles from the main Gate at Oceanside, California. Upon reporting to the Training Command, I was assigned to the Camouflage Section of the Engineer Battalion. The Engineer Battalion consisted of a Headquarters Company, an Engineer Company that trained Heavy Equipment Operators, Road and Bridge Builders and a Demolitions Unit. There was also a Pioneer Company that trained people to mark landing zones when assaulting an enemy beach, to set up supply dumps, water supplies and to assist the Infantry Units to move across a hostile beach. I had operated heavy equipment and trucks and had been in charge of a Survey Party in the Civilian Conservation Corps. How I ended up in the Camouflage Section I never knew, since I did not have the foggiest notion of their mission. It was obvious that the Marine Corps Personnel Classification System could stand some improvement.

I was not prepared for what greeted me when I reported to the Camouflage Section. There was a Captain, a Warrant Officer, a Technical Sergeant, three Staff Sergeants and several Sergeants. These people did not look like Marines and they didn't talk like real Marines. I was really confused when I found out that none of them had been in the Marine Corps for more than three months. I had been in the Marine Corps for three years, had been in combat at Pearl Harbor, raids on the Marshall Islands, Wake Island, Marcus Island, we escorted the HORNET on the Doolittle Raid on Japan, the Battle of Midway and the battle for Guadalcanal, and most of these people outranked me.

I soon discovered that except for myself, all other members of the Camouflage Section were Hollywood Marines. They had been given a Commission as Officers or as Non-Commissioned officers because of their technical skill. I had never heard of this arrangement! The Captain was Richard W. Day a movie Art Director. The Warrant Officer and the Non-Commissioned Officers were various technicians, including the Movie Actor Glenn Ford. The mission of the Camouflage Section was to design camouflage patterns for vehicles and equipment, including buildings, tents and artillery positions. About 90 percent of the time, I did not know what they were talking about since they used technical terms and Hollywood language. I decided that I would make the best of the situation since it was a lot better than my last assignment in the 3rd Tank Battalion!

Christene and I decided that we would marry as soon as arrangements could be made. Since I was 12 miles back in the camp, it was a real problem getting into town. Transportation into Oceanside consisted of an open truck with semi-trailer that hauled Marines to and from our area to Oceanside like a load of cattle. You also had to stand in a long line to get aboard the "cattle car" as it was called. The train from Los Angeles to San Diego was usually so crowded that it did not stop in Oceanside. The only regular transportation to San Diego was the Greyhound Bus. The line to get aboard the bus was usually wrapped around the Bus Depot three times in Oceanside and when trying to get back to Oceanside from San Diego it was the same procedure.

Because of the unreliable transportation problem, it was decided that Christene would ride the train from Dallas to San Diego and then take a Taxi to the Brennan residence in San Diego. I had met the Brennan family in 1940. Bill Brennan was a World War I Marine and he was always willing to be friends with young Marines. I had kept in touch with them and always dropped by to see them when we were in San Diego. Bill Brennan was a Plumbing Contractor. In 1940 he did the plumbing work on three nightclubs in San Diego. It turned out that the owners couldn't pay him and as a settlement gave him partial ownership of the three nightclubs. When World War II came along with the large buildup of Navy and Marines in the San Diego area, he became quite wealthy because of his partial interest in the three nightclubs.

When Mrs. Brennan learned of my problem she told me to have Christene come to her house and stay as long as necessary. Mrs. Brennan's gracious offer was accepted and Christene stayed with the Brennans for a week because I could not get away to go to San Diego. The Marine Corps philosophy was that if they wanted a Marine to have a wife they would issue you one! We did not know how we were going to obtain a Marriage License. My old buddy Bob Livingston was stationed at the Marine Corps Base in San Diego. Since the License Bureau was open only from 8 to 5 it was decided that he and Christene would obtain the Marriage License. Being a good, honest and truthful Marine, Bob Livingston told the clerk that his name was Frank E. Graves, signed my name to the application and walked out with the Marriage Certificate. His good wife Ruth Livingston had arranged for a Preacher and had him standing by at his home to perform the marriage on Friday night December 17, 1942.

In the meantime, I was trying to get from Camp Pendleton to San Diego. I stood in line for hours to get aboard the "cattlecar" for Oceanside. More hours to get aboard the Bus from Oceanside to San Diego. We were married at 11:00 p.m., Friday, December 17, 1942. Bob and Ruth Livingston stood up for us as Witnesses. There were no photographers or other activities by today's standards, but the Preacher tied the knot good and tight! We spent the night in San Diego, and the next day Mrs. Brennan drove us back to Oceanside and turned their Beach Cabin over to us to use as long as we needed it.

Transportation from Oceanside to the area of Camp Pendleton where my unit was located still involved many hours waiting my turn to ride the "Cattle

Truck". My luck took a turn toward the bright side in a few days. While eating lunch in the Mess hall, I ran into a Marine named Richard Martin who had been on the ENTERPRISE when I went aboard in 1940. He was being shipped overseas in a few days and did not know what to do with his car. He owned a 1934 Chevrolet four door sedan that he agreed to sell to me for $125.00. I wired the Banker in Ladonia to wire my last $125.00 from my savings account. He did so and I was the proud owner of a 1934 Chevrolet. The car turned out to be in good condition and solved my transportation problem.

Ruth Livingston found a two-bedroom house for rent in Mission Beach (near San Diego). She and Bob invited us to share the house and expenses with them. We took them up on the offer and moved to Mission Beach. All of our personal belongings did not fill the back seat of the 1934 Chevrolet! Gasoline was rationed, but if you had as many as four riders, they could sign your request and you could obtain a "C" Ration Card that provided adequate gasoline for the trips from Camp Pendleton to Mission Beach. It was easy to find four regular riders since transportation was a problem for everyone.

Chris obtained a Civil Service job at Lindberg Field where Ruth Livingston worked and she worked there for about three months, until morning sickness prevented her from working. Back at Camp Pendleton, things took a turn for the better for me. One morning when I was bored stiff working in the Camouflage Section with the Hollywood Marines a Captain that looked like old father time to me walked in. I saluted smartly while the Hollywood Marines stood around with their hands in their pockets. The "old" (must have been at least 50) Captain announced that he was looking for Sergeant Graves! In my best Marine Voice, I said "here sir". He introduced himself and shook my hand and said he would like to talk to me outside. I did not have the foggiest notion of what was going on but held the door open and followed him outside. He told me that he was a World War I Marine and that he had been called back to active duty.

The Colonel had decided that the Engineer Troops that we were training needed some basic Infantry Marine Training and that he was assigned the job. He told me that he had been looking at my record and noted that I had been to Machine Gun School and that I had acted as an Instructor of basic weapons aboard the U.S.S. ENTERPRISE. I stated that I believed that I was well qualified in those areas. He wanted to know if I would like to work for him. I did not tell him that I was extremely anxious to get away from those Hollywood types and work with real Marines! My reply was a hearty "yes sir". I checked out of the Camouflage Section, bid farewell to the Hollywood Marines and reported to the "old" Captain the next morning.

The Captain must have worked all night, for he presented me with a training schedule and told me to get busy. I got the last word in, I saluted smartly and said Yes Sir! My schedule required that I teach the .45 Caliber Pistol, M-1 Rifle, Browning Automatic Rifle, .30 Caliber Machine Gun,

Squad and Platoon Infantry Tactics and lead the trainees through the Obstacle Course on a daily basis. I was extremely busy and happier than I had been in a long time. I did not know what a good situation I had fallen into.

We soon learned that the "virus" that was causing Chris so much trouble was called Pregnancy! We started really looking for a place to live in Oceanside so that I could be home every night. In addition to my work schedule, the drive to Mission Beach and back using only park lights on the car was a nerve chilling experience. You could not use headlights because of the "blackout" along the coast. It was frequently foggy along U. S. 101 and it was difficult to see more than 10 feet. We finally located a small apartment in Oceanside and moved there immediately. It was still necessary to drive 12 miles to my assignment at Camp Pendleton, but this was a great improvement over driving 32 miles to Mission Beach on U.S. 101.

After about a week in my new assignment, the "old" Captain came to see me again. He said that he had been looking at my record again and noticed that Captain Randall had recommended me for Platoon Sergeant while I was still aboard the ENTERPRISE. He wanted to know why I had not been promoted! I said, "That is a mystery to me. When Captain Randall recommended my promotion, all promotions were made from Marine Corps Headquarters, but it is my belief that they no longer do that". He stated that he would see what he could find out and departed. In about a week he again came by where I was conducting class and told me that I was now a Platoon Sergeant! I was delighted, and told him so.

This promotion not only increased my basic pay, but this rank also recognized a Marine's right to a wife and provided an extra allowance called a Quarters Allowance for the top three enlisted ranks.

As soon as my class was over, I Went to the Supply Department and drew my allowance of Platoon Sergeant Chevrons. I took them home to Chris so she could sew them on my uniform while I was at work.

When I arrived home the next night, Chris proudly presented me my uniform with the new Platoon Sergeant Chevrons sewed on by hand with tiny almost invisible stitches, she must have worked on it all day. There was only one thing wrong with them, they were sewed on up-side down! She was crushed! With my peculiar sense of humor, I thought it was funny. I stated that if we had an Eagle to put on top of the Chevrons, I would be a Navy Chief Petty Officer. I think we both learned a lesson in assuming. I assumed that she knew how the Chevrons should be sewn on and she assumed that the arrow should point down and that the rocker belonged on top. After all these years, we can still laugh about it.

By this time, it was March 1943. The war was serious business and the troops that we were training would be assigned to units to go to the Pacific as replacements for troops killed or wounded in the Island Campaigns that were really heating up by 1943. An amusing incident took place that I shall always remember. There were two really sharp (smart) Privates First Class who were assigned as training assistants. These two guys were forever bitching to go fight the Japs! I kept telling them that this war was going to last a long time and they would have time to fight all the Japs they wanted to fight before it was over. These guys were eager, so every Monday morning they would request to see the Colonel. The Colonel, like my "old" Captain, was also a World War I "retread they were called". (The term "retread" came into use because the old slick automobile tires were recapped with a small amount of rubber to provide new treads and extend their useful life). The two eager PFC's would see the Colonel to request assignment to the next replacement unit for combat duty. The Colonel would listen to their story and then run them out of his office. This routine went on every Monday morning for about two months.

Finally the Colonel had enough, he threw them out of his office and told them not to come back. When he decided that they should be assigned to combat duty he would let them know. The next Monday morning, the two eager PFC's were absent. We could not find them and they were declared absent without leave. About three weeks later, we received a report that our missing PFC's were with a replacement unit headed for combat duty! The report stated that an investigation revealed that our two PFC's showed up on the Dock in San Diego where a Transport was tied up loaded with a Replacement Unit that was to sail on Monday morning. Because the Replacement Unit was headed for combat duty, the troops had been given a final weekend liberty in San Diego.

Our PFC's marched down the Dock to the Gangway of the Transport. When they were in speaking range of the Sentry on the Gangway one of our smart PFC's announced in a loud voice where the Sentry would be sure to hear him, "I have changed my mind, I am not going overseas and they cannot make me". The other one said, "you and I have been buddies since High School, if you are not going overseas, neither am I". The Sentry, ever mindful of his duty, placed the two of them under arrest and called for the Sergeant of the Guard. They threw our two PFC's into the Ship's Brig and the Ship sailed on Monday morning. After the Ship had been at sea for a few days and everyone had been accounted for, someone said "what about those two guys in the brig?" It was at this time the unit learned they had two extra people aboard. They released them from the brig and requested that we transfer their records to the Replacement Unit.

Our Colonel was not pleased when he received the report. In fact you could hear him all over the building. Between wars, he was the City Engineer of the city of Oakland, California. He was yelling that he had been outsmarted by young Engineers before, but he could not believe that he could be outsmarted by two PFC'S. I have often wondered if these two guys made it through the war. One thing that I am certain of is they encountered all of the Japs they wanted to see!

About two months after Chris had sewn the Platoon Sergeant Chevrons on all of my uniforms and shirts, I was walking through the Battalion Headquarters one morning when a young Major who was the Battalion Executive Officer stopped me. He stated that the Marine Corps had started a new promotion method for Senior Non-commissioned Officers. Starting immediately, there would be area wide promotion tests which would include all Marines at Camp Pendleton, Camp Elliott (near San Diego) and the Marine Corps Base at San Diego. He said he realized that I had been a Platoon Sergeant for only a short time but that the Captain in charge of the Training Unit had reported that I was doing an outstanding job and he had recommended that I be permitted to take the examination for Gunnery Sergeant. I was very pleased and told the Major I would continue to do a good job, that I was happy in my present assignment and thanked him for his confidence in me.

The area promotion examination was conducted the following week. The test consisted of about 150 questions, most of which were the very things I was teaching! The remaining questions were general things that most Marines should know. I thought I would make a good grade on the examination. The results of the area promotion examination were published the following week. Much to my surprise, I was number 2 on the list of about 150 people who had taken the test. In about three days, the authority came through for my promotion to Gunnery Sergeant! I couldn't have been happier, my pay would now be about $90.00 per month! I obtained the appropriate chevrons and took them home to Chris. She was happy to remove the Platoon Sergeant Chevrons and sew on the new Gunnery Sergeant Chevrons.

By the end of May, 1943 Chris was feeling much better and had started to gain some of her weight back. She weighed about 115 pounds when we married, but with the morning sickness, in fact she was sick most of the time, she was unable to eat and as a result her weight was less than 100 pounds. My normal weight of 165 had returned and I was getting lots of exercise on the obstacle course. Our eating habits increased and we developed a bad habit that was to make fatties out of both of us. The Drug Store in Oceanside had plenty of Ice Cream but no cones. We would take a large bowl to the Drug Store several times each week and have them fill it with Ice Cream. We would bring it home and eat all of it because there was no way to keep it overnight. We had a small, inefficient Refrigerator but it would not keep Ice Cream. This routine accelerated our weight gain.

My training assignment was going great and I was really happy, but I had a feeling that things were too good to continue. The War in the Pacific was getting cranked up and I had a feeling I would be transferred back to the Pacific soon. In early July, the Battalion Sergeant Major called me in and said "pack your bag, we have to send a Gunnery Sergeant to the First Sergeant's School in San Diego and you are it". I protested that I didn't know anything about being a First Sergeant and that I was happy being a Gunnery Sergeant. He told me the purpose of the school was to teach me how to be a First Sergeant and the issue was not debatable. I was to report to San Diego on Friday and the 6 week class would start on Monday, his final word was "get going".

When I checked into the First Sergeant's School, I discovered that my old buddy from the ENTERPRISE Bob Livingston was the First Sergeant and the First Sergeant from the ENTERPRISE Bill Parham was now Warrant Officer Parham and he was the Officer in Charge of the School. I thought that I could negotiate a deal with these two old friends to change my assignment and avoid the First Sergeants School. Their reaction was "don't be so stupid, you can do the work and if you work at it, the top 50% of graduates will be promoted one grade, that would put you in the top enlisted grade".

Chris and I were expecting our first baby in September and we could use the additional money that the promotion would bring. Because of this, I decided to put forth my best effort. This meant that I would go home only on Wednesday night and weekends. The other nights would be devoted to study. The First Sergeant's School consisted of all types of Marine Corps Administration, daily personnel reports, monthly Muster Rolls to Marine Corps Headquarters, calculating monthly Payrolls for the troops, supply and legal procedures. We had to type and prepare all of the reports.

I had taken a typing course in 1938 while in the CCC Camp at Wolfe City, Texas. I had not touched a typewriter since 1938 and had difficulty finding the home keys. Much to my surprise, a few days later my typing skill returned. I thought, this is just like riding a bicycle, once you know how to do it, you never forget. I must have put forth more effort than most of the students. Beside that, I kept my mouth shut and listened to the Instructors.

Many of the students were former Company Clerks who thought they knew more than the Instructors and frequently argued with them. One of the Instructors, an old time First Sergeant, would stop all debate by announcing, "Son, if you don't think that is right, just wait until you get your test paper back". I used the same statement many years later as a Teacher when one of my students wanted to argue a point.

About 10 days prior to graduating from the First Sergeant's School my friend Bob Livingston came into the Classroom and asked me to come with him to his private office. My grades in class were excellent and I wondered what this was all about. He told me to sit down and then handed me a piece of paper. It was a telegram from my Uncle Jack Chaney saying that my father had killed my Stepmother and himself. While I had not been really close to my father since I was a child, I was totally devastated. Bob Livingston told me to take the rest of the day off.

I went home to Oceanside and Chris knew that something was wrong when I walked into the Apartment. We tried to figure out what to do. It would take three days to get to Texas and Chris was unable to travel since the baby was due in September. There were only about 10 days left in School and since I could do nothing to change the situation, we decided that I would not try to go to Texas for the funeral. This was a most traumatic period in my life, so much so that I never tried to find out the details of the tragedy and never discussed it with my own children because it was too painful to think about, much less discuss. I discovered that hard work was the best therapy for grief and trauma. I returned to the First Sergeant's School and put all of my energy into the class work.

My efforts were effective. There were 40 of us who had survived the rigors of the First Sergeant's School at graduation the following week. My class standing was No. 9 out of 40. I was promoted to First Sergeant immediately. This was now the middle of August 1943. I could not believe that I had been promoted from Sergeant to First Sergeant in a period of six months! I was not yet 21 years of age and was one of the youngest First Sergeants in the entire Marine Corps.

I returned to Camp Pendleton and was assigned duties as First Sergeant of the Pioneer Company, Engineer Battalion, Training Center. This was a complete change of pace. I no longer spent all of my time with the troops, but instead spent most of my time in the office doing paperwork. Chris continued to fix me a good breakfast, and a large evening meal. I would usually eat lunch in the mess hall. I had a Company Clerk, PFC Francis X. Gibbons. He was about 40 years old and had been a successful manager of a Loan Company in Portland Oregon. He was extremely efficient and was the biggest con artist and scrounger that I ever knew. He would con the cooks out of eggs, bacon, bread, butter and cheese. He had a hot plate in the back room. Every morning about 10 a.m., he would bring me a toasted bacon, egg and cheese sandwich. I was not getting a lot of physical exercise and with Chris' good cooking and Gibbons morning sandwiches I started to gain weight rapidly. Chris was also gaining weight rapidly. There were no Navy Medical Facilities for dependents at Camp Pendleton but there was a good little Community Hospital in Oceanside. Chris had been seeing a lady Doctor in Oceanside and she was to deliver our baby in the Hospital there.

The name of the Lady Doctor was Kelley. Dr. Kelley's fee for the pre-natal care, delivery and the care of Chris and the baby through the 6 week checkup would be $75.00. My pay as a First Sergeant was now $125.00 per month. As I recall, Dr. Kelley agreed to accept a down payment of $15.00 and $10.00 per month for the balance. A private room in the Hospital would be $7.50 per day. Dr. Kelley stated that Chris would be in the Hospital for 10 days. This created another big bill, but it was better than driving all the way to the Naval Hospital in San Diego.

By the time Chris was to go to the Hospital she weighed 160 pounds. The Doctor was not concerned, said she would lose the weight after the baby was born. I might mention that I was up to 180 by this time. After we had eaten dinner on September 28, 1943 Chris said she thought that we should go to the Hospital. Dr. Kelley checked her and told me to walk her around the inner courtyard of the Hospital for about an hour. While we were walking (the windows to the rooms surrounding the courtyard were open), there was a blood curdling scream from one of the rooms. A young girl who was about to deliver, suddenly decided she did not want to have a baby and wanted to call the whole thing off. This was somewhat unsettling for Chris, but like the good trooper she has always been, she soon settled down. When the hour of walking was up, we went back into the Hospital and Dr. Kelley told me to go to the waiting room and promptly escorted Chris to the Delivery Room.

I had been out in the boondocks working with the troops for several days and was very tired. Instead of pacing the floor like expectant fathers are supposed to do I fell asleep in a chair. Sometime later a Nurse came in, shook me and announced that I was the father of a healthy baby girl. Mother and daughter were doing fine. The baby had a full head of dark hair and we named her Sharon Kathleen. She weighed 8 pounds 14 ounces. We were both very proud of her. I visited Chris and Sharon every night after I came home from work at Camp Pendleton. The Doctor made Chris stay in bed for 10 full days. As I recall she was not permitted to get out of bed until the 10th day. That was the way they did things in 1943. When I took Chris home, she was as weak as a kitten. The 10 days in bed along with the trauma of childbirth had taken its toll on her strength.

She eventually gained her strength back and there were no serious problems. We managed to pay the Doctor and Hospital Bills and to save a few dollars each month. Christmas and New Years came and went. Chris was beginning to want to go home to visit her parents and to show our Sharon to everyone at home. By March 1944 we had saved enough money to buy round trip bus tickets from Oceanside, California to Wills Point, Texas. I managed to get leave and we left for Texas by bus. This was quite an experience. The trip took three days and nights. Each day when the bus would stop long enough for the passengers to eat, I would take care of Sharon while Chris went into the kitchen at the bus stop. She would talk them into letting her borrow a pan to use to sterilize the bottles for Sharon's formula. After she had sterilized the bottles, she would mix enough formula to last one day. In the meantime I would eat whatever I could while taking care of Sharon and get a sandwich or hamburger for Chris to eat on the bus.

The bus was filled to capacity and at El Paso we had to change busses and we spent hours waiting for the next bus. To make matters worse, because of the crowds waiting at the Bus Depot, I had to stand in line for several hours to claim our seats on the bus. I was wearing my uniform and military personnel were given priority in boarding the bus. We finally got aboard the bus and departed for Dallas.

The bus was late in getting into Dallas and we missed the last bus that would take us to Wills Point. The next bus for Wills Point would be about

10:00 a.m., the next day. We decided that since we were both exhausted and getting a little ripe, that we would find a Hotel, get a bath and try to get some sleep. We found a Hotel near the Bus Depot and obtained a room. Soon after we got into the room Sharon went to sleep. While Chris and I were in the Bathroom getting ready for bed, Sharon woke up and must have thought that she had been abandoned. She started crying and there was no stopping her. We did everything that we knew to keep her from crying, including going outside the hotel and walking up and down the street, still she cried. We finally decided that we were disturbing everyone else in the hotel and decided to check out and go back to the bus depot. After some time back in the bus depot, Sharon settled down and went back to sleep. There was no sleep for her parents!

We managed to get a seat on the bus the next morning and arrived in Wills Point by noon and were met by Mr. and Mrs. McDonald. They had spent most of the night waiting for us at the bus depot in Wills Point. We spent several days with Chris'parents and then borrowed their car to go to Ladonia to visit my folks. We spent a few days visiting in Fannin County and then went back to Wills Point.

Shortly after we arrived back at the McDonald's, Chris' Aunt Lottie and Uncle Tommy Alsop and their young son Little Tommy arrived for a visit. They were living at a place called Oak Ridge, Tennessee. Tommy was working at a Defense Plant, but he did not know what they were making. He was a pipefitter and he said they would run pipes up to a wall and someone on the other side would continue the work and that he never talked to the people on the other side of the wall. He said they could not discuss what they were making, but that was easy because he did not have any idea what they were doing. He said that it must be something very powerful because the officials were always telling them their work was very important and the work they were doing must be very accurate. He said to convince them there must not be any leaks in the pipe joints one of the officials brought in a container of some substance and put a large piece of meat into the container and the meat disappeared! Tommy said what confused him was that there were carloads of material coming into the plant, but he never saw anything going out.

Right after VJ Day they announced that Oak Ridge, Tennessee was the main Uranium processing plant which produced material to make the Atomic Bombs that were used at Hiroshima and Nagasaki to bring World War II to an end.

Lottie Alsop was always a worrier and could become excited very easily. When they announced they had been producing material for the Atomic Bombs at Oak Ridge, Lottie stampeded! She loaded Little Tommy and their belongings into the car and told Big Tommy that they were getting out of there! They moved back to Texas in a hurry. As far as I know they never went back anywhere near Oak Ridge, Tennessee.

We also visited my half brothers and sisters who had been placed into Buckner's Orphans Home in Dallas. It was not a very happy visit, considering the reasons that they were there. After a few more days in Wills Point, we again boarded the bus for Oceanside. The return trip was a repeat of the trip to Texas, with a long lay over in El Paso. We arrived back in Oceanside late at night and obtained a taxi to take us back to our Apartment.

We met a young lady on the bus who was the bride of a young Marine stationed at Camp Pendleton. When we arrived in Oceanside there was no one to meet her and she was stranded with no money and no place to stay. I figured that her husband was unable to get liberty or was out in the boondocks training. We invited the young lady to come home with us as we had a couch that made into a bed and she could sleep there. She took us up on our offer and the next day I managed to locate her husband. We never heard from them again, but Chris and I were glad that we helped them because we well remembered how helpful Mrs. Brennan and Ruth and Bob Livingston had been to us.

A short time after returning to Oceanside, we made a trip to San Diego and traded the 1934 Chevrolet in on a 1937 Ford two door sedan. It was a good move, because the Chevrolet was getting a little tired.

Back at Camp Pendleton, rumors were making the rounds that the Engineer Battalion, Training Center would soon be disbanded. By early July, the rumors were confirmed and the entire Battalion was deactivated. Personnel were scattered to other units. Gibbons (my company clerk) was sent out with a Replacement Unit. Someone along the way decided that he was a little old for "foxhole duty" and they dropped him off at Camp Catlan, near Pearl Harbor. I had a letter from him and he indicated that he was bored with his assignment.

For some unknown reason, my orders were a little late in arriving, and to my surprise they directed that I be assigned to the Sea School at the Marine Corps Base, San Diego as First Sergeant! I couldn't believe that my streak of good luck was still running!

When I checked into the Sea School, I was greeted with open arms by the Captain in Command. He stated that the former First Sergeant was doing a sloppy job and that he couldn't figure out a way to get rid of him. There was a very bright PFC Company Clerk who was quite capable of running the office by himself if left to his own initiative. To say that I was happy to be the First Sergeant of this organization would be an understatement! I had graduated from this school in January 1940 and the Trash Can that we used to polish until it looked like a mirror was still in place in the Barracks. I applied for Base Housing and was looking forward to moving Chris and Sharon to San Diego. I could only manage to go home to Oceanside on Wednesday night and on weekends.

The Sea School Training was well organized and efficient. When the troops finished their training they would be placed into what was called a Sea

Pool. When orders came in to transfer one or more men to a certain ship, the ones who had been graduated the earliest would be sent out first. This worked quite well until one day we received orders to send 20 men to a certain ship. The bright young PFC Company Clerk had been giving me the names of the men to be assigned to the various ships. When the orders came in to send another 20 men out at the same time, I started checking the records and discovered about 15 men who had finished their training more than a year earlier, still hanging around the barracks (seemingly doing very little) and waiting for an assignment to Sea. I put their names on the list to be transferred. The efficient young PFC said "Top you can't send those men overseas. I said "why not, the written directive is very specific, the first graduated, the first out". He said "yes but those guys are the Colonel's Basketball Players". This really upset me. I well remembered the many times aboard the ENTERPRISE after I had pulled my own duty and would be getting ready to go on liberty the First Sergeant would grab me and say "Graves, the Whaleboat Crew has to practice and you have to stand their duty". To add insult to injury, the Whaleboat Crew had a special training table it was called, and as the rest of us would be lined up for breakfast in the ship's mess. We had to pass the Whaleboat Training table. Those guys would be eating steak and eggs for breakfast and they would give us the "raspberry" as we passed their table. This was before World War II and the Navy always served Beans and Cornbread for breakfast on Wednesday and Saturday morning. I could handle the beans, but those Navy Cooks always put sugar in the cornbread. I couldn't handle that!. As a result of this, I developed a keen dislike for Athletes that survives to this day.

The Colonel's Basketball Players departed and I told the PFC that from now on, we carry out the orders exactly as written. He said "OK but remember, I Warned you". I realized later that the PFC was the smarter of the two of us. He no doubt spent the rest of the War as Company Clerk of the Sea School.

The following week, the "roof fell in". At 11:00 a.m., one morning the Base Sergeant Major called me and said "Graves there is a train leaving at 10:00 a.m., tomorrow morning and you are going to be on it. It is going to Mare Island, at Vallejo, California. There is a Cruiser there waiting for you. The name of the Cruiser is the U.S.S. MONTPELIER." I told the Captain what had happened and he said "we will see about this". A short time later, he came in and said "the orders are firm, you had better pack your bag".

I packed my bag, and left for Oceanside to tell Chris the news. There was no time to waste. We knew where the MONTPELIER would be headed, for MacArthur was getting ready to invade the Philippine Islands.

We had taken many small photographs with our camera, but since we did not know when or if I would be back, it was decided that we would have a family photograph taken of the three of us at a Photo Studio in Oceanside that afternoon. Chris managed to contact her father who agreed to come to

Oceanside and drive she and Sharon back to Texas where they would stay until I returned.

Chris, Sharon and I said our good-byes and I departed on the train at l0:00a.m. the next morning. This was late August 1944. On the Train to Vallejo I reflected upon the events of the last few days. Sent overseas with 23 hours notice! I had no way to know for sure, but over the years, I have harbored a strong suspicion that sending the Colonel's Basketball Team overseas brought about my quick transfer to the MONTPELIER. It could have been mere coincidence, but my suspicions remain and it did not improve my view of Athletes in general.

Upon my arrival in Vallejo, I took a taxi to Mare Island and was told by the Sentry on the Gate of the Navy Yard where I would find the U.S.S. MONTPELIER. As ships go, the MONTPELIER was relatively new. It had been commissioned in 1942 and had been fighting the Japs ever since.

I was escorted to the Marine Detachment Office. I quickly realized that the Marine Detachment was in complete disarray. The Commanding Officer for the past two years had been promoted to Major and was being transferred. The First Sergeant had been promoted to Warrant Officer and had already departed. The Detachment Clerk was being transferred in a few days and the young PFC who had been assigned the duties of Detachment Clerk could not find the home keys on the typewriter!. A check of the remaining members of the Marine Detachment revealed that none of them could use a typewriter. (At least no one would admit that he knew how to type). I soon realized that in addition to my other duties, I would get to type all of the various reports. I was used to the efficiency of Francis X. Gibbons and the young PFC at Sea School (that I had concluded was much smarter than myself.)

As ships go, the living accommodations were not too bad. I had a bunk in the office. In fact there were three bunks in the Marine Office, one on top of the other. The Detachment Platoon Sergeant occupied the bottom bunk, I had the middle bunk and the Blackfoot Indian Gunnery Sergeant occupied the top bunk. In addition, there was a lavatory and a locker for each of us. The shower facilities were nearby in a Compartment occupied by Navy Personnel. The three of us ate in the Chief Petty Officers Quarters located in the aft portion of the ship. The balance of the Marine Detachment were quartered in a Compartment where the Detachment Office was located. They used the same shower facilities that we used but they ate in the crews' mess.

When I was not otherwise occupied with the duties of the Marine Detachment, I spent my time getting to know the U.S.S. MONTPELIER. I learned that she was a Light Cruiser. Not "light" in terms of displacement (she was 10,000 tons, about 1/2 the tonnage of the ENTERPRISE) but because the largest guns were 6 inch. To be classified as a Heavy Cruiser required that the Main Battery be 8 inch guns. The Montpelier was equipped with 12, 6" guns in the Main Battery and 12, 5" guns mounted in dual mounts. These were the exact type 5" guns that we once manned on the

ENTERPRISE, except that these were enclosed in steel containers called mounts.

In addition, there were sixteen 40 Millimeter Anti Aircraft Guns in open mounts with two guns in each mount. There was an additional sixteen 20 Millimeter Guns located in various parts of the ship from the bow to the stern. These guns were manned by the Marines and were exactly the same as those on the ENTERPRISE.

The MONTPELIER carried a crew of about 1200 sailors and 60 Marines. The ship was 600 feet long and only about 80 feet wide. It was long and sleek and capable of doing 35 knots (about 38 mph).

When I reported aboard the MONTPELIER, it was in Dry Dock. I remembered that when the ENTERPRISE went into Dry Dock, in Bremerton Washington, in 1940 that the entire crew went over the side on boards called stages and we scraped the bottom of the ship and painted it by hand. It took at least two weeks to complete the job. I noticed that the workers in the Navy Yard were sandblasting the sides and bottom of the MONTPELIER when I went aboard. Two days later they had not only completed sandblasting, but had painted the entire hull and the ship was moving out of Dry Dock.

The Marine Major departed and that left a young 2nd Lieutenant Byron C. Turner and myself as the senior Marines aboard the ship. Lieutenant Turner was a nice enough guy. He was a 1944 Graduate of the Naval Academy and this was his first assignment.

Having spent almost three years on the ENTERPRISE, I knew that the Executive Officer of the Ship ran the internal operations of the Ship. The Captain was in Command of the Ship, but the internal day to day operations were under the direction of the Executive Officer. I had not been aboard the MONTPELIER more than 24 hours when the Executive Officer sent for me. I soon learned that he had no use for Marines! It was obvious that my life would be miserable as long as he was aboard ship. He ordered that either the Gunnery Sergeant or myself would be under arms on the Quarterdeck of the ship at all times. I protested that we had other duties, but he said that is the way it was going to be! To me, this was living proof of the old saying there are more Horses Asses than Horses!

In a few days, a Marine Captain named Thomas T. Grady reported aboard. He was from Georgia and had an accent you could slice with a knife. It took me several days to get my ears tuned into his accent. He was fresh from the Jungles of New Britain with the First Marine Division. He had obviously been taking his Atabrin regularly to avoid Malaria because he was as yellow as a Chinaman.

The Navy, Yard workers were swarming over the ship like ants. Rumor had it that we had taken some losses in Leyte Gulf in the Philippines and it was obvious they wanted the MONTPELIER back in the war as soon as possible.

I had asked Chris to come to Vallejo for a few days, but when it became obvious that we would not be in the Navy Yard much longer, I sent her a telegram telling her not to come. She had already departed from Wills Point when her parents received my telegram. They contacted the Railroad and she turned back at Midland.

Two days before we were due to sail from Vallejo a fire broke out in a critical part of the ship, destroying electrical cables that were critical to the operation of the ship. This delayed our departure from the Navy Yard for at least one week.

As soon as repairs had been completed, we sailed from the Navy Yard at Vallejo, passed under the Golden Gate Bridge at San Francisco and set sail for Hawaii. Just before we left the Navy Yard, my luck took a turn for the better. The (Horses Ass) Executive Officer of the Ship was transferred. As he departed the ship, I was on the Quarter Deck as he had directed, instead of wishing him luck in his new assignment, I was cheering. Captain Grady wanted to know what that was all about and I explained what he had been doing to the Marines since I had reported aboard. The new Executive officer of the Ship turned out to be the best friend that the Marines could ever want. For this I was truly grateful. If we had a problem he was always willing to help us.

One big job that I accomplished while the ship was in the Navy Yard was to check the clothing size of all of the Marines and prepare requisitions for the Supply Depot in San Francisco to provide us with a two year supply of clothing, underwear and shoes. This was no easy task, since there were no computers to do this type of work. As it turned out, we were gone for a year and a half and our supplies were more than adequate.

Enroute to Pearl Harbor, all Departments of the ship conducted training exercise. There were many new men in all Departments. The Marines were a part of the Gunnery Department. The "Gun Boss" was a full Navy Commander, an old timer who knew what he was doing. He put us through some rigid and time consuming training exercises that would come in handy very soon.

In my spare time (there was very little of it) I researched Marine Corps Regulations looking for an obscure regulation that permitted a swap of personnel from a Ship's Detachment to a ground unit as long as a mutual swap could be arranged. What I had in mind was to swap PFC Schmidt (the Detachment Clerk who could not find the home keys on the typewriter) for PFC Francis X. Gibbons if he was still at Camp Catlin. I discussed my plan with Captain Grady and he gave me the go ahead. He also realized that PFC Schmidt was about as useful as "teats on a bull".

When we arrived in Pearl Harbor, the crew was not allowed to go ashore on liberty, however I made arrangements through Captain Grady and the friendly Executive Officer of the ship to go ashore on "official business". I went looking for PFC Gibbons. I found him at Camp Catlin. He was bored with his job and would be happy to transfer to the MONTPELER if it could be arranged. Our next stop was to visit the Commanding Officer of Gibbon's Unit. The Commanding Office was an "old time" Major who was also bored with his job, he also wanted to go "fight the Japs". He said he would not stand in the way of anyone who wanted to "fight the Japs" and he agreed that the MONTPELIER would do that in short order. He said "send me a warm body in exchange for Gibbons". I told him I would send him a young PFC who was supposed to be a Clerk, but that he could not find the home keys on the typewriter, and that he was absolutely useless around the office. The Major said he could find something to keep PFC Schmidt busy. There were a lot of commodes that needed to be scrubbed every day. I helped Gibbons pack and took him back to the Ship with me. Captain Grady was a little surprised that I had arranged the transfer.

PFC Schmidt was not happy to be moving to Camp Catlin but I told him there were more urgent needs than his happiness. We sent him to Camp Catlin and that was the last I heard of him. PFC Gibbons was somewhat of a curiosity not only to Captain Grady but to the rest of the Marines as well. Most of us were in our early to late twenties and Gibbons was 40. He finally told them that he had been a successful business man, but that he and his wife of 12 years had divorced. He said he gave her all of their property and joined the Marines. He had no difficulty in adjusting to life aboard ship and made friends with the rest of the Marines in short order. My life was much easier because I did not have to personally prepare and type all of the various personnel, supply and pay reports.

After taking on supplies of food and fuel, the MONTPELIER departed from Pearl Harbor for the Gunnery Range on one of the small Hawaiian Islands. As we came around Ford Island I had an opportunity to observe the Harbor. I was amazed at the progress made in restoring the Harbor to Pre War conditions. Except for the remains of the ARIZONA, all of the other damaged ships had been raised and repaired. We spent two days firing at targets on the small island and calibrating the fire control systems that controlled the guns. When this was completed we went back to Pearl Harbor, topped off the fuel tanks and took up a course to the west. Everyone knew where we were going but there was no official word until we cleared the Hawaiian Islands. The Captain (Captain Harry Hoffman) came on the PA system and announced that we were headed for Leyte Gulf in the Philippine Islands with a fuel stop at the Atoll of Ulithi, located south of the Island of Guam.

The ship set a zig zag course to confuse any Jap Submarine that might be lurking in our path and we conducted extensive gunnery drills all day, and part of the night. We would go to General Quarters (maximum alert, with all hands at their assigned battle stations) one hour before daylight and one hour before sunset each day. We would secure from General Quarters after about two hours and then conduct routine training the remainder of the day. By the time we arrived in Ulithi, the crew was working like a well oiled machine. We received a supply of food and topped off the fuel tanks at Ulithi. The anchorage at Ulithi was full of ships of all descriptions. I saw my old ship ENTERPRISE in the distance. Early the next morning all ships got underway heading west toward Leyte Gulf. The MONTPELIER was assigned to the 7th Fleet Bombardment Group. This meant that our job was to shell the landing beaches before the troops landed and to stand by to shell any Jap gun positions or other targets as requested by the troops ashore. We carried two old obsolete, fabric covered float planes. These were biplanes (two wings) that were launched from the Catapult located on the stern of the ship. They could do about 90 miles per hour when they were in a hurry, but they served their purpose as spotters for our naval guns.

While we were at Ulithi I was struck by the number of ships of all types anchored in the Lagoon. I counted at least 10 Aircraft Carriers, several new Battleships and Cruisers and more Destroyers and support ships than I could count. This was a different war than the one that I had known two years before. In 1942 every time we would go on a strike, we would have at least one ship sunk or damaged. That meant the next operation we went on would be short the number of ships that were sunk or damaged on the last trip. There were no replacements. We had more ships in our 7th Fleet Bombardment Group than we had in the entire Pacific Fleet in 1942. In our Task Force, there were 4 relatively new Cruisers like the MONTPELIER, several Old Pre-War Cruisers and about 10 Destroyers. In addition, at times we had 6 "Jeep" Aircraft Carriers. These were small Carriers built on a Cargo Ship Hull. They were commonly called Kaiser Coffins because they were mass produced by Henry Kaiser. They carried 12 FM-2 Fighters (these planes were just like the Grumman F-4-F's that we had on the ENTERPRISE except they were built by General Motors). The Grumman plant was turning out the new Grumman F-6-F Fighters that were more than a match for the Jap Zero's. The new Fighters were assigned to the large Carriers of the Fast Carrier Task Force. The Jeep Carriers also had 12 Grumman TBF Torpedo Bombers that could carry Bombs or Torpedoes. Once the planes were in the air it made no difference where they came from. We really appreciated the air cover they provided. The Kaiser Coffins were called that because they had no water tight compartments and if they took a hit, even a relatively small one, they would sink. The regular ships such as the Large Carriers, Battleships, Cruisers and Destroyers could take a lot of damage because they were designed with many Watertight compartments (rooms) and would stay afloat even when severely damaged. After evening General Quarters, the Captain of the ship would get on the PA system and tell the crew what we would be up against when we reached Leyte Gulf. The Japs had what they called a Special Attack Corps of Kamikaze (Suicide planes). They were giving the U.S. Fleet a bad time and many ships had been badly damaged or sunk. The bombs they carried would do extensive damage and the gasoline would spread fire over a large area. The only way to stop them was to destroy them in the air. If they were damaged, even on fire they could still crash into a ship, kill many people and sink or severely damage a ship.

We arrived in Leyte Gulf in late November. The next day, we were introduced to the Suicide Planes. About 30 of them made runs on the ships in our group. One of them hit an old pre war cruiser on the stern where the float planes were stored. The damage from the bombs was severe and the gasoline from the float planes created a large fire. I never did learn how many people were killed. The Cruiser did not sink but had to go home for extensive repairs.

The Captain of the Ship (Captain Hoffman) really knew how to handle a ship. I think he was an old Destroyer Sailor. He ordered "Flank Speed" (this is as fast as a ship will go). He performed violent tums, would have two engines flank speed forward and the two engines on the other side of the ship flank speed reverse and full rudder. The ship would shake violently and seem to move sideways in the water. They claimed we shot down several of the Suicide Planes, but it looked to me like we ran out from under them.

This was to be the Captain's standard procedure any time that we were under attack. The crew, including this young Marine First Sergeant thought that Captain Hoffman was the greatest Captain in the entire U.S. Navy.

All of the ships in the group were running low on fuel. Soon a Navy Tanker appeared in Leyte Gulf. All of the ships in the formation formed a huge circle around the tanker. The tanker was dead in the water (stopped). The tanker could fuel two ships at a time, one on each side of the tanker. The other ships continued to circle (it was like Indians circling a wagon in the old western movies) the tanker at 25 knots. When it was time for two other ships to fuel they would peel off from the formation and head for the tanker while the ships that had just refueled would take their place in the circle. The ships in the circle would fend off attacking planes to keep them from hitting the tanker, because ships without fuel are useless.

When it came time for the MONTPELIER to fuel we approached the tanker, tied up to it and took on fuel. The entire crew was nervous. If a suicide plane should break through the formation and hit the tanker, it would not only destroy the tanker but the two ships taking on fuel as well.

Shortly after we finished taking on fuel we rejoined the circle and a few minutes later a group of suicide planes made a run on the formation. Captain Hoffman immediately ordered "Flank Speed" while the rest of the formation remained at 25 knots. We remained in our same relative position in the circle but at times we would be twisting and turning, skidding sideways and going in the opposite direction from the rest of the group.

Four suicide planes made a run on the MONTPELIER. I saw three of them crash close by and thought the 4th plane had also crashed. There was smoke from our guns and flames and smoke from the burning planes that littered the water everywhere you looked. All of a sudden the 4th plane popped through the smoke a short distance from the ship. He was headed directly at my gun position amidship on the Port (left) side of the ship. We continued to fire all of the automatic weapons (40 and 20 Millimeter) guns at him. He was too close for the 5 Inch Guns to bear on him. The last thing that I remember was seeing his left wing catch fire and collapse!

The next thing I remember was members of my gun battery pulling an airplane wing off of me. I was cold and could not understand why I was cold because it was extremely hot and humid in Leyte Gulf.

The next thing I saw was an arm severed between the shoulder and elbow lying beside me. I thought that it was mine and picked it up and tried to replace it on my shoulder. It would not fit! At this point, I realized that the arm did not belong to me. There were several other body parts scattered around me. I stood up and was checking my legs to see if they were still in place. I must have been a sight to behold because my gun crew started laughing at me. All members of my gun crew were accounted for with no serious injuries.

The arm and other body parts were that of the pilot of the suicide plane. The reason that I was cold was that I was soaked in Jap aviation gasoline from the plane. I was told that when we hit the plane and knocked his wing off and set him on fire, he crashed into the Water putting the fire out. The bomb went off in the water blowing the plane up onto the ship. God must have been on our side that afternoon for there was no one killed on our ship. There were several injuries but it could have been a disaster. It would have killed half of the people on the Port side of the ship if the fire had not been extinguished and the bomb exploded in the water. It was many years later before I could discuss this incident without becoming emotional.

We were not bothered by any more suicide planes and it was soon dark. We secured from General Quarters and the evening meal was served. I did not attempt to eat because my stomach was still queasy from the recent attack. I attempted to sleep that night but every time I closed my eyes I could still see burning airplanes trying to crash into us.

There were more suicide plane attacks the following day, but we now had fighter air cover from the Jeep Carriers. We were really glad to see those Navy Pilots. We had previously been provided air cover by Army P-38's. They remained at high altitude and the very first burst from our 5" Anti-Aircraft Guns, they would clear the area. The 5" AA Guns made a lot of noise and the air burst from their projectiles created a lot of smoke, but as far as I was concerned they were largely ineffective. On the MONTPELIER and when I was aboard the ENTERPRISE the 5" Guns were not nearly as effective as they were supposed to be. By the time the suicide planes were within range of the 40MM and 20MM Guns, they were too close for comfort. Those Navy Pilot's in their little FM-2 Fighters were not afraid of our 5" AA Guns. The suicide planes would be making a run at us, we would be blasting away with the 5" Guns and the Navy Pilots would stay right on their tail with the leading edge of their wings winking as they blasted the suicide planes with their .50 Caliber Machine Guns.

I never saw one of our planes shot down by the 5" AA Guns. The Navy Pilots were a nervy bunch or else they knew we couldn't hit anything with the 5" AA Guns. We were so busy with the suicide planes, we were not assigned the task of providing close support for the troops on the Island of Leyte. Other units of the Fleet were taking care of this important mission, including some of the old Battleships that were severely damaged at Pearl Harbor on December 7, 1941.

Some of the old, recently repaired and modernized Battleships were able to get revenge on the Japs in October right after the landings on Leyte. The Japs decided to throw everything they had available to break up the landing operation. They approached Leyte Gulf from three different directions but their operation was not as well coordinated as it might have been. Two of our Submarines spotted their fleet in southern Philippine waters and as elements of their fleet were navigating the narrow waters of the Surigao Straits (Between Leyte and Mindanao) they were first attacked by our P.T. Boats then by our Destroyers. As the Japs were about to clear Surigao Straits into Leyte Gulf, the old Battleships were waiting for them. Many of the Jap ships were sunk or damaged by the old Battleships. The survivors turned tail and started back through Surigao Straits where they were again attacked by our Destroyers. The Jap forces that were coming around the northern end of Leyte were spotted by our Carrier Planes and pounded severely. Many of their ships were sunk, including the giant Battleship Musashi.

We continued operations in Leyte Gulf for several more days. The Jap suicide planes would attack two or three times each day, but there were not quite as many as before. We were credited with shooting some of them down, but I still say we ran out from under them, because the Captain continued his violent evasive maneuvers. The Chief Engineer complained to the Captain that he was going to tear the ship up, that it was not designed to be handled like a Destroyer. The Captain told him, "better me than the Japs. If we wear this one out, the taxpayers will give us another one. Your job is to see that you provide flank speed when I call for it. 'My job is to carry out my mission and get this crew home alive if at all possible." This information went through the ship like wildfire and the crew was further convinced that Captain Hoffman was the greatest Captain in the U.S. Navy.

All of the ships in the group were burning up ammunition rapidly and we were running low on ammunition. A few days later an Ammunition ship appeared in Leyte Gulf. The same procedure for loading ammunition was followed as was taking on fuel. The Ammunition Ship stopped in the middle of Leyte Gulf, the ships in the formation circled at a safe distance. We thought being tied up to a fueler was bad enough, but an Ammunition Ship was something to make the hair stand up on the back of your neck.

When it became our turn to take on ammunition, Captain Hoffman eased the Montpelier alongside the Ammunition Ship and a crane was used to load a cargo net full of ammunition from the Ammunition Ship to the deck of the MONTPELIER. Captain Hoffman got on the PA system and announced that all hands not engaged in critical duties bear a hand stowing ammunition. The quicker we load and stow our ammunition, the quicker we will pull away from the Ammunition Ship! You never saw such eager workers in your life! I am unable to recall ever having seen Senior Officers perform manual labor. We had full Navy Commanders and many other officers of lesser rank working like ordinary sailors and marines carrying ammunition down the deck to the Ammunition Hoist to be lowered into the ammunition storage area below deck.

We had a very smooth operation, working like a well oiled machine because everyone knew what would happen if a suicide plane should break through and hit the Ammunition Ship. Fortunately for us, either the suicide pilots did not know what was going on inside the circle of ships or else they had orders to go for the larger ships. Our ammunition was loaded and stowed below in record time and we departed from the Ammunition Ship in a hurry.

In early December, we departed from Leyte Gulf. We were happy to get away from the suicide planes, even for a few days. We went to the Pelau Islands, about 600 miles southeast of the Philippine Islands. The Marines had landed on the Island of Peleliu in September and had a really tough time taking the Island from the Japs. We dropped anchor at a place called Kossel Passage at the Island of Babelthaup, the largest Island in the Pelau Island group. We finally received mail. We had been moving so often our mail could not catch up with us. There were many letters from Chris. She had written almost every day, I lined her letters up by postmark date to read them. I was happy to learn that she and Sharon were doing well. They had obtained a small apartment in Wills Point. I had made out an allotment of my pay to her and she was receiving it every month. I kept $10.00 per month for myself which was adequate for my needs.

We knew there were still many Japs on the Island of Babelthaup, but they had no way of getting at the Marines on Peleliu because the Navy had sunk all of their barges and landing craft. At night, we could see many small fires on the Island. After the war was over, I read an Intelligence Summary that said there were 40,000 Japs removed from the Island of Babelthaup. If they could have gotten across to where the Marines were on Peleliu, they could have given the Marines a lot of trouble.

We departed from Babelthaup after two days and set course back toward Leyte Gulf. We soon joined a large Task Force that contained many troop and supply ships. The Captain came on the PA System and announced we were going back to the Philippines and we would provide support for the troop landings that were to be made on the Island of Mindora. There was still fighting going on at Leyte Island but it appeared that the Island would be secure soon. We were under the overall command of General MacArthur and he was eager to kick the Japs completely out of the Philippine Islands. His idea was to bypass many of the Philippine Islands and land our troops on the Island of Mindora. This is a large Island off the Southwest coast of the big island of Luzon. He could build airfields on Mindora and the planes from these airfields could provide air cover for the landings that would be made on the main Island of Luzon.

We continued our training and always went to General Quarters (all hands at battle stations) before daylight and before sunset each day. This would normally last for at least two hours. We were cruising at a slow pace, because the formation could only move as fast as the slowest ships. In this case it was the LST's. Their official name was Landing Ship Tanks, but their crews referred to them as Large Slow Target. They had a flat bottom and clamshell doors at the bow. When it was time to land the Tanks or trucks, they would run up onto the beach, open the clamshell doors, lower and ramp and the Tanks or Trucks would drive onto the beach.

We reentered Leyte Gulf. As we approached the west side of Leyte Gulf all of the ships in the formation lined up like ducks in a row in a single column. We soon discovered why as we entered Surigao Straits. This is a narrow passage between the Island of Leyte and the large Island of Mindanao to the south. As there were mountains on each side of the straits, our guns would not be very effective against any Japs that might be up on the mountains looking down upon us. We could see planes from our Aircraft Carriers bombing and strafing ahead of us, keeping the Japs busy while we navigated the narrow straits. There were many small islands in the straits. If there were Japs on them they kept quiet as we passed. Once we cleared the Surigao Straits, we were out into open water again in the Sulu Sea. This is a large body of water sitting almost in the middle of the Philippine Islands. We by passed the Islands of Cebu, Bohol and Negros to our north. These are rather large Islands and we knew they contained Jap airfields.

Our Carrier Airplanes had really worked them over and there were not as many suicide planes around as there were a few weeks earlier. We were all surprised at the number of small Islands. They were everywhere. The Captain said there were 7,000 islands in the Philippine Islands and about two thirds of them were unoccupied. Some of them were nothing more than large rocks or Coral Reefs sticking out of the water. Many others were quite large.

We arrived at the Island of Mindoro in the middle of December and provided gunfire support while the troops went ashore. General MacArthur landed shortly after the beach had been secured. The fighting on Mindoro was not as severe as it had been on Leyte. Apparently General MacArthur put one over on the Japs because they had not expected him to make a landing on Mindoro so soon.

Our Radar System, while much improved from those we had in 1942, still did not work very well when there were mountains around. The Jap suicide pilots would frequently come in very low between the mountains and the fleet and be on top of us before we knew they were around.

Early one morning off Mindoro, there was a low overcast. All guns were manned but it was quiet and no one expected an attack. All of a sudden a large twin engine Jap suicide plane dropped out of the overcast and headed straight for one of the small Jeep Aircraft Carriers. It looked like there was no way he could miss the small carrier. He was out of range of the 40MM and 20MM Machine Guns. We all watched with our mouths open. When the suicide plane was within a few yards of the small carrier, a gunner on a 20MM Battery on the Carrier came alive and got off three rounds, pop, pop, pop.

The Jap Plane pulled up and just barely skimmed over the Flight Deck of the Carrier. He must have been within 10 feet of crashing into the Carrier. The gunner on the Carrier must have hit the pilot and caused him to pull back on his controls for after skimming over the Flight Deck of the Carrier he continued to climb. He eventually climbed straight up for a few thousand feet, stalled out and fell off on one wing toward the surface of the Sulu Sea. He hit the water midway between the small Carrier and the MONTPELIER. There was a terrific explosion. Parts of the plane went out in all directions. Several seconds later a wheel from the main landing gear landed near the MONTPELIER.

By this time everyone was fully alert, including Captain Hoffman. He got on the PA system and said, "What is wrong with those 5" guns this morning? Are they all constipated?" I personally think everyone was so surprised, not expecting an attack through the low overcast that it took several seconds for them to respond and in a few seconds it was all over. By this time everyone on the ship was a little punch-drunk due to the stress and lack of sleep.

There is something strange about the crew of a ship. I first noticed it much earlier on the ENTERPRISE and now the same thing on the MONTPELIER. If a man had a "Battle Station" topside on one of the guns or below deck in the Engine Room, when the General Quarters alarm sounded he would run at top speed for his "Battle Station".

Aboard the ENTERPRISE off Guadalcanal in 1942 I saw a Navy Warrant Officer knock himself out cold when the General Quarters alarm sounded. Everyone was tired and more or less punch drunk from stress and a lack of sleep. This Warrant Officer ran toward a hatch (door) and missed it, crashing into the bulkhead (wall) and knocked himself out cold.

Aboard the MONTPELIER off the Island of Mindoro a Navy Chief Petty officer from the Engine Room was up on the main deck getting some air one afternoon. Suddenly out of nowhere, two suicide planes dove on the MONTPELIER. One landed amidship off the starboard side and the other on the port side. I don't know how they missed us. The Chief Petty Officer was so anxious to get back to his Engine Room he dove head first down the ladder going down to the next deck. He was knocked out cold and had a lot of bruises and cuts. He took a lot of kidding from the other Chief Petty officers. Not from me. I had learned early in the war not to blame a person for anything he did in a situation like that.

After a few more days at Mindoro, the Captain announced the situation on the Island was in good shape and we would be going to Manus Island in the Admiralty Group, just north of New Guinea.

We were running low on food and ammunition. The fuel supply was adequate since Tankers were usually available. We certainly used our share of fuel while dodging suicide planes at flank speed during their frequent runs on the MONTPELIER. There were rumors that we would pick up a large invasion fleet at Manus Island for an invasion of the main island of Luzon. Everyone was hoping we would have mail waiting for us at Manus.

We arrived at Manus Island a few days before Christmas. Manus Island is below the Equator and really hot and humid. As we crossed the Equator the crew put on the (I call this really stupid) ceremony to make "Shellbacks" of the men who have never crossed the Equator. It is an ancient ritual and there is a King Neptune Rex that is supposed to come aboard. What it boils down to is an official sanction of abuse and beating of the new men. It is supposed to be harmless but they make up canvas clubs stuffed with rags or cotton which would ordinarily be harmless, but the usual idiots in the group would soak the clubs in water which made a rather lethal weapon out of them. They required the new men to run the gauntlet and they would beat them as they ran down the deck. I was not very popular in the Chief Petty Officers Mess because I would have no part of the ceremony. I referred to it as Neptune's Nonsense. Fortunately the nonsense only lasted one afternoon.

When we arrived at Manus Island we noticed there were many ships in the harbor of all types. There was a continuous coming and going of ships. We received a large collection of mail and there were many letters from Chris which I spent some time reading and was happy that she and Sharon were getting along all right.

We received a generous supply of food and loaded ammunition until all ammunition storage spaces were filled. Some of the men were permitted to go ashore to a Recreation Area, but I stayed aboard ship to try to catch up on the paperwork that had been neglected while we were in the Philippine Islands. It is difficult to concentrate on doing paperwork and report preparation while being attacked by suicide planes.

Earlier I described our living quarters aboard the MONTPELER. There was a 40MM Battery on the main deck above our compartment. I soon realized when our Radar picked up a contact the 40MM Gun directly above us would swing out in the direction of the Radar contact.

I could be asleep but when the gun trained out the electric motor noise that powered the gun would immediately awaken me. I knew General Quarters would be sounded in a few minutes so I would get out of bed, put my clothes and shoes on and head for my battle station by the time the alarm sounded. The Gunnery Sergeant (Blackfoot Indian from Montana) who occupied the top bunk would sit upright in his bunk when the alarm sounded and about 9 out of 10 times would bang his head on the overhead. As I went out the hatch for my battle station he would be rubbing his head and swearing at the Japs, blaming them for causing him to bang his head. He could never understand why I was such a light sleeper.

We departed Manus Island the end of December. The rumors were confirmed, we were headed back to the Philippine Islands and would, according to Tokyo Rose., invade the Island of Luzon on January 9, 1945. It was obvious this was to be the "big one". I did not know there were that many ships in the entire Navy. There were ships of all types as far as you could see. Beyond the horizon where you could no longer see the ships there were ships masts. The masts looked like a forest of trees that had no leaves. We were told there were 800 ships of all types in the invasion fleet.

While we were moving at a slow pace so we would not run off and leave the ships that could only make 8 knots, we received word Admiral Halsey and his fast Carrier Task Forces were hitting the Jap airfields in the Philippines, Formosa and the coast of China about 600 miles West of the Philippine Islands. This was good news for us, because we believed we would need all the help we could get when we hit Luzon. The Japs would obviously use everything they had to defend Luzon.

They knew if we controlled the Philippine Islands, we would cut off the supply of raw materials they were getting from Borneo, The Dutch East Indies (now Indonesia), French Indo China (now Viet Nam) and the Malay Peninsula. In addition, they had many thousands of troops in those areas that would be cut off from the home islands of Japan.

There were about a dozen small Jeep Aircraft Carriers assigned to this operation to provide air cover for the invasion fleet and for close support for the troops on the ground once they were ashore. There were several of the old prewar battleships, many cruisers and destroyers plus a new type ship called a Destroyer Escort. These new ships were smaller than a Destroyer and were good to have around to keep the Jap Submarines away from the fleet.

By this time, PFC Francis X. Gibbons had made friends with all of the sailors that were in strategic assignments, especially the cooks and bakers. He would con them out of fresh baked bread and butter. For some reason the Navy would not serve fresh baked bread but would leave it on the shelf for at least two days before serving it. It was quite a treat to see Gibbons show up with fresh hot bread from the ships bakery. He was generous and shared with all of the Marines.

He also managed to con the Pharmacists Mates out of a few ounces of 190 proof Alcohol on a regular basis. At times it was necessary for him to trade some Marine Corps shoes, socks or underwear for critical items like

Sick Bay Alcohol. I looked the other way because we had a storeroom full of Marine clothing. He always shared the critical items he promoted from the Navy. This made it easy to overlook his breach of regulations.

On the way back to the Philippine Islands, we received authority to promote two PFC's to Corporal. I convinced Captain Grady one of the promotions should go to PFC Gibbons. He agreed and our chief con artist was now a Corporal in the U.S. Marine Corps. Gibbons was happy and more determined than ever to make life a little easier for the Marines.

When we arrived back in Leyte Gulf, we were greeted by more suicide planes. We now had operational airfields on Leyte and the recently occupied Island of Mindoro. The Japs were still able to sneak a few suicide planes in on us.

The Japs were beginning to get desperate, so they added a new wrinkle. They now had suicide boats and small Submarines. The suicide boats looked a lot like what we now know as Ski Boats. Very trim and fast. Our PT Boats would engage them and do a good job keeping them away from us. Late one afternoon, one of them managed to get near the MONTPELER and before we could hit him his engine conked out. The Captain called for a cease fire. He wanted to capture the Jap and hoist the boat aboard the MONTPELIER. The Jap would have no part of being captured. He jumped overboard and would not be rescued. This was fine with the Marines, for we all knew the Marines would have to man the ships brig if the Jap surrendered. We had enough work to do manning our battle stations without having to guard the brig on a 24 hour basis.

The boat was hoisted aboard the MONTPELIER and it was discovered there was about 800 pounds of explosives aboard the boat. The explosives were thrown overboard and the Navy Machinists repaired the boat and overhauled the engine. They painted U.S.S. MONTPELIER on it and later used it as a runabout when we were in a rear area. That boat could really move. The crews of the other ships were very impressed with the MONTPELIER runabout.

After our arrival in Leyte Gulf, General MacArthur moved his Command Post to one of the Cruisers in our group. At times, we could see him through our Binoculars on the open Bridge of the Cruiser smoking his corn cob pipe. Word came back from the Cruiser that while we were under attack by suicide planes, he would stand on the open Bridge and watch what he called "the show." If he was afraid of the suicide planes like the rest of us he certainly put up a good front.

It took some time to move all of the ships through the narrow confines of the Surigao Straits. On this trip we had continuous air cover not only from the Jeep Carriers but from airfields on Leyte and Mindoro. It was certainly a different war from what it had been in 1942.

We all listened to the Japanese Propaganda put out by Tokyo Rose. Her broadcasts were not as scary as they were in 1942. A lot of her information contained enough truth to make one wonder what her source of information was. We had many ships hit by suicide planes, but she reported more ships sunk or damaged than we had in the area. She continued to report that we would invade Luzon on January 9, 1945. She said there were thousands of brave Japanese waiting to throw our troops back into the sea when we landed on Luzon.

The invasion fleet moved out of the Sulu Sea and into the South China Sea and worked its way up the West Coast of Luzon to Lingayen Gulf. The invasion of Luzon would be made at the exact spot where the Japanese landed in 1942! The MONTPELIER, along with the Cruisers CLEVELAND, COLUMBIA and DENVER (all identical to the MONTPELIER), plus many Destroyers were assigned the task of patrolling the South China Sea to the North and West of the landing area to stop any Jap ships that might try to interfere with the landing of the troops.

This operation was the largest operation we had ever been a part of. There were many Army Divisions in the initial assault and would be followed up immediately by many additional Divisions. This was the second largest Amphibious Landing in History so we were told, exceeded only by the Normandy landings in Europe. From what I could see, I completely agreed.

The landing at Lingayen Gulf was different from Leyte. The terrain was more open and not as much rain and mud to contend with. The Tank Units could move much better. In a few weeks they had freed a lot of our prisoners that were still held at Cabanatuan and had recaptured Clark Field and soon had it back in operation. The number of fighter planes increased dramatically. Soon we were seeing fewer suicide planes.

After the Army had taken Manila, we were assigned to shore bombardment duties on Bataan Peninsula. The Army made landings in that area, after we had shelled the beach and they would frequently call for gunfire support against Jap strong points. We would frequently provide fire support all night. This was usually very slow firing that I suspect was designed to keep the Japs awake. I don't know if it always kept the Japs awake or not but it sure kept me awake.

Our mail was beginning to catch up with us by the time we moved down to the Bataan Peninsula. I had a large stack of letters from Chris. She would keep me informed about how rapidly Sharon was growing. I am sure my letters to her left a lot to be desired. All outgoing letters had to be censored. We were not permitted to say where we were or what we were doing.

Chris knew where I was located because we had worked out a very simple coding system, assigning names to various places I would likely be assigned. By reading the papers and listening to the news on the Radio she had a good idea what we were doing.

After working over the Bataan Peninsula, we started shelling the Island of Corregidor. This is a small tadpole shaped island sitting in the entrance to

Manila Bay. The Army soon cleared the Japs out of Subic Bay, located on the Bataan Peninsula and not too many miles from Corregidor. We would drop anchor in Subic Bay, leave at daylight and go down to Corregidor and blast away at Corregidor all day and return to Subic Bay at night. This went on for several weeks. Corregidor was almost solid rock. Many of our shells did very little damage, however once in a while we would hit an ammunition storage dump and there would be quite an explosion.

There was also Fort Drum across the channel from Corregidor. This was commonly called the concrete battleship. It was solid concrete with a large turret on top which looked somewhat like a battleship turret. We did not waste ammunition on this because the concrete was so thick our shells would bounce off. They never fired the big guns at us. It was thought our troops disabled the big guns before they surrendered in 1942 and the Japs were not able to put them back into operation.

After we had been returning to Subic Bay at night for a couple of weeks, I noticed our Lt. Turner was walking around like a zombie. I had noticed that PT Boats would come alongside shortly after we dropped anchor in Subic Bay. They would obtain fresh water and some food from us. I happened to be walking around on the stem of the ship one evening and spotted our Lt. Turner going down a rope ladder to board one of the PT Boats. The next day I caught him at a quiet moment and asked him what he was doing going aboard the PT Boat. He made me swear I would not tell Captain Grady what he had been doing.

He said the skipper of the PT Boat was one of his buddies from the Naval Academy and he had invited him along to have some fun. Some fun! The PT Boats carried torpedoes, but in addition, they had a 40MM, some 20MM and .50 Caliber Machine Guns. They had also promoted (stolen) a Mortar and ammunition from the Army. They would leave Subic Bay after dark and slip between Corregidor and Fort Drum with engines idling so the Japs would not spot them. They would proceed on into the dock area at Manila, shoot up the dock area and any Jap vehicles or positions they could find. After they had expended most of their ammunition, they would move out of Manila Bay at full throttle right under the guns of Corregidor. A PT Boat running full throttle would go about 45 miles per hour. As far as I know they never did get hit.

They would return to Subic Bay long after midnight and Lt. Turner would climb the rope ladder back aboard the MONTPELIER. We would have early reveille and go back and bombard Corregidor all day. No wonder the Lt. was walking around looking like a zombie, he was getting very little sleep. As far as I know, Captain Grady never found out our Lt. Turner was doing double duty!

In addition to our shelling, the Army Air Corps started hitting Corregidor at least twice a day with B-24 Heavy Bombers. It was obvious that a landing would be made on Corregidor pretty soon. Our forces needed access to Manila Bay and the dock areas at Manila. As long as the Japs held Corregidor they could block the entrance to Manila Bay and the city of Manila.

We spent part of one day shelling the tip of Bataan Peninsula. Located there is (was) a small town of Marivales and Marivales Harbor. We almost lost two Destroyers on this mission. There were small wood ships called Minesweepers that were used to clear Jap mines from the areas we were going to hit. The Minesweepers were made of wood so they would not set off Magnetic Mines. They missed some of the mines in the Marivales Harbor area.

When our Destroyers moved in for some close in firing, one of the Destroyers hit a mine near the stem as they were swinging around to get into a firing position. The Destroyer started to settle into the water by the stem. Another Destroyer rushed to their aid and also hit a mine that blew part of his bow off. He started settling into the water by the bow. We never found out how many men they lost, but they finally managed to get things under control and to limp back to Mindoro where temporary repairs could be made permitting them to make it to the Navy Yard at Pearl Harbor or the West Coast for a complete overhaul.

Around the middle of February, the pace of our bombardment of Corregidor picked up. Early one morning right after we had finished with a heavy barrage, a large group of B-24 Bombers hit the island. As soon as their last bombs had exploded, a large flight of A-20 fast twin engine bombers came over and hit the island. They were flying so low there were parachutes attached to their bombs to prevent the planes from being blown up by their own bomb blast.

While this was going on, the small landing craft were circling in front of Corregidor in a manner indicating they were going to make a frontal landing against the cliffs. The high part of Corregidor faces seaward and the Japs probably thought they would face a frontal assault. We were only about a mile from Corregidor and I was watching everything through my Binoculars.

Just as the last bombs from the A-20's exploded, the sky was full of C-47 Transport Planes. They were flying at a very low altitude. As soon as the first planes were over Corregidor, Parachute Troops started spilling out of the planes. No doubt the idea of the low altitude was to get the troops on the ground while the Japs were still in their holes from the bombing runs.

As I watched, I soon realized I was seeing a tragedy unfold right in front of me. The old 3 story Barracks and Hospital building on top of Corregidor were nothing but skeleton buildings with steel beams and concrete walls sticking up in the air. Many of the Paratroopers were slammed into the steel beams and concrete walls that were still standing. Many others missed the Island and were smashed against the cliffs before falling into the water. Several were never able to get their parachutes open before they hit the ground. I never heard or read about how many of the Paratroops were killed in the jump, but I would guess there were more killed in the jump than were killed by the Japs.

In the meantime, the landing craft circling in front of Corregidor moved around toward the tail of the Island and landed where there were no cliffs to scale. The high command announced the invasion of Corregidor was a success, but they never announced the number of killed and maimed.

We were back to patrolling the area to prevent any Jap ships from slipping in and disrupting the operations on and around Corregidor and Marivales. After two days, we again returned to Subic Bay. The Army Engineers had cleared a small island in Subic Bay, called Grandee Island. Areas not cleared had been marked with tape and warning signs to keep out.

Captain Hoffman decided the crew needed a change of pace. Part of the crew would be permitted to go ashore on Grandee Island to play softball and relax. Each man was furnished two cans of warm beer! In spite of the warning signs some wise guy went beyond the off limits area and encountered a booby trap. He was killed and his buddy lost an eye. So much for recreation for a while!

We operated out of Subic Bay for a few more days and then went back to Mindoro. This area was a beehive of activity by now. There were many landing craft type ships in the Harbor. It was not necessary that one be a Rhodes Scholar to figure out that another landing would be taking place. We soon pulled out of Mindoro headed west. We learned we would be part of the landing on the Island of Palawan. This is a long narrow island with the east coast facing the Sulu Sea and the west coast on the South China Sea. In fact Palawan completes the box of Philippine Islands that surround the Sulu Sea.

This was a much smaller operation than the other landings that had been made in the Philippines up to this point and would set the pattern for future landings on other islands in the Philippines and to the south in Borneo.

The MONTPELIER would provide close in support for future landings. The island would be pounded by Army Bombers and by Navy Carrier Planes from the Jeep Carriers. The Cruisers and Destroyers would move in for close in bombardment of the landing area. Our Float Planes would be launched from the Catapult to provide spotters for our Bombardment. One gun would be fired until we were on target and then the spotter in the Float Plane would call "fire for effect".

All guns would open fire and literally smother the target. We were close enough to shore to see what was going on. On the day of the landing, before daylight, the underwater demolition teams would move in from small rubber boats and plant demolition charges against underwater obstacles. They had to work fast and clear the area before the timing devices set off their explosives. As soon as the men were picked up, there would be explosions near the beach where they had planted their charges. The minesweepers would then move in to sweep the landing area of mines. While the minesweepers were doing their job, we were standing ready to cover them if a Jap shore battery should open up and fire on them. When this happened, we would open up with everything we had and literally smother them. Our main battery of 12, 6 inch guns and 8, 5 inch guns (there were actually 12, 5 inch guns on the ship but 4 of them would always be on the wrong side of the ship to fire), at one mile distance could have three projectiles in the air before the first one hit. This is what I mean when I said we would smother them.

After the minesweepers had finished their sweeping operations, the landing craft would head for the beach. We would stand by with our Float Planes in the air to provide additional gunfire support for the landing forces if needed.

On the smaller operations, General MacArthur did not come ashore with the troops. Instead, just prior to the troops hitting the beach, there would be a lone B-17 show up on the scene. It would continue to circle the landing area until the troops were ashore and things were going as planned. General MacArthur was always in the lone B-17.

The landing on Palawan went quite well and after two days, we returned to Subic Bay. We had mail waiting for us and there was good news and bad news. The good news was the mail, the bad news, as far as the crew of the Montpelier was concerned, was that Captain Hoffman had been promoted to Admiral and would be leaving to go back to his new assignment in the states.

Our new Commanding Officer was Captain William A. Gorry. The ships crew was suspicious of the new Captain for they all believed we would never have another Commanding Officer who put the safety and welfare of the crew above all else.

My battle station was changed from the Portside 20MM Battery to the 40MM Fire Control Director located high up in the superstructure of the ship right behind the open bridge. This is where the Captain controlled the ship when we were at battle stations. My job was the remote control of the 40MM Battery located on the portside of the ship about five decks down from the Fire Control Director. My office and sleeping quarters were one deck below the main deck. This required that I run up eleven ladders to get to my battle station when General Quarters sounded.

The heat, stress and lack of sleep the past few months had melted the excess fat that I was packing when I came aboard the MONTPELIER, instead of weighing 195 pounds I was sure that I was now about 160. I was to lose more weight and become quite a sprinter, running up those eleven ladders to my battle station.

Since my new assignment was in close proximity to the Captain of the ship, really only a few feet from him, I was able to observe him at close range. His ship handling technique was quite different from that of Captain Hoffman. In fact I was very apprehensive the first time we encountered a suicide plane. The Captain ordered 8 Knots instead of the "Flank Speed" that Captain Hoffman always called for. Instead of violent twists and turns we maintained a steady course. We were sitting ducks. We could not run out from under a suicide plane at this speed!

Fortunately during the next suicide plane attack the plane was blown apart before he could hit us. The crew was really upset and wasted no time in complaining to their officers. Some of the Senior Officers took the complaints to the Captain but he informed them he was commanding this ship!

Back in Subic Bay, things had quieted down to where we could have movies on the main deck! By this time, the Army had cleaned the remaining Japs out of Manila and arrangements were made to send part of the crew into Manila on a sightseeing trip.

We were transported from Subic Bay to Manila aboard a Destroyer. The harbor at Manila was a shambles. There were sunken Jap ships at almost every dock. The warehouses and the dock area in general had been bombed and shelled. All of the buildings in the dock area were in shambles. The town of Manila was in no better shape. The Japs died fighting. There were still many bodies under walls of building that had been knocked down. The stench was the worst I had ever encountered.

All of the modem buildings were badly damaged and most of them burned out. For some reason, the slum area north of the Passig River was untouched. We got into the infamous Bilibid Prison where many of our men captured in 1942, were held. The survivors had been removed, but there were many shallow graves in the prison yard where our people were buried. They had either starved or were beaten to death by the Japs. The Army troops told us the Filipino riff raff was stealing everything they could get their hands on and we had better hang onto our wallets.

The trip into Manila was an experience I shall never forget. I was happy to return to the Montpelier where we had a clean place to live, could take a hot shower and had clean clothes to wear.

We received information that B-29's from Tinian were hitting the main Islands of Japan on a regular basis and that carrier planes from Halsey's 3rd Fleet were launching air strikes against the Jap home islands as well. We all knew the tempo of the war was picking up and everyone was hoping the war would be over before Christmas. There was, however, a lingering suspicion that the closer we got to Japan the more difficult it would become. People who believe they will go straight to heaven if they die for the Emperor are difficult to deal with. From what I had seen of the Japs, I was convinced they really believed their own propaganda.

The MONTPELIER moved back to Mindoro and covered more landings in some of the lesser Islands: Cebu, Panay and Negros. Late one evening a lone suicide plane slipped in on us.

We were doing our usual 8 knots! We knocked this guy down just before he hit the ship. In fact he was so close the blast from his bomb shattered the Plexiglas in the Open Bridge right in front of Captain Gorry. At that moment, he learned how to say "Flank Speed, full right (or left) rudder". From then on, anytime we came under air attack, we went immediately to flank speed.

This really pleased the crew. Except for the fact that it was almost a disaster, they were delighted the Captain had finally understood the reason for full speed and violent twists and turns.

We returned to Mindoro and around the middle of April there was a large collection of ships including transports and landing craft. It was obvious this would be a large operation. An Army General and his Staff came aboard for a conference and we soon put to sea. It was learned that this time, we would hit the big southernmost island of Mindanao. We were to land troops at the southern end of the Sulu Sea on the north shore of Mindanao. The night before the landing, a small dugout canoe, like the native Filipinos used, appeared near the ship. As it came close to the ship we observed the scroungiest looking white man I had ever seen. It turned out he was an Army Colonel who had slipped into Mindanao aboard one of our Submarines in 1943 to organize a guerrilla band to resist the Japs on the island. This he had done. He pointed out the location of the Jap gun positions for our Gunnery Officer. He was given a hot meal and departed after telling our Gunnery Officer, "You hit them on the beach and when they move back into the Jungle, we will hit them from the rear."

The landings went smoothly and we were soon released for another assignment. We received information there was fierce fighting going on at Okinawa and the suicide planes were really giving our ships a bad time. We were just as happy we were supporting the landings in the Southern Philippines.

Our next assignment was a landing on the far southwest tip of Mindanao called Zamboanga. By this time, the landings had become a rather routine operation. The same routine used at Palawan was used. General MacArthur would fly over in his B-17, circle the landing area until things seemed to be going as planned and then head back to Manila.

As soon as things settled down at Zamboanga our group moved east along the underbelly of the large island of Mindanao to Davao. This is one of the larger cities on the underside of Mindanao.

The landings were more or less routine, that is, as routine as something as complex as an Amphibious landing ever gets. First the bombardment or softening up process, not only Naval gunfire but air strikes as well. This is followed by early dawn Underwater Demolition Teams, then the Minesweepers, more shelling by Cruisers and Destroyers followed by the actual landing of troops. Instead of throwing the troops into a frontal assault against heavily fortified positions (this is what the Navy High Command always did to the Marines), General MacArthur always put the troops ashore at the Japs' weaker points.

In the early days of World War II the Marines referred to General MacArthur as "Dugout Dug". We all picked up on this. However as a result of being a part of the Philippine Campaign, I changed my mind, and fell under the MacArthur mystique of believing he was either a genius or smart enough to surround himself with a good Staff! The intelligence information furnished prior to every landing was usually accurate and up to date.

The Army had things under control by the middle of May and we were relieved of our bombardment duties. We went back around the long tail of Mindanao at Zamboanga and headed north toward Subic Bay. We were again short on everything, fuel, food and ammunition. These would be readily available at Subic Bay.

On the way back to Subic Bay, I was walking around the main deck. As I approached the stern of the ship I noticed the cook from the Chief Petty Officers Mess throwing cases of something overboard. I discovered it was Honey. I ordered him to stop!

Honey had always been one of my favorites and I could not understand why anyone would be dumb enough to throw opened oases of Honey overboard. The cook said the Honey was spoiled. I called him a "dumb ass" and said Honey was nature's perfect food and it would not spoil. He opened a case and held up a jar of Honey. He said, "see it is white and spoiled". I again called him an uncomplimentary name and told him that Honey always turned white when it aged. It was good to eat as is but could be restored to its original appearance by putting it in a pan of hot water on a low fire for an hour or so. He was a non-believer, but since I was a member of the Chief Petty officers Mess I ordered him to come with me to the CPO Galley and to bring some of the Honey with him. I put the jar of Honey into a large pan, put it on the fire and ordered the cook to retrieve the cases of Honey that were still up on the main deck and to return them to the storeroom. After about an hour, the honey had returned to its original state. I told him from now on, I wanted to see a jar of Honey on the table at Breakfast every morning. He finally understood and for several months, I enjoyed Honey on my bread at Breakfast.

When we arrived back at Subic Bay, there were many sacks of mail waiting for us. As usual, I was happy to receive a bunch of letters from Chris. This was the one thing that kept me going. After a short time in Subic Bay, the ship moved into Manila Bay and the crew was permitted to go ashore in Manila.

An additional trip to Manila did not appeal to me, and Gibbons and I were behind in our paperwork. Each month, we had to submit a Muster Roll to Marine Corps Headquarters, listing the name of each member of the Detachment by rank showing their duty assignment for the month, calculate and prepare a payroll showing the gross pay for the rank of the individual, deductions for allotments and the amount of money retained on the books.

Each man was allowed to draw only $10.00 per month. The balance would be carried on the books until the person was transferred or when the war ended. This prevented the men from being taken in by the card and dice hustlers present in every military organization.

We also had to prepare a report giving the status of our clothing and other supplies, showing the number of items issued during the month and to whom. The monthly issues were sometimes padded when Gibbons needed underwear, socks or shoes to barter for special items like 190 proof alcohol that was used by the Navy for medicinal purposes or the cleaning of special equipment.

We spent about three days in Manila Bay and then returned to Subic Bay. In a few days, about a dozen Australian soldiers came aboard. Rumor was our next operation would involve the landing of Australian Troops on the island of Borneo. These guys would coordinate our Naval Gunfire support. Again, good thinking on the part of General MacArthur. The Australians claimed THEY spoke English and WE butchered the language. Be that as it may, there was a language problem, especially with Radio Transmissions. Radio communication leaves something to be desired under ideal conditions, but to throw in a language barrier as well could lead to disaster.

We departed Subic Bay and headed south through the Sulu Sea. The Sulu Sea was glassy smooth. The only ripples were caused by our ships. A short time later, it became overcast and the sea started to kick up. There was a Typhoon sweeping up out of the South China Sea between Indo China and the Philippines. This was early June and the start of the Typhoon season. We were soon taking water over the bow of the ship. I was on duty at my battle station, the Fire Control Director near the Open Bridge. Pretty soon, the ship was not only pitching fore and aft, but was rolling from side to side. The Captain directed all hatches secured and all loose gear tied down. We were in a very bad storm. We were taking green water (waves) over the number 1 Turret located on the main deck. The Marines manning the 20MM Guns on the bow had been relieved and sent below deck as soon as the water started to break over the bow. Many men were seasick including myself, I had seen rough seas before but this one was the worst ever. After several hours of this, the Typhoon finally passed and things started to calm down. We were ready for some calm water.

When the War ended in Europe, we were informed that many of the troops and equipment in Europe would be sent to the Pacific to help in the war against Japan. This was welcome news, for the closer we came to Japan, the more violent the war was becoming. The news from Okinawa was not good and we thought we would be sent to Okinawa as soon as our mission in Borneo was completed.

The second week in June, we covered landings by Australian Troops on the northwest coast of Borneo at a place called Brunei Bay and also at

Sandakan. Borneo is an oil rich island about the size of Texas. This island, along with the Dutch East Indies to the south of Borneo, was the field supply for the Jap war machine. They were not eager to lose this source of raw material and resisted with what forces they could scrape together. Due to the fact we now controlled the Philippine Islands, it was not possible for them to bring in additional troops or supplies. They were beginning to be in the same predicament our troops were in early in the war when they had to do with what they had.

There were not many Jap troops in the Brunei-Sandakan area and the Australians soon had everything under control. We were released for our next assignment. The next landing was to be made halfway down the east coast of Borneo at Balikpapan. To reach Balikpapan took some time. It would be like going from Lubbock to Corpus Christi, Texas by way of Amarillo, Oklahoma City, Texarkana, Beaumont, Galveston. We met a tanker at Tawi-Tawi and took on fuel. This is a group of small islands between the tail of Mindanao at Zamboanga and the northeast coast of Borneo.

We had no more than dropped anchor at Tawi-Tawi when many native dugout canoes arrived alongside the ship. They had all kinds of stuff to sell and trade. I had to laugh at two of the sailors who were negotiating with the natives for the junky trinkets they had for sale. The sailors would pass a string down to the natives with a dollar bill attached, the native would attach the string to his trinket and the sailor would pull it aboard. This routine continued for some time, and it appeared that the only English the native knew was "one dollar". After a while one of the sailors said "boy is that guy stupid, he can only say one dollar". The other sailor looked at the junk they had been buying and said "he is not stupid, we are the stupid ones, this junk isn't worth a quarter". The natives also had some scrawny pigs and chickens but the ships Doctor would not permit the pigs and chickens aboard ship.

The next day, our force sailed south for the invasion at Balikpapan. This took two days and when we arrived there we found several Oil Refineries. They looked like the ones back in the States. Around the Harbor there were also large storage tanks for crude oil and refined products.

It soon became apparent this operation was not going to be as easy as many of the others had been. The Japs not only had large coastal guns but numerous artillery positions that we were able to spot. We did not have air cover since we were well out of range of our fighter planes in the Philippine Islands.

General MacArthur's Intelligence network was working quite well. We were notified at 2:00 p.m. to expect an air attack by Japanese Heavy Bombers at sunset. Just before sunset, nine Jap Betty Bombers attacked the fleet (The Betty was the Japs largest and best land based bomber. It only had two engines but could carry a lot of bombs and was very fast). We threw up all of the Anti-Aircraft fire we could muster and kept them at high altitude.

We were thankful these guys were not the suicide types. The Admiral in command of the operation requested air cover to keep the bombers away while we tried to eliminate the Jap shore batteries.

We kept one of our two float planes in the air during daylight hours to spot the Jap shore batteries. We finally knocked out their large guns along the shore but not before they sank one of our Minesweepers and took several shots at us. By this time, Captain Gorry had learned to keep the ship moving at a good speed and their shells landed behind us or fell short. We could not spot their Artillery. The pilot of the float plane said they were dug in on the reverse slope of the hills. Our guns could tear up the front of a hill but could not hit anything on the reverse slope.

One of the pilots (a really crazy guy) convinced the Captain to allow him to carry bombs. The float plane could carry a 100 pound bomb under each wing. This goofy pilot wanted to be a Dive Bomber Pilot but instead had been assigned to a Cruiser flying an old obsolete, fabric covered bi-plane. He always wanted to carry bombs but had not been permitted to do so until now. The Captain of the ship and the Admiral in charge of the operation were becoming frustrated about not being able to knock out the Jap artillery positions.

The float plane was launched and this was the darndest sight I ever witnessed. This goofy pilot used that old bi-plane like a dive bomber. He would climb up several thousand feet, and roll over into a dive, straight down. Everyone watching was sure he would pull the wings off of the old plane. He pulled out after dropping one bomb. He again climbed up and pulled the same stunt with his other bomb.

We did not know the Japs had float planes of their own hidden in the jungle foliage. They did not like having their artillery positions bombed and soon had a float plane of their own in the air that started making passes at our guy. The Jap float plane was also an old bi-plane our identification pictures called a "Pete".

The Jap pilot must have been as goofy as our guy because these two guys got into a dogfight! This looked like something out of a World War I movie. Two old bi-planes zooming up and around, each trying to shoot the other down. The Jap plane was faster than our 90 miles per hour plane, but our pilot could out maneuver the Jap.

After some time, they called the show off. Our guy was low on fuel and the Jap did not follow him back to the fleet. He was smart enough to stay out of range of our anti-aircraft fire.

The nightly bombing attacks by the Japs continued. They would come over at high altitude, out of range of our 40MM and 20MM guns. I actually witnessed the 5" Guns finally shoot a plane down. They hit one of the large Jap bombers and set him on fire. The plane went into an arch toward the water. He was burning badly and it looked like he would never hit the water.

When he finally crashed, there was a big explosion which lit up the area in a large circle.

Our air cover finally arrived in the form of an Army Air Corps Night Fighter called a P61. It was a large twin engine plane and looked more like a bomber than a fighter. It was a single plane that flew down from Zmboanga. He would circle the fleet for about 15 minutes and then head back to Zamboanga. We thought he would make mincemeat of the Jap float plane but he did not bother with the Jap.

The Army started sending daily flights of B-24's (large 4 engine bombers) over to bomb the beach area and hit the oil Refineries. We had also been shooting up the Oil Refineries. This did not make sense to me because they would be in Allied hands in a few days if everything went as planned. The guy that scheduled the B-24 Bomber flight must have been a Dr. Pepper fan because about 12 B-24's would show up around 10, 2 and 4 each day. They would be at about 20,000 feet altitude and would scatter bombs over a large area. When they first started hitting the Oil Refineries, they would start a lot of fires.

I overheard the Captain cussing and was surprised to learn there was no way to communicate with the Army Bombers. They were flying up from New Guinea and should have been hitting the Jap Airfields on Sumatra, south of Borneo, to keep the Jap Bombers from hitting us. It appeared the Army and Navy High Command were still fighting each other and would not share radio frequencies.

We were pretty well informed about what was going on in the world because our radio operators monitored news broadcasts from Honolulu and would put out daily mimeograph "Press News" to the crew. After two days, the Army was reporting fires were still raging from the bombing attack at Balikpapan.

We noticed that shortly after the 4:00 p.m. air raid the smoke would die down and before sunset there would be no fires or smoke over the beach area or at Balikpapan. The next morning the area would be clear and smoke free. About 9:00 a.m., we would see fires start up and by 10:00 a.m. when the first Bomber Strike of B-24's arrived, there would be black smoke billowing up 10,000 feet into the air. We could watch this with our binoculars.

The Japs had put oil drums filled with crude oil all over the place and they would light them off around 9:00 a.m., and put the fires out around 4:00! The Japs were certainly not stupid. They were putting one over on the Army. The Admiral in charge of the operation was furious! He could not communicate with the Army and his complaint to the Navy at Pearl Harbor was probably lost in the paperwork shuffle.

This routine continued for more than a week. The Jap bombers continued to come over at night and the Jap float plane would also keep us awake. The invasion was at a virtual standstill. We continued our shelling during the day but still could not get at the Jap Artillery.

The Admiral finally got someone's attention. The main war effort was concentrated against the heavy fighting on Okinawa and all of our large carriers and main elements of the fleet were hitting Japan. In a few days, four Jeep Aircraft Carriers and several Destroyers showed up.

The little Navy FM-2 Fighters and TBM Torpedo planes from the Jeep Carriers soon finished off the Jap float plane and artillery. The Torpedo planes could carry 2,000 pounds of bombs when not armed with Torpedoes. They would go in low following the Fighters and sprinkle bombs all over the Jap artillery positions.

Two days later, the Australian Troops landed. The Jeep Carrier planes furnished close air support and we provided Naval gunfire. After a few days, we were relieved and headed back to Subic Bay.

We thought we were going back to Subic Bay. Instead, we returned to the island of Leyte where we had first encountered the suicide planes in Leyte Gulf.

Upon reaching Leyte we found, instead of the feared suicide planes, Leyte had been transformed into a large military base. There were ships, especially supply ships and tankers coming and going on a regular basis.

There were many bags of mail waiting for us and I was happy to receive my supply of letters from Chris. My letters to her were in bunches because mail from the ship would be sent only when we were in port which did not happen very often.

We took on fuel, food and ammunition. Our ammunition supply was extremely low after firing for about 20 days in Borneo. We received a new type of ammunition. The Anti-Aircraft projectiles for the 5" guns contained a recently developed fuse called a VT fuse. This was a small radio device and would explode when it came near the target. This was touted as a great improvement over the timer controlled fuses that we had been using.

There were also new powder canisters that were supposed to be flashless. The powder we had been using would light up the entire ship when we fired the 5" or 6" guns at night.

The High Command decided the crew of the MONTPELIER was in need of a few days of rest and relaxation.

The Navy had developed a recreation area on the island of Samar. Samar is a large island near Leyte and forms the northern end of Leyte Gulf. We dropped anchor at Samar and all of the ships crew was permitted to go ashore to the (more or less) recreation center on Samar.

There were picnic areas and rough baseball fields. The beer ration was increased from 2 cans to 3 cans per man. This was something to see, the sailors and marines trying to open the steel cans of warm beer. The beer was called POS for Philadelphia Old Stock. The men swore the name was misspelled! It was pretty terrible. Once opened you had two choices: watch about 2/3 of the beer go 15 feet into the air or put your mouth over the opening and try to swallow as fast as the beer came out. Some of the people could handle it but most ended up strangled, with a lot of coughing and hacking taking place.

I could not work up an interest in the softball game; instead, I thought about the recent violence and terror in Leyte Gulf. It was a peaceful place now with only the coming and going of supply ships and tankers to disturb the calm waters. I also spent some time looking and exploring the island of Samar thinking what a terrible "Hell Hole" this must have been for the Marines and Soldiers that served here during the Philippine Insurrection. Samar was hot, humid and mostly jungle. The mosquitoes were thick and a constant problem. There were also all kinds of biting bugs to make life miserable.

We had been required to study Marine Corps History in Boot Camp. It explained that after Admiral Dewey defeated the Spanish in Manila Bay in 1898 the United States occupied the Philippine Islands. Not all Filipinos wanted to go along with this and there was an uprising on the island of Samar called the Philippine Insurrection. It lasted for several years and a lot of Marines died on the island, both from disease and from the bolo knives of the Moro Tribesmen.

The Marines and Soldiers were armed with old rifles and .38 caliber pistols. The story was that the determined Moro Tribesmen could not always be stopped and many Marines and Soldiers died at the hands of the Bolo wielding Moro Tribesmen.

The Bolo Knife was more or less like a machete and in the hands of a determined Moro was a mean weapon. The .45 Colt Automatic Pistol was later developed as a result of experience of the Marines on Samar.

After walking around on Samar, I decided that while we had a tough time in Leyte Gulf, other Marines must have had a worse time on Samar some 45 years earlier.

The day was soon over and I left my thoughts about Samar on the Island and returned to the MONTPELIER. After all hands had spent a day on Samar, we departed for Manila. We anchored in Manila Bay near the dock area and all hands were again given a day off for sightseeing in Manila.

Many of the sunken ships around the dock area had been removed since our earlier visit and a lot of the rubble of the fighting had been removed. The smell of the place had improved remarkably.

I met Gunnery Sergeant Woodbury (our Blackfoot Indian) near the dock area and he was driving an Army Jeep. I was afraid to ask how he had obtained the Jeep for fear he had stolen it!

We spent most of the day sightseeing. The Jeep really came in handy, however I expected to be arrested at any time for running around in an Army Jeep.

Almost all of the modem buildings in Manila had been destroyed but their remains indicated Manila was once a modem city. It was not necessary to go very far into the rural areas to discover they were very primitive. While the Philippines were a very old country, they had not made much progress except in the main cities. When it was time to return to the ship, Woodbury dropped the Jeep off at an Army Motor Pool. I was relieved to learn he had conned them into letting him borrow the Jeep instead of stealing it.

After bringing more food aboard and topping off the fuel tanks we cleared the harbor and started up the coast of Luzon. We joined another group of ships that included two new Battlecruisers, the ALASKA and the GUAM. Everyone spent a lot of time gawking at the new ships. There were only two of them in the entire Navy and both were with us.

They were shaped like a Cruiser, long and relatively narrow, but with lots of fire power and the latest Radar and fire control technology. They were as fast as any of our present Cruisers and were armed with 12" Guns in four turrets, three 12" Guns in each turret plus they were covered with 5", 40MM and 20MM rapid fire Anti-Aircraft Guns. They would make up the backbone of our present Task Force.

We were on our way to Okinawa, but were told our operating area would be in the Yellow Sea, between Korea and the Coast of China. We were to clear the area of any Jap shipping. Our High Command believed the Japs would be pulling troops out of China and Korea to protect the homeland of Japan proper, since it was obvious we would be invading their home islands soon.

We arrived at Okinawa the middle of July. We topped off the fuel tanks and dropped anchor in the bay. By this time, we had new airfields on Okinawa and lots of fighter plane cover during the day.

An occasional suicide plane would slip through the fighters during the day but they concentrated their attacks at night. There were fighter planes in the air at night, however their Radar was not well developed and by flying low on the water the suicide planes could and did attack at night.

Our 5" Guns were permitted to fire using their new smokeless powder and the proximity fuses. The 40mm and 20mm Guns were not permitted to fire at night because the tracers lit up the area and exposed our position.

The Captain occupied what was known as his Sea Cabin when we were in an area where we could expect a Jap attack (which was most of the time). This Sea Cabin was one deck below the Open Bridge where he controlled the ship.

My Battle Station was the 40MM Fire Control Director located a few feet behind the Open Bridge. I had become quite fast when it came to climbing the ladders from my office which doubled as my living quarters.

When the 40MM Gun on the Main Deck, directly over my bunk became active the noise of the Electric Motor would radiate through the steel deck and I would be wide awake immediately. I knew the General Quarters Alarm would be sounded in a few seconds. I would get dressed and start running up the ladders to my battle station. I would always be at my station when the Captain emerged from his Sea Cabin half asleep.

One night after he had observed me at my station for weeks, he stopped and said, "Sergeant do you live up here"? I told him, "No sir, I am just fast on my feet". He said, "You sure are".

Almost every night, one of the ships would be hit. The suicide Pilots were not too particular what type of ship they hit as long as they hit one.

Tokyo Rose was always bragging about how many ships the suicide planes were sinking. According to her, they sunk more ships than we had in the area. Our propaganda was also pretty bad. The only information we had was what we could see for ourselves and the daily news broadcasts that were picked up on the ship's Radio and Broadcast over the ship's PA system. Our High Command would always report "superficial" damage to one of our ships.

Many ships were severely damaged and losses among the crew were extremely high when hit by one or more suicide planes. The bomb blast would cause a lot of damage and the burning gasoline killed many more.

I did not learn the full truth of the losses until after the War. The Navy lost more people at Okinawa and in operations off the coast of Japan than in any other campaign in the Pacific.

There were more than 5,000 Navy and Marine Personnel killed aboard ships in the area by suicide planes. There were many thousands more injured. Losses ashore by ground troops were also extremely high. It required three Marine and three Army Divisions to secure the Island of Okinawa.

The famous War Correspondent Ernie Pyle was killed on the small island of Ie Shima while serving with Marine Corps Troops. Lieutenant General Simon Bolivar Buckner was killed by Jap Artillery while observing a Marine Corps Unit. I believe he was the highest ranking Army Officer killed in combat in World War II.

As our troops squeezed the Japs on Okinawa into a narrow pocket in the final days of the campaign, almost 2,000 of them committed suicide by jumping over a cliff rather than surrender.

After a few more days and miserable nights at Okinawa, we left to make a sweep up through the Yellow Sea between China and Korea. This was fine with me. I would prefer to take my chances on the open sea rather than anchored as a sitting duck in the bay at Okinawa.

Besides that, we had lots of company. There were two additional cruisers like the MONTPELIER, those two beautiful Battlecruisers ALASKA and GUAM and several Destroyers.

We believed we could take care of anything we were likely to encounter on our sweep through the Yellow Sea. The ALASKA and the GUAM could hit a target more than 20 miles away with their 12" Guns.

Late evening and early morning, we were furnished scouting air cover from Okinawa by a Navy long range Patrol Bomber called a Privateer. The Privateer was almost identical to the Army B-24 Bomber except instead of the twin tail of the B-24, the Privateer had a large single tail. Unlike the experience at Balikpapan where we could not communicate with the Army B-24's, we had Radio contact with the Privateer at all times when he was scouting ahead of us.

We went up the west coast of Korea circled over to the coast of China and encountered some Jap small ships near the Yellow River off Shanghai. We also found out why the Yellow Sea is called yellow. There is so much silt carried by the Yellow River that most of the Yellow Sea is a dirty yellow color.

We continued on down the coast of China for about 200 miles and then returned to Okinawa. At Okinawa we took on fuel and food and were told we would make another sweep up through the Yellow Sea.

The Japs came up with a new wrinkle for their suicide pilots. They developed a Rocket powered plane called a Baka Bomb. I found out later that Baka in Japanese meant "crazy". This was really a crazy device. They flew so fast it was difficult to tell what they looked like. I saw plenty of them on the ground in Japan later. The Baka looked like an elongated bomb, about 3 feet in diameter and about 25 feet long. There was a tiny cockpit for a pilot, a primitive rocket in the tail that provided power for a few minutes. There was no landing gear but a device that could be hooked under the wing of a Jap "Betty" Bomber. This was the Japs best bomber and we had encountered plenty of them in the past.

The Baka carried almost a thousand pounds of explosives in the nose. The Betty bomber would carry the Baka under the Wing. When a ship was sighted the Baka would be released and his Rocket would kick in for a few minutes and build up a speed of about 500 miles per hour.

Our fighters were unable to shoot them down because of their high speed and small size. They also had small wings and either they were difficult to control at their high speed or else the pilots were picked up off the street and not trained properly. For this, we were thankful.

A few ships were hit by the Bakas but most of them either crashed because they ran out of fuel or due to poor control.

Our stay at Okinawa was short and for this we were thankful. Some nutty Admiral had decided the best defense against the nightly suicide plane attacks was to move all ships into a tight area in the bay, drop anchor and have small ships circle the formation from just before dark until daylight, making smoke. The smoke looked like a very thick fog and it was possible to see only a few feet. The idea was the suicide planes would not be able to see us.

The Japs may have been crazy but they were not stupid! Most of us, including the Captain, thought the Admiral responsible for this smoke routine was stupid!

As for me, I was just plain scared. I never wanted to be below deck during an air attack and spent most of the time on the main deck at night.

The suicide planes would come in and fly through the smoke until they hit a ship. If they did not hit a ship, you could hear him pull up, circle around and make another pass. When you heard a loud bang and saw a flash of light, you knew that someone had been hit!

This was about the worst situation I could think of. At sea or even while anchored in the clear we might get a shot at him and a lucky hit would knock him down. At least we would have a chance. Sitting in the smoke, all you could do was wait and hope you were not hit.

Two days later, we started our second sweep of the Yellow Sea. The entire crew, including Captain Gorry was happy to be out of the trap we were in at Okinawa.

There were still a few Japs hiding out in the hills at Okinawa but the island was now ours. Okinawa was a beehive of activity. It was quickly being converted into a full-fledged operating base. This was the last obstacle standing in the way of the invasion of Japan. You did not have to be a genius to figure out we would be launching an invasion of Japan in the near future.

The rumors (they were accurate enough to scare hell out of you most of the time) were that our bombardment group would begin bombarding the southernmost Japanese island of Kyushu on September 15 and would continue to do so until November 15 when landings would take place. There would also be 'round the clock air strikes against factories and airfields in Japan. The large Carriers had been hitting Japan with as many as 1,000 planes and the Army was sending hundreds of B-29's over all of the main Islands of Japan. The tempo of the war was continuing to accelerate. Troops, equipment and additional planes were pouring into Okinawa.

We received reports from new men reporting aboard ship that Guam was covered up with people and equipment. Troops and equipment were being concentrated in the Philippine Islands. It was obvious the main push against Japan would soon be at hand.

Our second sweep of the Yellow Sea was routine. I had too much time to think while manning my Fire Control Director during the long hours on duty. Something that had been gnawing at me for some time took hold of me. I had been in nine major battles and many small ones. I had had a very close brush with death in 1942 at the battle of Guadalcanal and again in Leyte Gulf. I was getting the feeling that my luck was about to run out.

The thought of spending two months bombarding the beaches on Kyushu and then being on hand to provide fire support for the landings on November 15 was most unsettling. The thought of starting the War at Pearl Harbor which seemed like so long ago and having come so far, the thought of being killed in the final stages of the war was something that no matter how hard I tried, I could not keep from thinking about. I was having difficulty sleeping and very little appetite for food. My weight was somewhere around 150 pounds. The ship's Sick Bay (Medical facilities) were near my office. One of the Hospital Corpsmen I had been friendly with for some time started slipping me two ounces of Sick Bay alcohol about twice a week. This helped put me to sleep for a few hours when I was not on duty and had a calming effect on my nervous system.

The MONTPELIER never fired a shot on our second sweep of the Yellow Sea. Our Destroyers sunk a few small craft along the coast of China. We returned to Okinawa the first part of August. We again huddled with the other ships in the bay and near sunset the small ships started the dreaded smoke routine. I was really getting jumpy about this routine because every night, some ship would be hit by a suicide plane flying through the smoke. I don't know why we manned our battle stations because we were not permitted to fire. Even when not on my duty station, I continued to remain on the main deck. If a suicide plane should slam into us, I did not want to be below deck when it happened.

On August 6, we received word that a new type of bomb had been dropped on the city of Hiroshima on the main Japanese Island of Honshu. The word was a single bomb had wiped out an entire city. We were told the new type bomb was an Atomic Bomb. We did not know what an Atomic Bomb was but we were glad it was ours and not the Japs. If one bomb could wipe out an entire city, we thought that was great as long as it was our weapon!

Information was broadcast over the ship's PA System that President Truman had demanded the Japs surrender. No reply to his demand had been made. That night, the suicide planes were out in force. We were again sitting in the smoke. You could hear the Jap planes flying through the smoke. One came very close to the MONTPELIER, pulled up and came around for a second pass through the smoke. There was a terrific explosion and flash nearby. It turned out to be the old Battleship PENNSYLVANIA which was sunk at Pearl Harbor, had been with us in Leyte Gulf and now she was hit again. The official broadcast admitted that one of our Battleships had suffered superficial damage.

When the smoke cleared the next morning, I looked over at our old friend the U.S.S. PENNSYLVANIA. If that was superficial damage I did not know the meaning of the word. There was a large hole near the stem of the ship and she was obviously seriously damaged. The PENNSYLVANIA was sitting low in the water by the stern and frantic efforts were being made to keep her afloat. A large seagoing tug came upon the scene and took the PENNSYLVANIA in tow. They disappeared over the horizon and we learned later she had been towed to Guam where temporary repairs could be made.

It was apparent the Japs were becoming desperate. During the night suicide plane attack, a Jap Betty Bomber (their large twin engine very fast bomber) crash landed on our air strip with a squad of Jap troops aboard. They succeeded in destroying a number of our airplanes with satchel charges before they were all killed.

On August 9th we received word we had dropped another Atomic Bomb. This time on the city of Nagasaki on the southern island of Kyushu. This was the island where we were to start our bombardment on September 15th for the landings on November 15, 1945. This was an operation I was not looking forward to at all!

On the night of August 10th word was received over the radio that the Japs had agreed to surrender. The troops on the beach and on the small ships near the beach apparently heard the same broadcast. All hell broke loose! Those idiots started firing their weapons into the air and there was more firing than when there was an air attack in progress. No doubt every weapon that could be fired into the air was being fired. Captain Gorry ordered everyone to "battle stations".

By the time I reached my battle station, there was a series of splashes and explosions nearby. Captain Gorry realized that what goes up must come down and immediately ordered all personnel in exposed gun positions to go below deck on the double. It did not take me long to seek shelter from all the shrapnel and spent bullets.

August 11th we learned the broadcast concerning the surrender of the Japs was premature. The wild shooting on the night of the 10th resulted in many casualties both on the beach and on ships in the area. The stupidity of man is beyond belief at times!

We remained at Okinawa and received information our B-29s and Navy Carrier Planes were continuing to pound the Jap cities and factories.

August 15th (14-th U.S. date) President Truman announced the Japs had indeed agreed to surrender and a cease fire was to be observed. The details of the surrender were to be worked out with General MacArthur in Manila. The Japs were to send their Emissary to Okinawa in a white Betty Bomber with a green cross painted on the fuselage. At Okinawa the Jap Emissary would transfer to a U.S. plane and be flown to Manila to arrange surrender terms with General MacArthur.

This time there was no wild celebration in the beach area. I was more or less in a state of wanting to believe the war was over but afraid something might go wrong at the last minute.

We remained in an alert status with morning and evening General Quarters. We were told not to fire unless fired upon. Things were quiet with no enemy activity. It appeared the cease fire was holding.

A few days after the announcement from President Truman, we received a radio report that the terms of the surrender had been worked out with General MacArthur and that the surrender ceremonies would take place in Tokyo Bay.

The Navy had one more mission for the MONTPELIER. Our ship along with another Cruiser, several Minesweepers, two transport ships and a Hospital Ship were to proceed to Japan to repatriate U.S. and Allied Prisoners of War being held in Japanese Prisoner of War Camps. The

Marines from the MONTPELIER and the other Cruiser were to provide security ashore in Japan for the Medical and other personnel involved in assembling and processing the U.S. and Allied Prisoners of War.

Prior to leaving Okinawa, some of us were permitted to go ashore to look the area over. We saw a large number of caves the Okinawans used to bury their dead in ancient times. Our troops had to flush the Jap troops out of them with grenades and flame throwers.

Upon reaching the crest of a small hill, I was startled to see one of the Sailors from the MONTPELIER sitting on an unexploded (dud) 14 inch shell! I called him an idiot and immediately put a lot of distance between the two of us. Marines were taught early on to stay clear of any unexploded bombs or shells. Two days after leaving Okinawa we entered the Inland Sea at the southern entrance between the islands of Kyushu and Shikoku. Our progress was extremely slow because the Minesweepers were out in front of us making sure there were no minefields we might stray into. We had taken on a Jap Pilot to guide us through the minefields but our Admiral had more faith in our own Minesweepers than he had in the Jap Pilot.

Many times during our passage through the Inland Sea we would come close to shore and it was easy to spot Jap Gun positions that could cover the area. It was several hundred miles from where we entered the Inland Sea to our destination at Wakayama on the main island of Honshu. I was struck by the number of fortifications and artillery positions all along the area. I gave thanks to the god that had seen fit to bring the war to an end for it was obvious our casualties would have been terrible had we invaded Japan.

Upon arrival at Wakayama teams fanned out to the various Prisoner of War Camps to rescue the Prisoners of War. We commandeered an undamaged Jap Hotel near the waterfront in Wakayama.

The Marines from the MONTPELIER were armed with all the weapons available to us along with sufficient ammunition. We were spread out around the Hotel and covered the area from the Railroad Station to the hotel. The Commanding Officer of the Marine Detachment, Captain Grady, decided he would move around in our assigned area should it be necessary to return fire if we were fired upon by dissident Japs. Since I was the senior Non-Commissioned Officer, he assigned me to take charge of the entrance to the Hotel and to maintain order in the immediate area of the Hotel. The Hotel was a beehive of activity. Additional showers were installed on the first floor. Cooks and large quantities of food were brought from the ships along with many Doctors, Hospital Corpsmen, and Chaplains. Japanese who could speak English were drafted to assist with many necessary details. I recall one young Japanese woman who spoke fluent English, and claimed that she graduated from the University of California! She was very helpful. When we told her to tell some Jap something she would repeat the order in Japanese and the Jap would really move. She said the Japanese propaganda had told the Japs Americans were bloodthirsty animals.

When the trains would arrive with the POW's they would be segregated into groups. Those who could walk under their own power would be guided to the Hotel. Those who were too sick or starved to the point where they could not walk would be moved to the Hospital Ship.

Upon arrival at the Hotel, the POW's wanted to hug us and shake our hand. As soon as this ritual was out of the way, they would be sent into the Hotel in small groups, told to put their personal effects in the room assigned and remove their clothes. At this point, the Hospital Corpsmen would spray them with DDT to kill any lice or other varmints they might be carrying. They would then be given a hot shower and new clothing and then sent to the dining area for a full meal. After their new clothes and hot food they would go up to the next floor for medical screening. Those who required medical care would be sent to the Hospital Ship for treatment and as soon as the airfields were operational they would be flown to the Island of Guam where we had a major base with complete Medical Facilities. Those that were in reasonable health would be sent up to the next floor where administrative details could be taken care of. They could draft a message to their next of kin for Radio Transmission or be given necessary writing materials to write letters.

Next came interviews to see if any of them wanted to charge Jap Prison Guards or Commanders with War Crimes. Many of them filed complaints, others just wanted to go home and they did not give a damn about anything else. After the processing had been completed, they would be permitted to recover their personal effects from the first floor storage area and then be sent to one of the Transport Ships.

The second day, I was startled to see a group of Marines approaching the Hotel, marching in step and wearing starched summer Marine Uniforms! They halted in front of me and demanded they be furnished weapons and ammunition so they could go out and kill a bunch of Japs! I said, "The damned war is over, who the hell are you people?" They informed me they were POWS. I said, "You people sure as hell don't look like any of the other POW's that have been through here. As a matter of fact you look like you are in better shape than my Marines."

They said they were captured on Guam, that they had been placed into a propaganda camp near Osaka and the only work they did was loading ships on the Docks in Osaka. They said they had all the food they could eat since they had learned how to steal the Japs blind while loading supplies on the Jap ships. I asked, "What do you mean, you were in a propaganda camp?" They said the Red Cross would come by once in a while and take pictures of them in uniform. That was the reason they permitted them to keep their uniforms. They figured the Japs would send the pictures to the International Red Cross and tell them they treated all of their POW's in a like manner.

I passed the word up the line to keep an eye on these guys as they wanted weapons to fight the Japs. They were processed through rather quickly and then moved to the Transport where they could not steal weapons and start a new war.

About 2:00 a.m. on the second day, my tail was really dragging and I was just about dead on my feet. I was suddenly jolted to full alert when the most emaciated, bedraggled group of men I had ever seen approached the Hotel. Their clothes were in rags and they all appeared to be on the brink of starvation. It turned out they were the survivors of the 4th Marine Regiment. They had been moved from China to the Philippines just prior to the outbreak of World War II.

They had fought the Japs on Bataan and Corregidor, had survived the infamous Death March in the Philippines where the Japs slaughtered many of their friends and had spent the War working in a Coal Mine in northern Japan. Many had died from starvation and the lack of medical care. The Coal Mine Shaft went down and out under the Sea of Japan. They said water seeped into the mine shaft constantly and the Jap Guards would not go deep into the mine with them. But if they did not send up enough coal for the day, they would be lined up and beaten with a bamboo stick and not given any food.

It appeared to me all of them should be sent to the Hospital Ship immediately. They were in such bad shape they would do anything they were told to do without question, much like a herd of sheep. All except one.

This turned out to be one of the most heartrending emotional experiences I ever encountered. When told to put their personal effects in the room provided for such items, all of them did so immediately except one. He held a small wooden box about the size of a cigar box.

It was painted white and had a metal handle the man held tightly in his hand. When I told him to place the box in the room along with the other items, he said, "This is my buddy, Sergeant (I regret that I did not write down the name). I am taking him home". In my exhausted state, I did not realize the full impact of what he was telling me and ordered him to put the small box into the room. He again said, "Look this is my buddy and I am taking him home". He then tugged at my arm and said, "Let me tell you about my buddy. We were in China together and moved to the Philippines just before the war started. We fought the Japs on Bataan and Corregidor and survived the Death March. We were moved to Japan and worked in the Coal Mines for three years. We survived the torture and slave labor, poor food and lack of medical attention. When the war ended, the B-29's started flying over the POW camp dropping pallets of food by parachute. My buddy ate a lot of canned peaches and became sick. He went back into the old barracks where we were housed to rest. When the next flight of B-29's came over to drop food, one of the parachutes did not open. The pallet of food went through the roof of our barracks and killed my best friend. We cremated his body and this box contains his ashes and I am taking him home. Neither you nor anyone else is going to take this box away from me".

I had seen an awful lot of death since Pearl Harbor, but this story made an emotional impact upon me that to this day causes me problems when I think about it. I wished the man good luck and told him to proceed with his friend through the processing routine.

The survivors of the 4th Marines also had a mongrel dog with them they had picked up along the Soochow Creek in Shanghai, China as their mascot. They smuggled the dog aboard ship when they were moved to the Philippines and somehow managed to keep the dog with them during their long ordeal. The dog's name was "Soochow" and they told me the dog was the thing that kept many of them alive. They said many of their comrades just gave up in despair, pulled a blanket over their head when they went to bed and died! They had lost the will to live.

After the experience I had just been through with the man taking his friends ashes home, I was not about to tell them they could not keep the dog, but instead told them to try to keep the dog out of sight when they went aboard ship. (Many years later, I read a story in Leatherneck Magazine concerning the dog "Soochow". They did indeed manage to smuggle him back to the United States where he died of old age).

In addition to the Marine POW's, there were also many Army and Navy Personnel, a lot of British Colonial Troops and a few Dutch Troops that had been captured in Dutch East Indies (now Indonesia). We processed about 3,600 POW's of all types. All of the POW's in our group were Enlisted Personnel. The officers had been sent to different POW Camps and were picked up and processed by another group.

Years later I served with some of the Marines who had been POW's. A number of them remained in the Marine Corps. Everyone I encountered had health problems and deep emotional scars as a result of their treatment by the Japs. They had what became known as a 1,000 yard stare. They did not look at you. They appeared to be looking through you when you talked to them. Remembering my experience in processing the POW's at Wakayama, Japan, I had nothing but sympathy and a deep respect for them. Many of them died at an early age and very few survived long enough to retire from the Marine Corps.

I have no first hand experience to know how the Americans who were POW's of the Germans suffered during captivity but to put it into perspective, I read a document many years after World War II which stated that less than 1% of the Americans captured by the Germans died in German POW Camps while 40% of the Americans captured by the Japanese died in the Jap POW Camps!

After all of the POW's had been processed and sent home, we turned the Hotel back to the Jap owners and went back aboard the MONTPELIER.

Our ship had not been invited to be present in Tokyo Bay for the formal surrender ceremonies, since we were occupied picking up the Prisoners of

War. We did, however, listen to the broadcast of the activities over the Ship's Radio.

We stayed at Wakayama for some time and had an opportunity to go ashore to look around. I had been too busy working with the POW's to pay attention to the surrounding area but with that job out of the way we were free to look the area over. Most of the city of Wakayama was in pretty good shape, however all of the factories in the area were bombed and burned out with nothing but burned machinery and steel skeletons of the buildings left.

I watched some Jap women harvesting rice. They were wading in muck up over their knees. They would reach down and cut a handful of rice (looks a lot like wheat) and carefully place it in a burlap looking container strapped to their back. They always placed the heads of the rice in the same direction. As soon as they had a large bundle of rice on their back they would wade through the muck to the edge of the Rice Paddy and carefully tie the rice to a Bamboo rack to dry, with the heads pointed toward the sun. They would remove the rice that had been allowed to dry from the rack and carry it to a small shed near the Rice Paddy. This turned out to be where they removed the Rice from the straw. There was a very primitive looking machine made of wood that one woman would walk up and down on. This was connected to a wheel that was connected to what looked like a part of a wood log with many nails driven into it. While the woman powered the treadle that made the wood log turn, another woman would take a bundle of rice straw and hold the heads against the spinning log. The nails would cause the rice to be removed from the straw and it would fall under the log onto a large straw mat. Another woman would remove the rice from the straw mat and place it on a large flat woven straw mat and throw it up into the air. The wind would separate the chaff from the rice in due course and she would place the rice into a basket and repeat the process. This labor appeared to be even worse than "picking cotton" which I had no desire to do ever again.

One of the more interesting things to watch was the Jap cars and busses. The Japs had some serious shortages of gasoline after we cut their supply convoys off from the Dutch East Indies. They had developed a Charcoal Burner to power their vehicles. This was a "Rube Goldberg" looking device, about the size of a garbage can for the automobiles, complete with a smoke pipe and a lot of plumbing. The Charcoal Burner for the trucks and busses was about the size of a 55 gallon steel drum. There was an opening near the bottom where they could stoke the fire with charcoal. The gas created by the burning charcoal was either sucked into the engine or pumped into it. The device contained a lot of plumbing but I could not understand the finer points of how the thing worked. It worked fine as long as the vehicle was going down hill or on level ground. It would stall out on hills and it was a riot to watch the busses. The Japs were not only packed into the busses like sardines in a can, but were on top and hanging on each side and on the front fenders as well. When the bus would stall out on a hill, all of the Japs would pile off and push the bus to the top of the hill, get back aboard, on top of the bus and on the front fenders and sides and away they would go to the next hill where the process would be repeated. The cars (what few there were) worked a little better but they also had difficulty getting up the hills. It appeared the charcoal gas did not develop enough power to keep the vehicles from stalling on the hills. What few trucks there were had two charcoal burners that gave them enough power to creep over the hills.

By the middle of September, the weather had cooled off to where it was comfortable during the day and quite chilly at night. It was obvious the weather was changing. A few days later, the sky became overcast and the ship started to roll from side to side. We were at anchor and the sea started to kick up large swells and soon it was raining and the wind started to howl through the superstructure and mast of the ship. The word was passed over the loud speaker to batten down all loose gear and to prepare for rough weather because there was a Typhoon (Hurricane) headed in our direction. Several large Flying Boats (Sea Planes) anchored nearby took off for parts unknown to us to escape the Typhoon. The wind and rain continued to increase and as darkness fell, the Captain of the ship' ordered the port Anchor be dropped since the Starboard Anchor was unable to hold the ship in position. The crew was served sandwiches for the evening meal because the ship was rolling from side to side so violently the cooks could not prepare the food for a regular meal. We had been in rough seas before in the Philippines but I had not experienced anything like this since 1942 aboard the ENTERPRISE after our raid on Wake Island and Marcus Island when I thought the ENTERPRISE was going to roll over.

There was very little sleep aboard the MONTPELIER that night. Those who tried to sleep would be tossed out of their bunk. The Captain spent the night on the Bridge. In addition to having both anchors out, he directed the Engine Room to tum up all four engines to keep us from dragging anchor. It became necessary to increase speed to 13 knots to maintain our position. The ship was designed to sustain a 45 degree roll and our maximum roll during the night was 38 degrees. There was concern we would roll over because additional weight had been added to the superstructure of the ship after it had been designed, with the addition of the Radar and Gun Fire Control Directors that were several feet higher than the Bridge. Around 2:00 a.m. the device on the Mainmast which measures wind speed was torn away and the last recorded wind speed was 115 knots! Before daylight, the wind and sea abated and everyone gave a sigh of relief. I heard more than one man say he thought it would be a hell'ova thing to survive the war only to be drowned in a Typhoon.

When daylight finally came, many people went topside to see what had happened to the other ships. There was a sad sight on the beach near the cliffs! There were four ships lying on their side on the beach. One of the Minesweepers that had preceded us through the Minefields in the Inland Sea was smashed against large rocks on the beach and broken in half. There were two LSD's (Landing Ships that hauled tanks, trucks, bulldozers and other heavy equipment) and one Transport Ship. We never did hear how many members of their crew was lost but the visible evidence indicated there must have been many.

The Typhoon that hit us at Wakayama also devastated the Island of Okinawa. Okinawa was the main staging area for the invasion of the home Islands of Japan. The 7th Fleet Bombardment Group, of which the MONTPELIER was a prominent member, was scheduled to start the shore bombardment of the Island of Kyushu on September 15, 1945 with landings to take place on November 15, 1945 had the war not ended. The invasion of Japan may well have been a catastrophe of the first magnitude. Our Bombardment Group would have no doubt suffered serious damages during the Typhoon but the invasion force on Okinawa was seriously damaged as well. We lost four ships at Wakayama in the Inland Sea. It is difficult to imagine what our losses would have been had we been bombarding the coast of Kyushu.

The Japanese place great faith in what they call the "Divine Wind". This was because a Typhoon wiped out the Invasion Fleet of Kublai Khan in 1274 and again in 1281 as they were attempting to invade the Island of Kyushu! In fact they called their suicide pilots the "Divine Wind". Had they used the same suicide tactics earlier in the War, the results may have been quite different. In that case, there would probably not be very many "Soft Headed" College Professors offering condolences for the victims of Hiroshima and Nagasaki and stating that we never should have used the Atomic Bomb on such cities. I never hear them say that the Japs should never have bombed Pearl Harbor or slaughtered our Prisoners of War on the Death March in the Philippine Islands. I must also admit I have regrets concerning the use of Atomic Bombs to end World War II. My regret is that we only had two Atomic Bombs available and they were not available much earlier before we lost so many good men at Peleliu, the Philippines, Iwo Jima and Okinawa.

In early October we left Wakayama for Hiro, Japan near the large city of Kobe and the huge Japanese Naval Base at Kure. Our job was to provide fire support to the Army Troops that were to land on October 6th. The Kure and Kobe area is about 240 miles southwest of Wakayama on the Inland Sea. The trip took two days since we had to work our way through many Jap minefields. The Army Occupation Troops landed without any difficulty and our fire support was not needed.

The Kure Naval Base was Japans largest Naval Base, many times larger than Pearl Harbor. The Base was a shambles. It reminded me of Pearl Harbor after December 7, 1941. There were ships of various types including the Battleship HARUNA that was supposed to have been sunk off the Island of Luzon in the Philippines in 1942. It was lying in shallow water with her main deck awash just like Battleship Row in Pearl Harbor so long ago. There was also the largest Aircraft Carrier I had ever seen lying on its side in the Harbor. There were many more ships of various types in a similar situation, sunk with their superstructure showing above the water.

The U.S. Navy Carrier Pilots really worked the place over. In two of the Dry Docks, I counted about 20 midget Submarines under construction. The larger type of midget Submarine carried a two man crew, two torpedoes and a space in the bow of the Submarine for additional explosives to be set off when the Submarine rammed an American Ship after firing the two torpedoes.

The smaller type carried only one man, had one torpedo and also explosives in the bow to explode when the Submarine rammed an American Ship. There were Airplane Factories, Machine Shops and all sorts of heavy industrial shops in the area. All of these were bombed severely and burned. The buildings were only steel skeletons of what theyonce were.

Once the Army Troops were in place, we were permitted to go ashore on sightseeing trips. On one trip several of the Chief Petty Officers and myself took picnic supplies and decided to have a picnic and softball game on what we thought was nothing more than a small deserted island in Kure Bay. To our surprise, the island was covered with extensive caves and artillery positions. Fortunately all of the Jap troops had departed.

Something else caught our attention. The island was covered with many hundreds of bamboo poles about 30 feet long and what today would be called Scuba Diving Equipment. This equipment consisted of a face mask and two air tanks with hoses from the tanks to the face mask.

We had never seen equipment of this type and could not figure out what the Japs were using it for. Some of the Intelligence Officers found out we had stumbled onto a training base for underwater suicide infantry.

They were to wade out into the water and wait for an American landing craft loaded with troops to pass over and then shove the long pole equipped with a 30 pound explosive charge into the bottom of the boat, killing 30 to 50 Americans and one Jap! We had encountered our share of Suicide Planes, some Suicide Boats in the Philippines, many more Suicide Planes and the Rocket Powered Suicide Baka Bomb at Okinawa. The Japs were prepared to use all of this plus the small Suicide Submarines and the Suicide Underwater Infantry against us when we invaded the Home Islands.

Everywhere I looked in Japan, I could see evidence of Artillery, Machine Gun and Coast Artillery positions. Had it been necessary to invade Japan, I fear it would have been a disaster even worse than that suffered by Kublai Khan in 1274 and 1281. Thank God for the Atomic Bombs that ended the War!

On one of our sightseeing tours, we ran across several "Baka Bombs" at one of the Airfields. This was the small rocket powered airplane carried under the wing of a Betty Bomber. When a ship was sighted, the bomber would kick the Baka loose. He would ignite his rocket motor and go over 500 miles per hour for a few minutes before hitting his target or crashing. Several of them hit ships at Okinawa. I looked these planes over carefully and was surprised at how crude they were. They were definitely designed to fly only one time. They did not have a landing gear and had very few instruments. They looked a little like our modern Cruise Missiles but used a Jap to more or less fly the thing. As a matter of fact the word Baka in Japanese means Crazy. The name was very descriptive because you would have to be crazy to try to fly one of them.

A few days later, some of the lower rank navy personnel were sightseeing on one of the other small islands in the Bay. Many of them returned to the Ship with what they thought was Japanese candy. One of them took a bite out of one and announced that was the worst tasting candy he had ever tasted! One of the more intelligent navy men looked at one of the "candy bars" and noticed some Japanese writing on the wrapper. We had a Navy Lieutenant (JG) on the Ship who could speak, read and write Japanese. The more intelligent type took his "candy bar" to the Lieutenant and said this was the worst tasting candy he had ever tried to eat. The Lieutenant said" My God!, this is Jap Dynamite! How much of this stuff was brought aboard ship"? The shocked sailor told him a bunch of the guys had some in their pocket when they returned to the ship. The Lieutenant took off in a dead run for the Executive Officer's Cabin. The Executive Officer got on the Ship's speaker system and called for the attention of all hands to listen to what he had to say.

He explained that Jap Dynamite had been brought aboard ship by men who thought they were bringing Jap candy aboard. He ordered an inspection of all areas of the ship, including in particular all trash containers since he thought most of the Dynamite would be tossed into the trashcan after the sailors had tried to eat it. It took several hours to round up all of the Dynamite and to interview everyone in the group that had been ashore that day. I was glad there were no Marines in the group and hoped they would not be stupid enough to bring anything aboard ship that even remotely resembled explosives. After the Executive Officer was satisfied all of the Dynamite had been collected, he had it moved to the stern of the ship and personally supervised the process of throwing it over board.

In late October we covered another landing of Army Occupation Troops on the Island of Shikoku. This is another of the main Japanese islands and is on the southeast side of the Inland Sea between the Islands of Honshu and Kyushu.

After the Army was safely in position on the Island of Shikoku we departed for the Island of Honshu. Our destination was the city of Hiroshima, or what was left of it. We arrived the following day and dropped anchor in Hiroshima Bay. The devastation of the city was apparent from the ship. We were sent ashore in small groups to observe the effects of the Atomic Bomb dropped on August 6.

The only thing we knew about the Atomic Bomb was that it packed the equivalent of 20,000 tons of TNT. We knew nothing of Radiation or the possible consequences of being exposed to Radiation. My first impression was the evidence of tremendous heat. The only thing left standing were smokestacks where factories had once existed and many safes that were no doubt in destroyed business buildings. There were a few of the earthquake proof buildings made of reinforced concrete. These buildings showed evidence of the extreme heat and the steel casement windows were torn loose from their mountings. The remains of what once had been trolley cars appeared to be fused together from the intense heat as well as what remained of automobiles that appeared to have been in a parking lot.

Unlike Manila where there were dead bodies buried under fallen buildings and lying in ditches and other areas with green flies everywhere and a stench that would "gag a maggot", what remained of Hiroshima was free of dead bodies and animals. There was no stench. The bodies had probably been turned to ashes. I also noticed there were no flies, birds or insects. The only noise was the sound of our feet as we walked through the area. The troops were also very quiet. I guessed every man was busy with his own thoughts and impressions. There were living Japanese in the outlying areas away from the blast area, but there were none in the area where we were located.

I left Hiroshima with no guilt feelings whatsoever. I had seen evidence of the cruelty inflicted upon our people by the Japs and realized the city of Hiroshima contained many factories that were turning out equipment to kill us when we invaded their Home Islands. In my view there were no "innocent civilians" in Hiroshima or Nagasaki! We remained in the area of Hiroshima and Kure for a few more weeks and on November 8, 1945 we set sail for the United States and home! Most of us finally realized the war was really over and we had survived! The Chaplain had a full house at Religious Services on Sunday.

We had about 450 extra Army Personnel aboard that were going home to be discharged. They put troops on every ship and plane headed for the United States in order to get the boys home as soon as possible. The trip across the Pacific was uneventful. The ship was extremely crowded with the extra Army Personnel aboard. There were long lines for showers and food and some bunks were used in shifts. However everyone was happy to be going home. After what they had been through, they could not be bothered by a little inconvenience. We stopped at Pearl Harbor for food and fuel. The Harbor did not look like the same place! All of the sunken ships except the ARIZONA had been re-floated and many of them saw combat against the Japs after they had been repaired. The next day we departed Pearl Harbor for San Diego.

We arrived at San Diego on December 1, 1945. As we entered the harbor we could see a large banner draped across the entire end of one of the large warehouses on the Pier. It said in large letters "Welcome Home Veterans, Well Done". As the Captain eased the Ship alongside the Pier, suddenly a Marching Band appeared on the Pier led by about a dozen very pretty young girls dressed in scant little uniforms that looked like they had been sprayed on! Just as suddenly 1,500 men ran over to the Port Side of the Ship to get a good look! Two "idiots" could not wait and jumped overboard and had to be fished out of the Water. With 1,500 men on the Port Side of the Ship, we took on a sharp list to port and started drifting away from the Pier. The Captain got on the "Bull Horn" and said, "You people are causing the ship to drift away from the Pier. I want exactly half of you to move immediately to the Starboard Side. I am as anxious to get ashore as you are but we are never going to get this ship docked until we are on an even keel". Everyone could understand that kind of talk. At least half of them moved to the starboard side. The ship eased into the dock and the gangway was in place in short order.

There was a mad scramble to get ashore and a flurry of activity on the dock since there were many wives and families waiting to greet their loved ones.

The MONTPELIER would remain in San Diego for a few days and then sail for the Panama Canal and then to the Navy Yard at Brooklyn, New York. Many of the Sailors and one-half of the Marines were given a 30 day leave with orders to join the ship in Brooklyn, New York at the expiration of the 30 day leave. I arranged to be in the group given leave immediately. Chris and Sharon were living in a small apartment in Wills Point, Texas. I got word to her I would be home in a few days. Two days later, I left San Diego by Greyhound Bus with a ticket to Dallas, Texas. The Bus was packed with some people sitting in the aisle on their baggage.

Things went reasonably well, considering the crowded conditions until we reached El Paso, Texas. At El Paso, we were informed all Bus Drivers from El Paso east to Dallas were on strike! The language was most colorful when we heard this news! This was late in the afternoon and the four of us going to Dallas were trying to figure out what to do next. Around midnight we located a man who had a 1940 Chevrolet 2 Door Sedan. He agreed to take the four of us to Dallas for $100.00. We quickly agreed, piled our luggage in the trunk of the car and departed from El Paso. We were exhausted and immediately fell asleep. Around 3:00 am, I awoke and decided something was wrong.

We were headed in a southeastern direction but my keen sense of direction told me that by this time we should be going northeast.

When I quizzed the driver, he said we were headed for San Antonio! I told him we were going to go to Dallas. He said San Antonio. I shook the other three guys awake and told them we paid this jerk $100.00 to take us to Dallas and he said we were going to San Antonio. We agreed we would remove the driver from his driving responsibility and one of us would take the wheel unless he had an immediate change of attitude. The driver quickly realized we meant just what we said. As soon as he could find a road that would lead us north to U.S. Highway 80 he turned north and we finally hit Highway 80 near Midland, Texas.

We arrived in Dallas late in the afternoon and I caught a Taxi to Blackburn Street where Mr. and Mrs. McDonald lived. Chris and Sharon were there waiting for me. What a happy day! I could not believe how Sharon had grown and changed. She was less than a year old when I left and now she was running all over the place, talking up a storm. I am afraid I had a little difficulty getting used to being called Daddy.

A short time after dinner, Christene's Uncle Roy Bristow arrived. He had recently been discharged from the Army Air Corps in California and was in the process of visiting his relatives. The next day, the three of us went to Wills Point. The 1937 Ford we had purchased in California in 1944 was still running and came in handy when we went to Fannin County to visit my Grandparents and Jack and Pauline Chaney.

After a few days in Fannin County we went to Hollister, Oklahoma to visit my Granddad Culbreath. We spent two days in Oklahoma and then back to Wills Point. All too soon my 30 day leave was coming to an end and it was necessary that I allow a few days to get to Brooklyn, New York to rejoin the MONTPELIER. I did not know what the future held but planned to have Chris and Sharon join me in Brooklyn if it appeared that we would be there for some time.

The trip from Wills Point to St. Louis was uneventful, but from St. Louis to New York City was terrible. The train was so crowded you could barely move. It was packed with servicemen on their way home. All seats were taken. People were sitting in the aisle and the open areas between the rail cars was jam packed with people. Today there would be a Congressional Investigation if a train were so crammed. Everyone was so happy to be going home they could care less how crowded things were.

After three days and nights on the train, we finally arrived in New York City. Everyone was getting a little ripe by this time and I was anxious to get back aboard the MONTPELIER, get a shower and some sleep.

Getting from the Railroad Station in Manhattan to Brooklyn was quite an experience, but I finally found the MONTPELIER tied up at one of the Piers at the Brooklyn Navy Yard. Half of the crew was on leave and many of the others were in the process of being discharged. No one, including the Captain of the Ship had an idea of what was in store for us. Since it appeared we might be in Brooklyn for some time, I started looking for an apartment so Chris and Sharon could join me. It appeared that as large as Brooklyn was, there was not an apartment available in the city.

It was extremely cold in Brooklyn, a lot of snow and ice. I spent most of my time aboard ship trying to keep up with all of the paperwork. Gibbons was on leave and I not only had to prepare all of the various reports but had to type them as well. I did get over to Manhattan a couple of times but it did not impress me at all. Too many people milling around. They were rude and always in a hurry. When a train pulled into one of the Subway stations they would run and push and shove each other trying to get aboard the train. I would usually stand back and watch since I knew there would be another one going to the same place in about 5 minutes. I decided I would not live there if they gave me the place!

After about a month, we received word the MONTPELIER would be assigned duties of transporting troops from Europe to the United States. Since all berthing spaces were needed, the Marines would be transferred from the Ship. We were to go by train to Portsmouth Navy Yard at Portsmouth, Virginia where the Marine Detachment would be disbanded. We were directed to discharge all members of the Detachment who requested a Discharge. All equipment and supplies were to be inventoried, packed and shipped to the Marine Corps Supply Depot in Philadelphia, Pennsylvania.

We still had quite a supply of clothing aboard. Before we left Mare Island, California a year and a half ago, I had been told to obtain enough clothing from the Supply Depot in San Francisco to last at least two years. I padded the request somewhat and as a result we had a good supply on hand to be inventoried and invoiced to the Philadelphia Supply Depot. We also had Landing Force Equipment aboard that had never been used. This was to be used if it became necessary to provide a landing force from the Marines aboard ship. This equipment consisted of additional weapons, field kitchen, tents and supplies that would be needed ashore. I was glad to see Sergeant Gibbons return from leave so he could relieve me of the typing job. It required about 10 days to complete the administrative details required to remove the Marines from the MONTPELIER and bid our farewell. We went from Brooklyn to Manhattan by subway. The MONTPELIER Marines were a sharp looking group of men and the civilians really gawked at us. They probably couldn't figure out why we were still in uniform. We boarded a train in Manhattan and arrived at the Navy Yard in Portsmouth, Virginia the next day.

We were not a welcome guest at the Marine Barracks! It was soon discovered that Marine Detachments were being transferred from ships all along the East Coast and they were all converging upon the Marine Barracks, Portsmouth, Virginia to be disbanded. The Marine Barracks was crawling with unemployed First Sergeants whose Marine Detachments had been disbanded. The First Sergeant of the Marine Barracks was so fearful one of them would steal his job he would not go ashore for any reason. He would neither speak to one of them nor provide them with the time of day!

Captain Grady finally located a room where we could set up our typewriter and get on with the paperwork involved in disbanding the Marine Detachment. All members of the Detachment except the Platoon Sergeant, Gunnery Sergeant and myself, were discharged. We prepared the final

Muster Roll and Daily Report. Captain Grady signed them and we mailed them to Marine Corps Headquarters. That was the end of the Marine Detachment, U.S.S.MONTPELIER (CL-57).

I am not sure where Captain Grady and Lieutenant Turner went. The Gunnery Sergeant and myself were transferred to the Naval Base at nearby Norfolk, Virginia.

When we arrived at the Marine Barracks, Naval Base, Norfolk, Virginia, we discovered there were no lower rank enlisted personnel and very few officers. They had all been discharged! There were however, plenty of First Sergeants, Gunnery Sergeants and Platoon Sergeants. Only one was employed as the First Sergeant of the Marine Barracks. Others were assigned guard duties normally performed by Privates and Privates First Class. One of the first things they did was determine my date of rank. Since I had been promoted to First Sergeant in August 1943, instead of walking post, I was assigned duties as Commander of the Guard. This would normally be done by a Second Lieutenant, but since there were no Second Lieutenants, this was my job. The job was not very challenging and I had lots of free time so I started looking for an apartment for Chris and Sharon.

I finally located a small place in Norfolk. Not very desirable but at least we could be together. The least desirable feature was a coal burning, pot bellied stove for heat!

Chris and Sharon arrived by train in about a week. We made do with the apartment for a few weeks until my name came up on the waiting list for an apartment in the Navy Housing Area. The only drawback was that the apartments in the Navy Housing Area were unfurnished. The occupants of the apartment assigned to us agreed to sell their furniture to us, and we were eager to leave the coal burning apartment in Norfolk. We were short on cash and agreed to have Mr. McDonald sell the 1937 Ford for us. This was accomplished in short order because cars were in big demand at that time. There was adequate public transportation in Norfolk, and we really did not need the car at the time.

In June 1946, I received orders transferring me to the Southeastern Recruiting Division in Atlanta, Georgia for further assignment to the Recruiting District Headquarters in Birmingham, Alabama as First Sergeant of the District.

We did not know what to expect housing wise in Birmingham but thought the best thing would be for Chris and Sharon to return to Dallas and stay with her parents until I could locate housing in Birmingham.

It turned out this was a smart move! I spent two days in Atlanta being briefed and then left for Birmingham. When I arrived in Birmingham, the Marines from the Recruiting Station were on hand to meet me at the Railroad Station. My thoughts were that things were improving.

The Major in Command of the Recruiting Station greeted me like a long lost friend and made my day as pleasant as possible. Finding a place to stay was a real problem.

We finally located a room in one of the Hotels, but there was a three day limit on how long they would permit anyone to stay. I finally located a room in a private home that I shared with a Tool and Die maker from one of the Steel Mills in Birmingham.

This was a most unsatisfactory arrangement and I spent my off duty hours searching for an apartment. After two weeks of searching for a place to live, I finally located a new little house on the northeast edge of Birmingham for $3,500 with a $500.00 down payment and a monthly payment of about $50.00 per month. The house was small with two bedrooms, bath, kitchen and living room. It was wired for an electric stove, but there was none to be had.

The house was plugged into the Tennessee Valley Authority Electricity and there was tremendous competition between TVA and Birmingham Electric. The salesman from Birmingham Electric was trying to convince me to discontinue TVA Power and plug into Birmingham Electric. I finally told him to find me an electric stove and he could pull the meter belonging to TVA and plug in Birmingham Electric. The next day he told me where to go to obtain a stove.

Chris and Sharon arrived in a couple of days and we purchased enough furniture to make do. We never did obtain a Refrigerator since they were not available! The little house was comfortable enough for the times but it was in an undesirable location. There was a Bus Stop about two blocks away and I would ride the Bus for about 20 minutes and then transfer to a Trolley for the remainder of the trip downtown where the Recruiting Station was located. The commute involved about one hour each way.

Grocery shopping was a chore for Chris and Sharon since they also had to ride the bus to the shopping area and then carry the groceries up the hill to the house from the Bus Stop. In late summer of 1946, Christene's parents and grandparents came to visit us. The little house was crowded but we managed to survive.

The house was not equipped with a heating system and as winter approached we started looking seriously for some means to heat the house. Most small houses in the area used a coal or oil burning space heater. We finally located and purchased an oil burning space heater. I did not care for coal because it was too messy.

Birmingham in 1946 was called the Pittsburgh of the South and for good reason. There were steel mills on the north and west side of town and a pig-iron plant on the east side of town. To make matters worse, all of the older houses used coal fired space heaters or coal fired furnaces to heat a boiler for steam heat. As a result Birmingham, in fact all of Jones Valley (where Birmingham is located), was a dirty place to live. My office was located in the center of downtown Birmingham and my desk was covered with an oily soot every morning when I came to work. The entire city was a dirty nasty place.

Where we lived out on the edge of town was a little better than the downtown area but we still had days when the air was terrible. The Birmingham Recruiting District covered the entire state of Alabama. We had Sub-Stations in Huntsville, Anniston, Montgomery and Mobile.

There were about 40 Marines all total and the Commander was Major O'Connel. In early 1947 we were assigned an additional Officer, First Lieutenant G. T. Annitage. I was not involved in actual recruiting as such. My duty as First Sergeant was to take care of the routine administrative details and paper work. We provided a Color Guard for every parade in the state of Alabama or so it seemed. It also appeared that every Marine Officer and Senior Enlisted Man from the state of Alabama decided to reside somewhere else. It was our responsibility to arrange to have their household goods and personal effects shipped to their new home of record. This required us to obtain bids from three moving companies, accept the lowest bid and see that they did the proper job of packing and crating the household goods for shipment.

The young First Lieutenant was a real "eager beaver". He was always dreaming up ways to obtain publicity for the Marine Corps. He became friends with a man who owned horses and cooked up a scheme to borrow the friend's horses and have a Mounted Color Guard for the next parade. The Marines worked very hard to make the Mounted Color Guard a success. The only problem was that it was too successful. Pictures appeared in every major Newspaper in Alabama and we were flooded with requests to have our Mounted Color Guard appear in just about every parade in Alabama. Unfortunately, we did not own the horses and had no way to transport them even if we could borrow them regularly. We spent a lot of time with correspondence fending off requests for the Mounted Color Guard.

In one of the parades, Admiral Halsey came to town and was the Grand Marshal. I had served as his Orderly (runner, messenger) aboard the ENTERPRISE in 1940. I was assigned the job of escorting him during the parade. He remembered me from the days on the ENTERPRISE and we got a lot of publicity mileage out of the event. That was the last time I saw him. He spent the remaining few months of his life trying to save the ENTERPRISE from the scrap heap but to no avail. The ENTERPRISE was the most famous ship in the entire U.S. Navy and would be a remarkable tourist attraction today. However when it was scrapped no one cared about preserving anything that would remind them of the recent War.

In early 1947, we located an Apartment in an old residential part of Birmingham. It was in an area of old very large homes. Our Apartment was servants quarters at one time and space wise was larger than our little house. I did not enjoy the long commute to work and we decided we would sell the little house and move into the Apartment. The Apartment had steam heat and supplemental heat was provided by a coal burning fireplace. I could ride the bus to Work and it only took about 15 minutes to accomplish. The grocery shopping was much easier for Chris and Sharon.

The young First Lieutenant was promoted to Captain and transferred to his own Command at Jacksonville, Florida where he earned quite a reputation for himself in Recruiting Circles.

In the Spring I managed to get a few days leave and Chris, Sharon and I rode the bus to Texas to visit our relatives. While we were visiting Mr. and Mrs. McDonald we met a man who wanted to sell his 1942 Oldsmobile for $1,000. We did not have any money but Mr. McDonald said he would loan us the $1,000 and we could pay it back at $50.00 per month. We took him up on the offer and after visiting my Grandparents in Ladonia and Aunt Pauline and Uncle Jack Chaney in Windom, we returned to Terrell for a few more days and then drove the Oldsmobile back to Birmingham. It was a very good car but the gasoline tank had a leak where the filler spout joined the tank and it was necessary to stop for gasoline about every 100 miles. If you put very much gasoline in the tank it would leak out. We had the tank repaired in Birmingham and drove the car until we bought our first new car about a year and a half later.

The Marines assigned to Recruiting Duty were usually Senior Non-Commissioned Officers. Many of them had been in the Marine Corps for many years and some of them had difficulty dealing with potential recruits and civilians in general. From time to time it became necessary to relieve one of his assignments and send him back to regular Marine Corps duties. Since this was a problem nationwide, the Marine Corps decided to start a Recruiters School at Parris Island, South Carolina. Captain Armitage (our former eager beaver Lieutenant) would organize and command the school. He was given authority to select his own staff of instructors.

PARRIS ISLAND

In early October 1947, the Chief Clerk opened the mail and orders fell out directing that I be transferred to Parris Island, South Carolina without delay for duty as an Instructor at the Recruiters' School that was being formed. I had not received any warning of a pending transfer but knew immediately Captain Armitage was responsible for it.

We fully expected there would not be housing available at Parris Island. We placed our furniture in storage and Chris and Sharon rode the bus to Texas to stay with her parents until I could locate a place for us to live. I drove the 1942 Oldsmobile to Parris Island. Upon arrival I learned there was a waiting list of about one year for base housing.

My job at the Recruiters' School was to teach typing and Business Correspondence. Other personnel would teach Recruiting Techniques and Captain Armitage would teach Public Speaking. The students were required to type 35 words per minute in order to graduate. Some of the old time Sergeants were all thumbs and teaching them to touch type was quite a challenge. Otherwise my job was pretty cushy as Marine Corps assignments go. After about three weeks on Parris island a Hurricane swept up the Coast. The wind was not too severe but it hit the Island during High Tide. As a result the entire Island was covered, except for about two acres around the Base Headquarters, with at least two feet of salt water.

I managed to park the Oldsmobile upon the sidewalk and did not get any salt water in the motor. Many automobiles were ruined because their owners left them in a low area. The water was in all of the Barracks and created quite a mess.

I was happy Chris and Sharon were in Texas. There were no civilian apartments or houses available in the area of Port Royal or Beaufort, South Carolina. The Marine Corps had converted an old bachelor Non-Commissioned Officers Quarters into living quarters for married personnel. Each family was permitted one or two rooms, depending upon how many children were involved. The shower and other facilities were located down the hall and all meals were taken in a common dining area. The cooking and cleaning duties were performed by the wives on a rotating basis with several women being assigned such duties for about one week each month. The cost of food was totaled up at the end of the month and each family would be assessed an amount equal to the number of family members residing in the facility. This arrangement was most unsatisfactory but under the circumstances it was the best that could be had.

Chris and Sharon rode the train from Dallas to Savannah, Georgia. I met them in Savannah and they were soon introduced to our living quarters on

Parris Island. They were not too thrilled with the arrangement but made the best of a bad situation. One of the students in my class had an apartment in an old Plantation about five miles from Parris Island. He would be leaving the area upon graduation from the Recruiters' School. He put in a good word for me with the owners and we soon went out for an interview. The owners were named Gray. The family consisted of the old lady, her son, his wife (both middle aged) and their small son.

The Plantation had once consisted of several hundred acres, but the family had fallen upon evil times and the land holdings had been reduced to less than 100 acres. The house was a large two story with brick walls at least two feet thick. A portion of the upper floor had been converted into an Apartment which they rented for $50.00 per month. They still maintained a working Plantation. By working plantation, I mean that Blacks did all of the work. There were the regular field hands plus a combination cook, maid and cleaning lady and an outside "boy" named Willie. The family did not lift a finger to work. The cook-maid had to answer the door when a guest arrived! This was a new experience for us. We passed their inspection and were happy to move into our own Apartment.

We really liked living in the country. Sharon had a large play area and she made friends with a little Black girl who was the daughter of the cook-maid. The house was about 300 feet from the road. The driveway was lined with huge Live Oak trees that also extended around the house. They were about 4 feet in diameter and probably 75 feet tall. Mrs. Gray (the old lady) informed us they were planted by her ancestors before the war. (She meant the Revolutionary War).

Chris and I both thought we were from the South but the South Carolina Plantation Mentality was a new experience for us. The wife of Mr. Gray taught school in Beaufort and they lived on her salary plus the $50.00 per month rent from the apartment. They maintained a façade of "Southern Gentility" as though they were well off financially. They appeared to make enough off of the land to pay the taxes and the hired help.

The Recruiters' School was located next to the Bay and during the lunch hour I would catch Sea Trout and Crabs. I purchased a crab basket and with this device, I could catch a bucket full of crabs as large as my hand during the lunch hour.

The first time I brought a bucket full of live crabs home for Chris to cook was quite an experience. I thought she would know how to cook them but she did not know what to do with them. We left them in the bucket and went to bed. During the night, they crawled out of the bucket and were scattered all over the apartment. There was a lot of squealing .from Chris and Sharon the next morning when we tried to round up all of the crabs. The next day, she learned from the Gray's cook-maid that you were supposed to put them into boiling water when they were still alive! We tried this in the apartment. What a stink! We learned it is best to cook them outside.

The humidity at Parris Island was terrible and I had problems with a sinus infection much of the time. Otherwise our tour at Parris Island was a good assignment. In the summer we spent almost every week-end at the beach. The beach was about 10 miles from Parris Island and was never very crowded. There was a movie theater on the base with free admission. We saw all of the latest movies. Chris shopped at the base Commissary and on Saturday afternoon we would go into Beaufort and just before going home we would go by the Bakery and buy fresh bread right out of the oven. Most of the time, we would eat the entire loaf before we arrived home.

In 1948, I took flying lessons-at the nearby Airport. After obtaining my Private Pilots License, I could carry passengers. The Airplane was a little Piper Cub, really fun to fly. I also flew the P-19 (World War II Army Trainer). One nice Saturday, I talked Chris and Sharon into going for an airplane ride with me. Everything was fine until we became airborne. Chris said she did not feel well. I circled the field and prepared to land. While we were on final approach to the runway, Chris got really sick when we started the letdown. In a Piper Cub, the Pilot flies the plane from the rear seat and the passenger is in the front seat. As we neared the end of the runway, Chris started to vomit! The prop wash blew it right into my face! I finally was able to see enough to get the plane down to a safe landing and we agreed that perhaps she should not take any more airplane rides with me.

After about a year living in the Gray's Apartment, we were assigned to quarters on the base. This was a two bedroom Duplex and was reasonably comfortable. The only problem was no insulation in the walls separating the two Apartments and the couple on the other side would go out every Saturday night and get boozed up. They would arrive home around 2:00 a.m. and get into a big fight that would last until dawn. They were nice and quiet the rest of the time but we knew we would be awake half the night every Saturday night.

Before Christmas in 1948, we purchased our first new automobile. It was a 1948 Plymouth 4-door sedan. It was a very comfortable car but it seemed that if you ran over a large cigar butt it would knock the front Wheels out of alignment. We also had to replace the universal joints at least twice. Otherwise it was relatively trouble free which was good for automobiles built during that time.

In 1949 my tour of duty at the Recruiters' School was coming to an end and it looked like I might be transferred to Camp Lejeune, North Carolina. Chris was pregnant and I knew if I were transferred to Camp Lejeune I would spend a large part of the time out in the boondocks on training exercises. I decided to see if I could arrange a transfer to the West Coast, preferably San Diego or Camp Pendleton. I had an old friend from my U.S.S. ENTERPRISE days in Marine Corps Headquarters in Washington. I took leave and paid him a visit. The only assignment on the West Coast that was available was with the 12th Marine Corps Reserve District in San Francisco.

It would involve 30 days special Schooling in Washington and 3 days in New York City before reporting to San Francisco with a 30 day leave enroute. I was delighted with this assignment. I returned to Parris Island and orders came through in about two weeks directing my transfer to San Francisco with temporary duty in Washington for a period of 30 days.

We sold our furniture before leaving Paris Island, shipped a few things to San Francisco, loaded our personal things into the car and departed from Paris Island. We stayed with our friends in Washington, the ones that stood up for us at our wedding, the Livingstons. The 30 days in Washington passed quickly. I was being briefed every day on my new duties and had to go to New York City for three days for special briefing. I did not enjoy New York any more than I did while stationed there on the MONTPELIER three years earlier.

On our way to Texas to visit relatives, we stopped off in Virginia to visit an old friend from the MONTPELIER. He worked for the Appalachian Power Company and lived back in the mountains at Grundy, Virginia in the Coal Mining area. We arrived on a Friday afternoon and had planned to leave the next morning. He would not let us leave until Sunday morning because the Coal Miners come out of the mines on Friday night and get boozed up and run up and down the two lane roads all day Saturday and Saturday night. He said I would be taking too many chances of being in a wreck unless we waited until Sunday morning and leave while they were sleeping off their wild weekend. They were telling us the truth because on Sunday morning when we left, we saw a number of wrecked cars on the road.

After leaving Virginia, we proceeded to Texas and spent several days with Christene's parents in Dallas and visited Jack and Pauline Chaney in Windom. Chris was pregnant and the heat in Texas bothered her. We were not looking forward to the trip through New Mexico and Arizona in the middle of the summer.

I found a device in Dallas they called an Air Conditioner that would fit the 1948 Plymouth. This device fit on the upper part of the window on the passenger side. It was about two feet long and about 12 inches in diameter. It had a wind scoop in front that forced air through a wet filter kept wet by water dripping from a tank. It held about a gallon of water. It worked like a present day Evaporative Cooler (swamp cooler). The device kept the car reasonably comfortable in Texas but when we hit New Mexico with the low humidity, we could not keep water in the tank. It would evaporate in a very short time. This let hot air into the car in great volume. We thought we were having a tough time.

A few hours later, we knew we were having a bad time. About 30 miles west of Las Cruces, New Mexico, we noticed a very dark, heavy looking cloud low on the horizon. A car with New Mexico license plates ahead of us suddenly made a U-turn and headed back toward Las Cruces at a high rate of speed. We thought, what is wrong with that guy? He must have never seen a cloud before. As we approached the cloud, we could see lightening and the cloud was still low and appeared to be rolling toward us. In a few minutes we figured out why the other car made a U-turn and headed back to Las Cruces!

Soon we were engulfed in a violent sandstorm! We both thought we had seen sandstorms in East Texas, but nothing like this. We could barely see the road 10 feet ahead and the sand was coming in through the Air Cooler and hitting Chris in the head. Her hair was a mess. I managed to remove the Air Cooler and roll the window up. This helped some, but the dust managed to enter the car from all directions. We drove in the dust for what seemed to be several hours at about 5 miles per hour. The thunder and lightning increased and the wind almost blew us off the road. Eventually it started to rain, very slowly. Instead of water, it was raining mud! I did not know it was possible to rain mud. In 1949, cars did not have windshield washers and pretty soon our windshield was covered with mud. The rain finally increased to a slow drizzle and we were able to see the road.

We arrived in Deming, New Mexico around 9:00 p.m., and found a Motel that had a vacancy. We all had baths and were glad to wash the sand out of our hair. The rain increased during the night and washed the sand and dust out of the air. We were really happy to see the sun and clear sky the next morning as we departed for California. The rest of the trip was uneventful except that Chris was very uncomfortable and suffered from nausea in the mountains.

For a long time, I had been telling Chris about what a beautiful place New Mexico was. I had been across there by train and bus several times and was impressed by the beauty of the place, especially the herds of Pronghorn Antelope browsing along the highway. She was not impressed, especially after the dust and sandstorm we had encountered. I told her, "Wait until you see the northern part of New Mexico".

SAN FRANCISCO

We drove up the beautiful Coast Highway in California to San Francisco. We found a Motel in Daly City on the Pacific Ocean on the west side of San Francisco. The next morning, I checked into my duty station at 100 Harrison Street. This was the Headquarters of the 12th Marine Corps Reserve District. The area included all of Northern California, most of Nevada and the state of Utah. My assignment was in the Personnel Department. My immediate concern was a place to live. The Motel was very expensive and it was miserably cold near the Ocean, even in the middle of the summer!

After a few days, we obtained quarters in a Naval Housing Area known as Guam Village. These were small individual buildings built during World War II as temporary housing. Since housing was still in short supply, they were still in use. The houses were sitting on blocks about two feet off of the ground and the wind whistled under the house and the floors were always cold. There was a small bedroom on each end of the house. The bath, kitchen, living room, dining area was in the middle. There could not have been more than 800 square feet in the entire house. The good part was the rent was only $38.00 per month, including utilities. No telephone, since these were not available. There was a large Farmers Market across the Boulevard and Chris always managed to serve fresh fruit and vegetables.

In a few days, I joined a car pool that required me to drive to work one or two days per week. This permitted Chris and Sharon to get acquainted with the area and to locate the School which Sharon would attend as soon as school started in the Fall. Chris had to drive across the Bay Bridge to Oakland, California to the Naval Hospital for her Prenatal care.

My job at the 12th Marine Corps Reserve District was to update and maintain the records of several thousand Officer and Enlisted Personnel within the three state area. There were many members of what was known as Active Reserve Units. Members of such units would meet once each week and earn one day's pay for each meeting. During the summer, they would go to Camp Pendleton for two weeks of active duty training. In the event of a national emergency, they would be the first people called to active duty. The entire unit would be activated and would be assigned to one of the Regular Marine Divisions. In addition, there were many thousand Inactive Reservists. These individuals did not belong to any unit, did not perform any drills or activities and would be called to active duty in an emergency only after all of the organized units had been mobilized.

Our daughter Catherine Louise was born September 14, 1949 at the U.S. Naval Hospital in Oakland, California. Unlike the little civilian Hospital in

Oceanside where Sharon was born six years earlier, they had Chris up walking around the first day. She had to spend 10 days in bed when Sharon was born.

Mrs. McDonald came out to stay with us for a few days until Chris was able to get her strength back. This was a great help for I was pretty useless around the house. I did learn to wash the diapers at the coin operated laundry about half a block from our house.

A few weeks after Cathy was born, I was sent back to Washington for 10 days of intensive training. The Marine Corps was in the process of adopting a new simplified Personnel Accounting System and they called in senior Non-Commissioned Officers from all over the world. There were about 500 assembled in Washington and it was like "old home week". It seemed that just about every old time Marine I had ever known was present. Some of the informal "bull" sessions were really lively.

Upon my return to San Francisco, it was necessary to brief other personnel on the new procedure. We spent several months converting the personnel records to fit the new requirements.

The climate in San Francisco did not agree with Cathy at all. She was sick quite often. It kept Chris busy taking her to the Navy Medical Clinic in the downtown area. Cathy would recognize the building and start to cry because she knew she would get another shot. She had so many Penicillin shots the Corpsmen called her the Penicillin Kid.

The routine of washing diapers and baby clothes every night gave me time to study a Correspondence Course called the Officers Basic Extension Course offered by the Marine Corps Schools in Quantico, Virginia. This course was quite involved and took two years to complete. It was the same course all new Second Lieutenants completed in nine months at the Basic School in Quantico. With the constant reduction in the size of the Marine Corps, I believed having this course on my record would help me to survive the next round of personnel cuts'.

Sharon and the other children in the housing area attended school in the San Francisco Public School System. The Elementary School was about one mile from the housing area. The School was old but adequate. Sharon was making good progress but she was not too thrilled about school.

We had along week-end over the Memorial Day Holiday in 1950. We rented a small travel trailer, hooked it behind the 1948 Plymouth and toured the Northern California area where I was stationed in the Civilian Conservation Corps in 1937. The camp located at Whitmore, California (about 35 miles east of Redding) looked like it did in 1937, except it had a fence around it and was being used by the California Youth Authority for young boys that had committed a crime.

We stopped by a beautiful stream near Lassen National Park. I noticed a man was catching Trout from the stream and since I had brought fishing equipment decided to see if I could also catch some Trout. After about 45 minutes without a strike the friendly fisherman said if I would go to the Country Store about 5 miles clown the road and buy some Salmon Eggs for bait and some tiny hooks my luck might improve. I followed his suggestion and caught a nice Trout on my second cast. Before long, I had caught six nice Trout and we decided we would spend the night where we were parked. Chris cooked the Trout and we had a feast.

The next morning we departed for Lassen National Park. I wanted to show them the 10,400 foot tall Mt. Lassen that I had climbed in 1937. At the time, this was the only active Volcano in the United States. In the lower areas, there were boiling mud pots, steam and hot water coming up out of the ground. I decided to take a shortcut that would save many miles of driving according to my map.

We started up the side of the mountain on the two lane, blacktop road. After several miles we were deep into a forest of large Ponderosa Pine Trees and the blacktop road turned into a dirt road! There was no way to turn around so we continued on up the mountain. Pretty soon we encountered several cowboys driving a large herd of cattle up the road. There must have been several hundred head. There was nothing to do but plod along behind them up the mountain. After about 45 minutes, another car pulled up behind us and as soon as the terrain flattened out so the woman driver could pass us, she started blowing her horn. This noise spooked the cattle and they scattered in all directions as fast as they could run. The cowboys were really upset and called the lady some names I had never heard before. Since the road ahead was now clear of cattle we speeded up and were soon headed down the mountain to Lassen National Park. It would be some time before I took any more shortcuts.

We spent the day sightseeing and camped in the park that night. Since the trailer was rather small, I decided to sleep outside under the stars. I did not sleep too well since deer kept milling around the area as well as other animals. The next day we returned to San Francisco.

In late May 1950, I managed to obtain a 30 day leave and we departed for Texas to visit Christene's parents and my relatives. I told Chris I wanted to show her the beauty of northern New Mexico and the Grand Canyon in Arizona. She was skeptical about New Mexico after the terrible dust and sand storm we had encountered on our way through New Mexico the year before.

Things went well until we were several miles east of Albuquerque, New Mexico. We encountered a violent thunderstorm with terrible wind and hail. I fully expected that at least the car would be severely damaged, however the storm finally let up and we proceeded to Texas without further trouble. To my surprise, the car was not damaged.

While we were in Texas, I traded the 1948 Plymouth in on a new 1950 Buick. This was a fine automobile for its day, the total cash price was $2,200.00. It was a two-tone blue, 4-door sedan with Radio, Heater and

Whitewall Tires. It had an in-line 8-cylinder engine, was very comfortable and would get 18 miles per gallon of gasoline. We kept this car for 5 years and it never required anything but routine maintenance.

On June 25, 1950 the North Korean Anny invaded South Korea. The news reports indicated the North Koreans were equipped with modern Russian Tanks and they were running through the South Korean Army with ease. At this point, President Truman stated he would commit United States troops to defend South Korea. I decided rather than wait to be called back to my duty station, we would start back the following morning.

Our trip back to San Francisco was uneventful. We decided to take a different route back. We turned north at Amarillo to Dalhart and then into New Mexico through Raton, New Mexico. From Raton we went into Colorado at Trinidad and then west through the San Luis Valley through Alamosa, Monte Vista, Del Norte and South Fork. For several years, I had wanted to know what South Fork looked like in the Summer. This was where I was in the Civilian Conservation Corps Camp in 1937 after they closed the Camp in California. The snow was almost waist deep where we worked in the mountains searching for Beetles that were killing the Ponderosa Pine Trees in the National Forest. As I had anticipated, the area around South Fork was beautiful. The snow fed streams were clear and looked like a good place to fish for trout. This would have to wait for a later date.

From South Fork, we proceeded over the Wolfe Creek Pass to Pagosa Springs and then to Durango. From Durango, we visited the Indian Cliff Dwellings at Mesa Verde National Park. We spent a rainy, stormy night at Moab, Utah. The next day, we visited the Arches National Monument and were impressed with the beautiful Sandstone Arches. We then proceeded across Utah through Salt Lake City, Reno, Nevada, across the Sierra Nevada and on into San Francisco.

When I returned to work at the Headquarters of the 12th Marine Corps Reserve District, word had been received there was a possibility some of the Organized Reserve Units would be called to active duty.

President Truman called the Korean War a "Police Action". He directed General MacArthur to commit U.S. Air, Land and Sea Forces in the Far East and to stop the North Korean advance into South Korea.

I cannot speak for the Army and Navy or Air Force, but the U.S. Marine Corps was still equipped with World War II equipment. President Truman had appointed a Secretary of Defense by the name of Louis Johnson sometime in 1948. Louis Johnson was always cutting "the fat" out of the military. By 1950 the Marine Corps consisted of two Divisions and two Air Wings on paper. In fact these units were merely hollow shells. The entire Marine Corps strength was only 68,000. At the end of World War II the Marine Corps consisted of more than 500,000 men in six Marine Divisions with supporting specialized Force Troop units. There were four Air Wings with additional specialized support units. It was my understanding the other branches of the service were in similar shape. Louis Johnson had not only cut "the fat" out of the military, but had also cut out the muscle and was working on the bone when the Korean War began. In addition, the Commissary Stores in the Bay Area had been closed and the Base Exchanges were reduced to a bare minimum of merchandise. I assume similar action had been taken throughout the United States.

It soon became apparent our Far Eastern Forces could not stop the North Korean advance into South Korea. The World War II Anti-Tank Rockets would bounce off the Russian Built Tanks and they continued to advance.

The Marine Corps was ordered to send the First Marine Division to South Korea. By combining all of the effective strength of the First and Second Marine Divisions and getting personnel from various Guard Detachments throughout the United States, the Marine Corps was able to scrape up a single Brigade consisting of two Regiments of Troops. In order to rebuild the First and Second Marine Divisions, all Marine Corps Reservists were called to Active Duty. This involved not only the Active Reserve Units, those individuals who had participated in training one day each week plus two weeks of training during the summer, but also those Inactive Reservists who had not worn a uniform or fired a weapon since World War II. To say this was a chaotic situation would be an understatement. We worked day and night preparing orders and chasing down some of the Inactive Reservists who were less than enthusiastic about returning to active duty. What happened to some of them should not happen to any man under any circumstances. Many had worked themselves into responsible jobs or their own business. Farmers could not stay to harvest their crops. Most Reservists had family responsibilities which could not be resolved on short notice.

By August of 1950 the Communist North Koreans had pushed the U.S. and South Korean Forces into a small pocket in South Korea known as the Pusan Perimeter. It looked like our forces would be pushed into the Sea of Japan. The lst Marine Brigade arrived in Pusan and was thrown into combat on August 17th. By some miracle our forces were able to hang on in the Pusan Perimeter until we could rebuild our own depleted forces back in the United States.

I have had a disdain for politicians for many years. I have strong memories of how we fought the early days of World War II with very little equipment, most of which was obsolete. Our politicians destroyed the strong, well trained, well equipped forces we had at the end of World War II. Then they turn around and commit us to fight a war in Korea with very few people and obsolete equipment.

After we had activated most of the Reservists in the 12th Marine Corps Reserve District, things settled down to a normal routine and I fully expected to be ordered to the Fleet Marine Force at any time. I continued my routine of washing diapers and working on my Officers Basic Extension Course every night at the coin operated laundry.

We purchased a small two wheel trailer and I spent weekends converting it into a camping trailer. It was small by Travel Trailer standards but two people could sleep in it. There was a door on one side and a window on the opposite side. The tailgate folded down and there was a Coleman stove mounted on the tailgate. There was also room for a box containing pots and pans and eating utensils.

Over the Labor Day Weekend we hooked the trailer behind the Buick and drove down to Yosemite National Park and camped out during the weekend. Chris and Cathy slept in the car and Sharon and I slept in the trailer. I did not dare sleep out on the ground because there were a number of Bear roaming the area breaking into the food supply of the campers. The Warning from the Park Rangers to keep a distance from the Bear was really not necessary as far as we were concerned. The Yosemite Valley was really a beautiful place and the waterfalls were magnificent. We also drove down to the area containing the giant Sequoia Trees and took a picture of the Buick sitting in the hollowed out portion of the famous giant Sequoia. We enjoyed the weekend of sightseeing and were impressed with the beauty of the place and the large number of deer and bear. The trailer worked fine.

After returning to San Francisco, we decided if I were to install a pipe inside the trailer from one side to the other, we could hang a lot of clothes on the rod and still have room for suitcases and boxes of clothing the next time we moved. There was always a delay in shipping personal items from one duty station to another and with the trailer we could take most of our clothing with us and would not have to put up with the usual delay in waiting for our personal things to arrive at the new duty station.

Most people had a rather "ho hum" attitude about the "Police Action", as President Truman called it, going on in Korea. The Word filtered back to us it was indeed a real war and our people in the Pusan Perimeter were hanging on by their fingernails. As the Reservists arrived at Camp Pendleton, they were thrown into the skeleton 1st Marine Division, given a few days of training and then shipped out to Korea.

In early September, 1950 the 1st Marine Brigade was pulled out of the Pusan Perimeter, put aboard ship and joined up with the remaining elements of the 1st Marine Division that had just arrived from Camp Pendleton.

On September 15, 1950 the 1st Marine Division landed at Inchon on the west coast of Korea. After heavy fighting they advanced inland and soon cleared the North Korean Troops out of the capital of Korea, Seoul.

The 1st Marine Division along with Army Units advanced across the peninsula of Korea. In the meantime the Army Units still defending the Pusan Perimeter broke out of the area. The North Korean Army, now caught in a pincer movement, fell apart and those who did not surrender fled northward into North Korea. The forces under the command of General

MacArthur chased the North Korean forces all the way to the Yalu River on the border of China. They also captured the city of Pyongyang, the capital of North Korea. General MacArthur announced that the war would soon be over and the American Troops would be home by Christmas.

There was no reason to doubt the statement made by General MacArthur. At the Headquarters of the 12th Marine Corps Reserve District in San Francisco plans were made to welcome the Reservists home and to reopen the Reserve Training Centers located in various cities in the District.

I learned a valuable lesson in World War II which was do not volunteer for combat duty if you are stationed in a non-combat assignment. I did not volunteer for combat duty in Korea and took the attitude that the Marine Corps had no difficulty in locating me when they wanted to ship me to combat duty. They knew where to find me if my services were required in Korea.

Things do not always turn out as planned. Instead of the Korean War being over by Christmas, in late November 1950, the Chinese entered the war on the side of the North Koreans. They sent hundreds of thousands of Chinese Troops into North Korea causing many casualties among the U.S. Troops. Many of them were cut off and captured. The 1st Marine Division fought their way from the Chosin Reservoir to the port of Wonsan where they were evacuated to South Korea.

The Marine Corps had suffered many casualties in the Korean War and with the entry of the Chinese on the side of North Korea it looked like a long war ahead.

Due to the turn of events in Korea, the Marine Corps was ordered to start an immediate expansion in early 1951. The Selective Service System (Draft Boards) would supply the enlisted personnel that could not be obtained by volunteers. All of the Reserve Officers had already been called to active duty and the Officer Training Program at Quantico could not produce Second Lieutenants in sufficient quantity to meet the immediate needs. Due to the urgent need for Second Lieutenants, they hung Second Lieutenant Bars on 500 Master Sergeants. I was one of the early appointees. The fact that I had completed the Officers Basic Course by correspondence no doubt played a part in my being among the first group selected for Second Lieutenant.

My appointment to Second Lieutenant was immediately followed by orders to report to the 3d Marine Brigade then being formed at Camp Pendleton, California by the old World War II and Korean War hero, Brigadier General Lewis (Chesty) Puller who had recently fought his Way from the frozen Chosin Area to Wonsan, Korea. Chesty Puller was to the Marine Corps what Patton was to the Army. He was always in trouble with the Press but when they needed a combat leader they always called on Chesty Puller.

We did not own any furniture at this time so we packed our clothing and personal belongings into the little trailer and moved to Oceanside. As usual, housing was in short supply. We spent a couple of days in a Motel and found our old landlord. He stated our old apartment was vacant and we could have it. This was the same place we lived when we were first married. With two children it was very crowded but we managed until we could make better arrangements.

I checked into the 3d Marine Brigade and was pleasantly surprised to be assigned to the 3d Service Battalion as Personnel Officer. I fully expected to be assigned to one of the Infantry Regiments as an Infantry Platoon Leader. I was further surprised when I checked into my new organization to discover that my office was across the hall and in the same building that I had occupied while stationed at Camp Pendleton during World War II some eight years before. After a few months in the tiny apartment, we were assigned a two-bedroom apartment in the Marine Corps Housing Project in Oceanside. This was not perfect but was a great improvement over the small apartment.

My job kept me very busy. We soon learned the "Draftees" had more problems than the usual volunteer Marines. Many of them were married with children and they had all of the financial problems associated with low pay. For that matter, our situation was not much better. The pay of a Second Lieutenant was no better than the pay I received as a Master Sergeant. In addition, I had to buy my own uniforms and other clothing which had been furnished free in the past.

The job of the Service Battalion was to support the other units in the Brigade. We had a number of bulldozers, cranes and other heavy equipment to support landing operations. There were also Machine Shop Trailers, Water Purification Units, food, fuel and ammunition transportation and storage units. We spent a lot of time out in the mountains training and at the beach conducting landing exercises.

After completing a full Brigade Training Operation, General Puller announced that the 3d Marine Brigade was now "Combat Ready". We were expecting orders to go to Korea very soon.

The Marines in Korea suffered many casualties in the winter of 1950 because of the cold weather. This was attributed to a lack of cold weather training and inadequate cold weather clothing. The Marine Corps started a "crash program" to develop both cold weather clothing and cold weather training.

The Marine Corps high command selected a training base in the high Sierra Nevada Mountains behind Yosemite National Park. The "old timers" that had cabins in the area told the Marines you cannot survive up here in the winter. They would board up their cabins and leave the area until late spring. The Marine Corps high command stated this is just the type of place we are looking for! They may still be using the same area. When I left the Marine

Corps in 1960 the Pickle Meadows Cold Weather Training Base was still in operation.

In late November 1951 the Colonel commanding the Service Battalion called me into his office and told me that everyone going to Korea must go through cold weather training at Pickle Meadows before being sent to Korea. He gave me a choice of going to Pickle Meadows the next week or in early January 1952. I volunteered to go to Pickle Meadows immediately (I violated my rule of not volunteering). I had been in the high country of the Sierra Nevada Mountains in the Summer and could well imagine what it would be like in January. I also remembered my days in the Civilian Conservation Corps in Colorado when we worked out in snow waist deep in -22 degrees weather. When I arrived home that night and told Chris I had volunteered to go to Pickle Meadows for Cold Weather Training and would be gone for a week, she was less than enthusiastic. When I explained the alternative of going in January, she agreed it would be better to go in November.

My assignment for the Cold Weather Training was as a Platoon Commander of an Infantry Platoon headed for Korea when their training had been completed. I did not realize the members of the Infantry Platoon thought I would be their permanent Platoon Commander and would be going with them to Korea. They were a fine bunch of troops and did everything exactly as they were told.

We traveled by bus from Camp Pendleton to Pickle Meadows and arrived at the Base Camp in late afternoon. The Base Camp consisted of two tents! One was used as an office, the other was used for storage of rations and had two stoves. This tent could also be used to care for sick or injured personnel. The Base Camp was located at 9,500 feet above sea level and our training assignment would be from there up to about 11,000 feet above sea level. There was about a foot of snow on the ground and the temperature was around 32 degrees. We were issued World War II Type C-Rations for five days, given maps of the training areas and told to get moving.

The training at Pickle Meadows was routine Infantry Tactics. We did not get much sleep since we were attacked by "Aggressor Forces" every night and we had to maintain constant security. The weather was not too bad. At night the temperature would drop to 5 degrees below zero but we were equipped with a new type thermal boot and mountain sleeping bags. When we returned to Camp Pendleton, I said good bye to my Platoon and returned to the 3d Marine Brigade. They soon sailed for Korea.

In early January 1952 the next group left for Pickle Meadows. I was happy to have my Cold Weather Training behind me. The second group did very little training. They spent their time just trying to stay alive!

Two days after the second group arrived at Pickle Meadows, the area was hit with a blizzard. This was the thing the "old timers" who lived in the area had warned the Marine Corps about. The temperature plunged to 40 degrees below zero. The snow drifts piled up over 8 feet deep in many areas.

The snow plows could not get through to Pickle Meadows. It was almost a disaster. They would run about 50 people into the tents for a few minutes to let them thaw out a little, run them out and send another 50 men in for a few minutes. I was told this went on for two days and nights. The blizzard finally passed but the roads were still closed and some of the men were coming down with pneumonia and frostbite. Someone decided they could lift the sick out by helicopter. This was a slow process since the helicopters in those days would barely fly at 10,000 feet altitude and they could only lift one person out at a time.

Meanwhile I was at sunny, warm Camp Pendleton congratulating myself for going to Pickle Meadows in November.

U.S. Forces in Korea had been pushed back to South Korea by the Chinese Forces. It looked like there was a long war ahead of us. Instead of sending the 3d Marine Brigade to Korea, word came down from Marine Corps Headquarters the 3d Marine Brigade would be used as the nucleus for formation of the 3d Marine Division. The First Marine Division was fully committed in Korea. The Second Marine Division at Camp Lejeune, North Carolina was being held for deployment to Europe should that be necessary. It was therefore directed that the 3d Marine Division be organized and trained for deployment to Korea. Under ideal conditions, it takes a year to organize, train and equip a Marine Division for Combat. The situation in 1952 was less than ideal. It was necessary to convert civilians into Marines. A Marine Division needed about 20,000 men. Equipment had to be procured, in many cases, manufactured. After the men and equipment were available, we had to start with small unit training and then work up to the training of larger units and finally training of the entire Division.

My new assignment was as Adjutant and Personnel Officer of the 3d Shore Party Battalion. We activated the Battalion at Camp Del Mar. This camp was located on the beach area near Oceanside. While I worked my rear end off in this job, it turned out to be one of the more pleasant assignments of my entire Marine Corps Career. This is the unit that opens up the beach area in an Amphibious Landing. We were equipped with bulldozers, cranes, road building equipment, supply and fuel handling equipment and other specialized equipment needed in an over the beach assault.

We were not overjoyed living in the housing project and since there was an excellent chance I would remain with the 3d Marine Division for a year, Chris and I decided to try to find a house to buy. We could not find anything we liked in Oceanside or Carlsbad that we could afford. We found a little Spanish Style house on 1/2 acre in Encinitas we liked and could afford the price of $10,500 with a small down payment and monthly payments of $87.00 per month. We loved the place. It was about 15 miles from my duty station. There were avocado, orange, lemon, apricot and grapefruit trees in the back yard. It was a perfect place for me to unwind after a wild week at Camp Del Mar. Sharon enrolled in the nearby School and was happier than she had been at San Francisco or Oceanside. We moved our church membership to the Encinitas Methodist Church and Chris became very active in Church Activities.

The large area in the back of the house was fully enclosed by a high woven wire fence. Cathy and Sharon could play in the back yard and Chris did not have to worry about them being run over by a car. The soil was excellent and I soon had a small garden growing near the back fence.

There was a wonderful couple that lived next door. Their name was Vossbeck. He was a retired Doctor who spent his time growing champion flowers. His wife puttered around with Bantam chickens and her own special flowers. Mrs. Vossbeck was over 80 years old and Dr. Vossbeck must have been almost as old. They used to amuse Chris and myself telling us about the "old" couple that did live in our house. Sharon and Cathy enjoyed talking to the Vossbecks almost as much as Chris and I. Dr. Vossbeck always talked about his goal in life which was to take a trip around the world on a Tramp Steamer. After we moved from Encinitas we learned he had pulled out into the path of a truck and Mrs. Vossbeck was killed. He later started his trip around the world by Tramp Steamer and died of a heart attack at sea.

The winter in Encinitas was perfect weather wise. There would be snow on the mountains 50 miles away and I would be out in the yard mowing our lawn, smelling the orange blossoms and dressed in shorts and a T-shirt. If the children wanted to play in the snow, Chris would pack a picnic lunch and we would drive up to Palomar Mountain. Sharon and Cathy would play in the snow for a few hours and then we would return home to the warm balmy weather in Encinitas Our house was about six blocks from the Ocean. There was a strip along the coast about 10 miles wide where the temperature did not vary more than 15 degrees all year.

When you crossed over the first range of mountains to the east at Escondido, about 18 miles east of Encinitas, the temperature would drop to freezing in the winter and hit 100 degrees in the summer.

The elderly couple that lived next to us on the south side were named Foote. The bell in our back yard was brought to California from Iowa by Mr. Foote's ancestors when they migrated to California by covered wagon. Mr. Foote died and Mrs. Foote sold the property to Howard and Ruth Eden who became our best friends. The bell passed to the Edens and Mrs. Eden later gave the bell to us and we brought it to Denison.

The little folding rocking chair that sits in the livingroom was given to us by Mrs. Eden in 1975. This is a very old chair. It was given to Mrs. Eden by an elderly neighbor when they lived in Oregon. Her ancestors brought the chair from Illinois to Utah in a covered wagon when the Mormons migrated from Illinois to Utah. We purchased the property in Encinitas from a wonderful couple by the name of Alva and Blanche Covert. We became very good friends and maintained contact with them until their deaths. They were in their 90's when they died. Many years after we moved from Encinitas we had a Christmas Card from Mrs. Covert. She said "We can't see or hear, but thank God we can still drive". That is how Chris and I came by that expression which we use today.

In October 1952, I was promoted to First Lieutenant. The prestige was minor but the small increase in pay was very welcome. Including allowances, my pay was now $360.00 per month. We managed to survive but did not live very "high on the hog".

In April 1953 I received orders, along with about sixty other officers and senior Non Commissioned Officers to report to Camp Desert Rock, Nevada as an observer in one of the Nuclear Tests being conducted. (It appears we should have been called Guinea Pigs instead of observers).

When we arrived at Camp Desert Rock, we discovered the camp was a very primitive "Tent City" and the Nuclear Test we were to observe was to be an air drop as opposed to the usual tower shot. There was some apprehension that the Air Force people doing the dropping might miss the target and we would be cremated. We also learned the purpose of the test was to see if troops could still function as a military unit after being exposed to a near-by Nuclear Explosion.

Deep trenches had been dug near the site of the test. These trenches were occupied by regular Army and Marine Units who were to move out through the area after the dust had subsided. (I have often wondered what ever became of these young men. Many of them probably died of cancer at an early age).

On the day of the test, our "observer" group was moved to the test site by bus. We were located some distance from the troops in the trenches and told we would remain in an open area! The busses departed and said they would return to pick us up after the test! They no doubt did not want to take a chance on damaging the busses!

A steel tower had been constructed on the Desert Floor. This was (hopefully) to be Ground Zero. The troops-were well hunkered down in their trenches when we spotted two B-50's approaching at what appeared to be an altitude of 20,000 feet. As the planes came closer, we were told to turn our back to the drop area and to close our eyes as tight as we could. With our eyes closed, there was the whitest light (seen through our eyelids) any member of the group had ever seen. When the "white light" had subsided, we were told to turn around.

The Atomic Bomb had exploded several hundred feet above ground. When we turned around, it was like looking into the sun. The brightness soon changed to bright red, then dirty red and started to take on the familiar "Mushroom" shape. It seemed to roll into itself for several seconds as it ascended into the clear blue air. It was sucking dirt and debris up from the desert floor. This formed the stem of the mushroom. Soon after we turned around the "shock wave" we had been told to expect arrived along with the noise of the explosion. I will never forget the white light of the explosion and the heat! The heat was very strange. It was not terribly hot to the skin but seemed to penetrate to our bones. The internal heat soon disappeared but it left me with an eerie feeling I had not experienced before or since.

As the mushroom cloud ascended, it turned color from the dirty red to white. A short time later it became a brilliant white, as the dust particles settled and the sun could hit the cloud. When the mushroom cloud reached higher altitude, the stem disappeared and the cloud created a perfectly shaped white dome on top. We were told this was an ice cap created by the difference in the heat of the cloud and the cold atmosphere.

A short time later as the cloud ascended further into the atmosphere, the ice cap started to break apart and we could see large chunks of ice break away and drift back to the surface of the desert. The pieces of ice melted and vaporized before striking the desert.

By this time, the "grunts" emerged from the trenches and started to form up for an advance through the impact zone of Ground Zero. The busses arrived in a short time and after having a guy wave a wand over us (said to be a Geiger Counter to see if we were Radio Active) we returned to the Tent Camp where we were told we would depart for Camp Pendleton the next day.

I was somewhat surprised that there was very little discussion of what we had just witnessed by the members of our group. I strongly suspect, like myself, they were so awed by the spectacle we had observed that they were not in any mood for discussion.

The test we had observed was in the 20 Kiloton range, slightly larger than the 19 Kiloton Bomb dropped on Hiroshima, Japan. Having seen what the 19 KT Bomb did to Hiroshima, I can well understand that the 5 Megaton Hydrogen Bomb tested at Bikini Atoll completely destroyed the Island and many ships anchored in the Lagoon.

Alter the heat of the Nevada Desert, it was good to return to Camp Pendleton. The Weather was pleasant and after what we had encountered in the Nevada Desert, even the rigid training we were doing seemed to be a lot easier.

Chris, Sharon and Cathy had been kept busy taking care of the menagerie I had created in the back yard. I had put a fence in the back that created an area of about 1/4 acre. I did not have the time or the energy to keep the entire 1/2 acre mowed. I had purchased a pair of geese to keep the grass down in back and four ducks to eat the snails under the Avocado trees. We soon had little ones that increased the numbers of geese and ducks.

Mrs. Vossbeck was always fussing about one of her little Bantam Hens that wanted to nest. One day when she was fussing at the little hen, I asked her if she would let the hen hatch some Pheasant eggs for me. She agreed and I found some Pheasant eggs and put them under the little hen.

I had to build a cage to confine the hen and the chick Pheasants when they hatched since they are able to run as soon as hatched and will depart for parts unknown right after they come out of the shell. We soon had a cage full of baby Pheasants. They had to be provided with food and water every day. The mother hen just about went crazy because her chicks would not pay any attention to her.

The 3d Marine Division was taking shape. We had completed all required unit training and began an intensive training period as a full Division. We would go aboard ship, mill around at sea for a few days and then stage an Amphibious Landing on the Beach at Aliso Canyon. The Tanks, Infantry and Artillery Units would move across the beach and advance inland into the mountains at Camp Pendleton. The Shore Party Battalion would remain in the beach area and move supplies of all kinds forward to the other units as they were unloaded from the Ships. When the exercise had been completed, there was a critique of all operations of the Division and the Commanding General announced he was pleased with the performance of all units. When the 3d Marine Division was formed from the 3d Marine Brigade, Major General Claude Pepper had been placed in command and Brigadier General Lewis B. (Chesty) Puller was assigned as Assistant Division Commander. I never met a Marine who had served under Chesty Puller who had a neutral opinion of him. They either hated him or would be willing to follow him anywhere because he was a leader who was always out front. He used to drive the Battalion and Regimental Commanders nuts. Normally when a General Officer is going to look in on a unit you know he is coming a few days in advance or if you do not have advance notice, you can see him coming a mile away because he will be in a Sedan or Jeep with his stars shining and flags flying. Not so with Chesty Puller. He never announced that he was dropping in on a unit. He always traveled in a non-descript Jeep, no stars or flags flying. He dressed like an ordinary marine and usually the first time a unit Commander knew the General was in the area was when someone reported that General Chesty was over in one of the barracks areas or the motor pool talking to some Pfc. or Corporal. This was his way of keeping his finger on things and finding out how the morale and effectiveness of the unit really was.

With the successful completion of the Division Maneuvers, it did not require a Rhodes Scholar to figure out we would be on our way to Korea very soon. In early July 1953, word came down that the Division would conduct another full scale Division Exercise. We had just completed a very successful operation and this operation sounded a bit strange. In addition to my duties as Adjutant and Personnel Officer, I was also in charge of Secret and Classified Files. I soon learned we were going to Korea rather than a Division Exercise.

I talked the situation over with Chris and we decided she and Sharon and Cathy would remain in our house in Encinitas while I was gone. I made out an allotment of $300.00 of my pay to her and kept $60.00 per month for myself since I would have to pay for my food, laundry and incidentals. Chris would make the $87.00 house payment, $50.00 car payment and send $25.00 per month to my Uncle Narnon to help support my half-brother John, Jr. That left her with $138.00 per month for everything else, taxes, insurance, furniture payment and food. It was obvious we were in for some very lean times. It had always been a financial struggle for us and we believed we could handle this problem one day at a time.

Back at the 3d Marine Division, things were going very smoothly. We were preparing to go aboard ship and morale was very high. The Division was well trained and equipped and we all believed we could handle whatever assignment was given to us.

One week prior to going aboard ship, the "roof fell in". Word came down from Marine Corps Headquarters in Washington that we would transfer all Personnel who had already served in Korea to the Marine Corps Base at Camp Pendleton! Replacement personnel would arrive from the 2nd Marine Division located at Camp Lejeune, North Carolina. I use the term loosely when I say this created a state of absolute chaos. I worked (along with my office personnel), 24 hours per day for three days processing the people going out of the Battalion and the incoming personnel from Camp Lejeune. Our Battalion Commander, Lieutenant Colonel Ralph Bohne, a Reserve who had been called to active duty for World War II, sent home and called up again when the Korean War started in 1950, stated he did not desire to take an untrained hodgepodge unit into combat. More than half of our Battalion had been transferred and new people assigned to most positions. Confusion reigned supreme.

Lieutenant Colonel Bohne was reassigned as Executive officer and we received a new commanding officer, Colonel Kenneth A. Jorgensen. I must have made a good first impression on him. As soon as he arrived, he called a Staff Conference. As soon as we were all seated, I promptly fell asleep in my chair. Lieutenant Colonel Bohne shook me awake and explained to the new Colonel that I had not had any sleep for three days. That explanation kept me out of trouble and I got along fine with Colonel Jorgensen until he was transferred about a year later.

I managed to get home one night before we went aboard ship. Chris and my girls took me back to Camp Pendleton the next morning. We said our good-byes and I did not see them again for 17 months. This was the second time we had been confronted with a long separation during our marriage. This time she had two children to take care of by herself. I know she did a remarkable job and must have had many long, lonely days. I missed them and was lonely, but they kept me so busy I did not have a lot of time to feel sorry for myself.

We spent the entire day loading aboard a troop transport. My people were busy preparing sailing rosters and last minute reports prior to sailing. Our office was two field desks set up on a hatch cover in one of the troop compartments. We sailed from San Diego the next day.

Our ship along with the other ships in the convoy were World War II vintage and badly in need of extensive maintenance. From my vantage point, I had the terrible thought that we were better equipped to fight a war in 1941 than we were in 1953. I was not looking forward to the landing above Wonsan on the East Coast of Korea since the balance of the Division was in the same shape as the Shore Party Battalion.

The convoy could move only as fast as the slowest ship and we wallowed our way across the Pacific at eight knots. The troops were restless and not very happy. They spent most of their time standing in the chow line or in line to use the Head (rest room facilities). The officers fared a little better. Not much, but we did not spend-quite as much time standing in line as the troops.

We were at sea for two weeks. The Chinese and North Koreans had been stringing the United Nations Forces along for some time in the Peace Talks. They spent most of their time arguing about the size of the table and the seating arrangements surrounding the Peace Talks.

The word must have leaked out there was a reinforced Marine Division at sea, combat loaded and preparing to make a landing on the East Coast of Korea. In any event, they decided to quit fooling around and get down to business on the Peace Talks. As a result of the change in the position of the Chinese and North Koreans, our orders were changed, land in Japan.

JAPAN

The United States had a large number of military bases in Japan, however there was not one large enough to accommodate a Marine Division. Because of this, the 3rd Marine Division would be scattered over the southern part of the main Island of Honshu. The Shore Party Battalion was assigned to an Army Base ten miles west of Yokosuka, Japan. The base was then known as Camp McGill.

We arrived in Yokohama around noon after being at sea for two weeks. We were immediately loaded onto a Japanese train for our trip to Camp McGill.

Yokohama was being rebuilt, but there was evidence of World War II damage where the fire bombing had destroyed the city. For several miles there was extensive evidence of the fires that had devastated the city.

The Japanese train reminded me of the cartoon "Toonerville Trolley", very tiny and primitive by U.S. standards (The Bullet Trains had not been invented yet). After a lot of starting and stopping, we arrived at Kinegasu about four miles from Camp McGill. We were met by Army Trucks and were transported to Camp McGill, arriving there about 3:00 a.m. Everyone was totally exhausted.

We soon discovered that Camp McGill had been a former Japanese Naval Base where they trained pilots for their float planes and Flying Boats. Two of the all metal hangars were assigned to the Shore Party Battalion to be used for our equipment maintenance shops. The balance of the base was of wood construction. The Barracks were huge. We put an entire company in each of the four Barracks assigned to us. The Japanese version of Air Conditioning was a four foot air space between the first and second floor of each building. This looked to me like a real first class fire trap.

As soon as we had settled in and everyone had been assigned to their particular job, Colonel Jorgensen started an intensive training program. While the heavy equipment required by our Shore Party Mission sat idle, we concentrated on Infantry training and the heavy equipment began to deteriorate for lack of maintenance.

The only personnel excused from the Infantry Training were the cooks and one clerk in the Battalion Headquarters. We had to do most of our paperwork and reports at night and on week-ends.

We did our training out in the Rice Paddies and along the country roads. The rice paddies were still flooded and we were forced to use the narrow dams between the rice paddies.

In the early fall, the Japs started the Rice Harvest. I was surprised to see how much of the labor was performed by women. There appeared to be a shortage of Japanese men, no doubt caused by the thousands of men lost in World War II. Their methods of harvesting the rice had changed little since I had observed them during my previous "trip" to Japan.

The more prosperous farmers had acquired a factory made harvesting device. It looked very much like the primitive "woman driven" ones but was powered by a small gasoline engine.

The odd thing about the gasoline powered model was that they were always operated by a Japanese man! The women performed all of the other work involved in the harvest. When the time came to mow the grass on the parade ground about 120 Japanese women would show up with small hand scythes. They would spread out about three feet apart in a line at one end of the parade ground. At a given signal from the male honcho (boss), they would all squat down and start cutting the grass. They would move at the same speed and when they reached the end of the parade ground, they would move over, reform and repeat the process. After several hours the job would be finished and the parade ground would be almost as smooth as a Golf Green.

One Sunday three of us decided to catch a Japanese Bus that came by Camp McGill and visit the old City of Kamakura about 15 miles away. This was the capital of Japan in ancient times and we wanted to see the large bronze Buddha we heard about.

Upon our arrival in Kamakura, we amused ourselves by watching a woman powered pile driver in operation. There were 12 women and one man, the honcho. The pile driver consisted of two A-frames connected at the top with two large pulleys. A large rope ran from each side of the drive head, up over the pulleys. About six feet from the pulley, the rope separated into six smaller ropes with six women on each side. The women would hold onto the rope and when the man gave the signal, the women would go into a little sing-song and at the proper note, all of them would pull on the rope lifting the heavy drive head into the air near the top of the A-frame. At the proper note in the sing-song routine they would drop the drive head, hitting the piling.

The process would be repeated in rapid fashion and the piling would be sunk into the soil very quickly.

I wanted to stick around and see how they took care of the next piling. It was very simple and efficient. They picked up the next pole, put it in the proper location, stood it on end and held it in position with ropes, picked up the A-frame pile driver, placed it over the pole and repeated the process. A modern power driven pile driver would be hard pressed to keep up with the Japanese women with their primitive pile driver.

We finally located the big Buddha. To say I was impressed would be an understatement. This appeared to be a solid bronze replica of Buddha contemplating his navel. It was 43 feet tall perched on a granite base and had been in Kamakura for almost 750 years. The detail of the structure was very intricate and I started trying to figure out how they made it. We went around to the rear of the structure and found out for the equivalent of 10 cents, we could go inside. Once inside, it became obvious the Buddha had been cast into large sections and then put together. The sections fit so perfectly that from the outside it appeared to be one solid piece of bronze. There was no information to explain how the structure was created. We soon tired of sight seeing in Kamakura and returned by bus to Camp McGill.

Mt. Fujiyama the highest point in Japan, more than 12,000 feet, could be seen from Camp Magill most of the time. The top part would be covered by clouds on a cloudy day, but on a bright clear day it stuck out in all of its glory. It is an extinct volcano and is an almost perfect cone shape with snow on the upper part. One morning in early October we had a warning of winter not too far away. Mt. Fuji was covered with snow about half way down from the top. It was a beautiful sight and the only way I can enjoy snow.

My cousin R.C., who was stationed with the Artillery Regiment about 40 miles away at Camp Fuji on the base of Mt. Fujiyama, came down to visit me one weekend. We talked about our growing up years and about how we missed our families. It was good to see him since we had always been good friends.

My old friend Bob Livingston from Boot Camp, the U.S.S. ENTERPRISE and First Sergeant's School was stationed on the west side of Camp McGill with the Western Pacific Troop Training Unit. His assignment was a three year tour and his family was able to accompany him. They had government quarters on the Naval Base at Yokosuka. I was invited to their Apartment on occasion for a home cooked meal which was very much appreciated.

The Naval Base at Yokosuka was not touched by World War II. Only one building was slightly damaged when one of our U.S. Navy Dive Bombers missed the ship he was making a run on in Yokosuka Harbor and hit a building instead. The Japanese had a joke among themselves during World War II that if you wanted to be safe from the war you should move to Yokosuka, because the Americans were saving it for themselves to use after the war. This was pretty close to the truth, since in 1953 it was our main Naval Base in the Western Pacific.

As winter approached, many of our Reserve Officers were sent home to be released to Inactive Duty. A number of new officers joined our unit. One was a Major I had served with in World War II when he was a young Lieutenant and I was a First Sergeant. Another Major, Tom Stirewalt who was an old China Marine and veteran of the Nicaragua Banana Wars, and I soon became close friends. He had been in the Marine Corps for 27 years and I was going on 15 years at the time. It seemed Tom knew about half of the people in the Marine Corps and certainly knew his way around. He was Assigned the job of Battalion S-4, which meant he was responsible for all equipment and supplies for the entire Battalion.

Colonel Jorgensen was bumped up to the job of Division Inspector and we received a new Commanding Officer, Colonel Stephen V. Sabol. With the departure of Colonel Jorgensen, I had hoped that our Infantry training would be a thing of the past and we could do some training with our heavy equipment.

Tom Stirewalt realized right away that our heavy equipment was in poor condition through lack of use and the non-availability of spare parts. The Army was capable of providing spare parts, but the Division G-4 (Colonel) would not permit the Army to provide the spare parts.

We were at the end of the Marine Corps supply pipeline and the spare parts were not to be had. Things finally got so bad some of the troops could not be furnished new footwear and had to have their boots repaired by Japanese shoe repair people at their own expense. Needless to say, morale was in bad shape and Colonel Sabol could not come to grips with the situation. Major Stirewalt cautioned Colonel Sabol that the Shore Party Battalion would not be able to carry out its mission if it were called upon to do so.

Winter arrived early at Camp McGill. The weather was cold with lots of snow. I had a room in the BOQ, an old Japanese Officers' Quarters. We had steam heat but the radiator was right under the window. The Windows did not fit and the heat from the radiator went up the window and to the outside. I finally scrounged a sheet of metal, placed it behind the radiator and bent it out into my room. This permitted the heat to circulate in the room before it escaped through the cracks. Tom Stirewalt laughed at my innovation, but at least I was more comfortable.

On one of our hikes through the countryside in the snow and ice, I spotted a Tangerine Grove. I regret that I did not find out how the Tangerines could survive in that climate. The climate in that part of Japan is about like North Texas. It never occurred to me at the time to find out more about their Tangerines. Christmas at Camp McGill in 1953 was an especially lonely time. Letters from Chris arrived on a regular basis and kept me going.

Early in 1954, I was promoted to Captain. This not only provided a boost to my ego, but to the pay as well. I was no longer tied to my $60.00 per month and was able to go into Yokosuka once in a while for a couple of beers at the Officers' Club. This was a very plush establishment and for 25 cents one could purchase a liter bottle of good German or Dutch beer. I also managed to send a few presents home to Chris, Sharon and Cathy.

In March, the 3rd Marine Division decided to hold maneuvers at Iwo Jima. This was to include an Amphibious Landing. The 3d Marine Division along with the 4th and 5th Marine Divisions, were the units that landed on Iwo Jima in 1945.

Unknown to the Division high command, Tom Stirewalt sent some of the troops to the Yokohama Salvage Depot where they scrounged enough spare parts to put our heavy equipment into operation for the maneuvers at Iwo Iima.

The Shore Party Battalion was responsible for the beach area, including marking the landing areas and opening up roads for the various units. We also provided supply depots, fuel and water as well as medical facilities. I met my cousin R.C. on the beach when his Artillery Unit landed.

My cousin, Master Sergeant R.C. Graves was with the 4th Marine Division on Iwo Jima in 1945. I told him I was glad I was on Iwo Jima in 1954 instead of 1945. He was one of the few men in his Artillery Unit not killed or wounded in 1945 and was awarded the Bronze Star for his part in the operation. To permit some perspective, about one third of all Marine Corps casualties in World War II occurred on Iwo Jima. Of the three Marine Divisions (75,000) men, over 26,000 were casualties and more than 6,000 killed. It was reported there were 23,000 Japanese on the Island. Approximately 1,100 surrendered in the final days. The rest of them died. Iwo Jima was probably the best defended area in the world. I inspected some of the bunkers of concrete and steel which had sustained direct hits by 14 inch naval guns and remained intact. There would be a chunk of concrete about six feet in diameter and three feet deep that would be blown away. The bunkers I saw were four feet thick and full of steel rebars. It appeared most of them were destroyed by flame-throwers and individual charges placed in the air vents. This meant some marine had to get real close to destroy them. The Island was a honeycomb of caves, some of them with as much as five levels. I was glad I was on a Cruiser in the Philippine Islands while the battle for Iwo Jima was taking place.

There were more Marines on Iwo Jima, 75,000 concentrated on an Island of about 8 square miles, about 4.5 miles long and 2.5 miles at the widest part, than at any other place in the history of the Marine Corps. Add to this the 23,000 Japanese and it is difficult to imagine the carnage that took place on this small Island. My cousin, R.C. could not get over the fact that Iwo Jima contained a large amount of vegetation in 1954. He said in 1945, there was not a blade of grass or leaf of a tree on the entire Island. It had been stripped bare by the violent nature of the battle. We climbed to the top of Mt. Suribachi to the area where the flag was raised. It was difficult to imagine how any man could climb Mt. Suribachi with some one shooting at him all the way.

After two weeks at Iwo Jima we returned to Camp McGill. The balance of the Division returned to their various bases scattered all over the Island of Honshu.

A few weeks after returning from Iwo Jima, I was sent to the U.S. Naval Hospital in Yokosuka for surgery on my legs. I had been having trouble with leg aches for quite some time due to large Varicose Veins. The Veins were removed from the groin to the ankles from both legs. I spent about two weeks in the Hospital and then returned to Camp McGill.

By the Spring of 1954 the lst Marine Division was still in Korea. Many of the troops were being returned to the United States for discharge or reassignment. The Korean War was over and as usual the Armed Forces started winding down. The 3rd Marine Division in Japan was more or less a training unit for replacements for the 1st Marine Division in Korea.

Major Tom Stirewalt was beside himself with frustration. This was my first experience with the conflict between the military services. The Army was ready and willing to furnish spare parts for our equipment but the Marine Corps would have none of it. Our old time Supply Officer, Warrant Officer Bud Elmore kept copies of all requisitions for spare parts and all correspondence from the Division Headquarters pertaining to supply problems. This later saved his neck. Even with the turnover in personnel, I was able to stay on top of my job as Adjutant, Personnel Officer and Custodian of Secret and Top Secret Files. After 15 years, I knew the whereas and wherefore of Marine Corps Administration.

In early Summer, Tom Stirewalt came in to see me and said he was going to get hold of his Rabbi and bail out of this outfit. (He was not Jewish, but had a friend in Washington he could call on for help. He referred to him as his Rabbi). At that time, the only way out of the 3rd Marine Division was to transfer to the lst Marine Division in Korea. Tom said this outfit (Shore Party Battalion) was falling apart and sooner or later something would happen and there would be "hell to pay". He said he did not want to be around when it happened. In about two weeks, he was transferred to the lst Marine Division in Korea.

About a month after Tom Stirewalt was transferred to Korea, the roof fell in. President Eisenhower decided he would send the 3rd Marine Division to French Indochina (later Viet Nam) to rescue the French who were on the verge of being kicked out of the country. The French did not have the capability for an effective evacuation of the area. We received a Top Secret message for the Shore Party Battalion to move out and to set up evacuation facilities at the Port of Haiphong to evacuate the French. About half of the Shore Party heavy equipment would not operate because we could not obtain spare parts. Because of this, the operation was canceled and the French were left to their own devices.

In a few days, all hell broke loose. The Commanding General of the Division and all of his senior staff swooped down upon us. The Commanding Officer, Colonel Sabol was relieved of Command immediately. In a few days the Lt. Colonel Executive Officer was relieved. A short time later, a new Colonel and Lt. Colonel were flown out from Camp Lejeune, North Carolina. The Major who had replaced Tom Stirewalt was relieved as well as the Battalion Training Officer and all of the Company Commanders. The only two officers left were Warrant Officer Elmore and myself. Each day after work, Elmore and I would meet in the Officers' Club and speculate on when we would be caught up in the "purge".

After a few weeks, the new officers were in place and Elmore and I were still on the job. We could not understand how the two of us had survived. The new Commanding officer confided in me that the senior people at Division Headquarters had stated Graves and Elmore were the only two people in the entire Shore Party Battalion that were on top of their job. I told him in my opinion the blame should be placed at Division Headquarters for not providing spare parts for the equipment. After checking Elmore's files, he agreed with me. The new Colonel, an old time experienced Shore Party Officer would not put up with the usual run around from the Division Staff. He went directly to the Commanding General and told him what he needed and he needed it right now. Soon, we were receiving spare parts and other supplies flown out from the United States. In a few weeks all equipment was operating and the Shore Party Battalion was functioning as it should be. Our Infantry Training was canceled. Tom Stirewalt in Korea heard about our problem and was congratulating himself for bailing out when he did.

As summer turned to fall, many of the people in the 3rd Marine Division who had not been rotated to Korea began to receive orders back to the United States. I had requested an assignment at Camp Pendleton, California. That was my favorite duty station. By October everyone else had been rotated back to the United States except me. I was beginning to think the Marine Corps had forgotten I was still in Japan. By November I was really becoming concerned. The second week in November we received a message from Washington directing that I be transferred immediately to Marine Corps Headquarters in Washington by first available government air transportation, with 30 days leave authorized. I was not thrilled about a three year assignment in Washington but was happy to be leaving Japan for the second time. It dawned upon me that it was about the same time of year I departed from Japan in 1945. The thought of being with Chris and my girls compensated for my lack of enthusiasm for the assignment in Marine Corps Headquarters.

I managed to get a message to Chris that I was on my way home and departed from Haneda Airport in Tokyo a few days later on an Air Force C-97 transport plane. This was the transport version of the famed B-29 bomber. We were scheduled for a fuel stop at Midway Island but due to a strong tailwind we went on into Hickam AFB in Hawaii. We spent the night at Hickam and departed at 8:00 a.m. the next day for Travis AFB about 40 miles from San Francisco.

Once on the ground at Travis AFB I was on my own. I rode a Bus into San Francisco and on to San Francisco International Airport. I had a terrible time getting a flight to San Diego. I finally managed to get a seat on a small Regional Airline. I called Chris and told her I should be at Lindbergh Field in San Diego by 6:00 p.m. We took off from San Francisco crossed the bay and landed in Oakland! We landed at about every airport between San Francisco and San Diego with a long stop in Burbank, and finally arrived in San Diego about 8:00 p.m. Chris and my girls had been waiting at Lindbergh Field for several hours. It was wonderful to be home!

We arranged to have our furniture packed and shipped, tried to sell the house but could not do so on short notice. We decided to rent the house and managed to do so at the last minute.

It was a trying time for Sharon. She would be going to a new school in Virginia in the middle of the year. She had attended school in San Francisco, Oceanside and Encinitas, California and would now have to attend a new school.

We spent Christmas in Texas with Christene's parents, visited my relatives and departed for Washington right after Christmas 1954. We rented an apartment in Falls Church, Virginia. I could ride the Bus to work and the school Sharon attended was in the neighborhood. The location of the apartment was great but we were not very happy with the arrangement. There was no place for the girls to play and our apartment was on the second floor with people above us on the third floor and below on the first floor. It seemed there was someone moving around all day and all night either above or below us.

My assignment at Marine Corps Headquarters was in the Personnel Accounting Section. This was the section that kept track of all Marines, worldwide. We were responsible for all statistical data and provided other departments and agencies with what seemed like hundreds of statistical reports on a constant basis.

My boss was a Marine Lieutenant Colonel. I had a Marine Gunnery Sergeant assistant and a Secretary. The Personnel Accounting Section also contained about 50 women Civil Service workers. I soon discovered my primary function was to keep peace and settle petty differences between the women. This was very frustrating.

I could identify the women in the Section in three categories. There were the young women with their husband and boyfriend problems, the middle aged "party girls" suffering from a hangover most of the time and the most difficult of all the frustrated old maids. All of the Civil Service employees had a very lengthy job description and were extremely jealous. If someone did something that intruded into the job description of someone else there would be a shouting or crying episode. They would frequently go for two weeks where they would not speak to each other. At times I wondered how we managed to put out any productive work.

I did not realize at the time, but a couple of things occurred which would completely change my life. The first thing was we used IBM Punched Card equipment to assist in maintaining our records and statistics. This was the forerunner of the computer and I found the punched card equipment much more fascinating than trying to keep peace between the various factions among the women in the Section. I spent as much time as I could with the punched card equipment.

The second thing I noticed was many of the Captains in the other departments were going to school at night at the University of Maryland and George Washington University. Both Universities offered night classes in the Pentagon, about one mile from Marine Corps Headquarters. I inquired about the possibility of enrolling and was told to contact the Director of Admissions and was given directions to his office.

A couple of days later, I told Chris I would be late getting home from work since I had an appointment after work with the Director of Admissions at the University of Maryland.

I wore my uniform to the appointment and it turned out to be the proper thing to do. The Director of Admissions was a retired Army Colonel, very friendly and gracious. I was very apprehensive when I told him I not only did not graduate from High School but never attended High School.

He looked me over carefully like he was holding inspection and said "do you mean to tell me you are a captain in the Marine Corps and you never attended High School". I replied in the affirmative. He said "well I'll be damned" or words to that effect. He informed me he "had authority to accept adult students on an individual basis. He would permit me to take one course and if I performed satisfactorily, I would then be admitted unconditionally.

I enrolled in one course in American History for the Spring Semester 1955. I was very apprehensive about taking a college level course. My anxiety soon vanished when I completed the course with an "A".

The following semester I doubled up and took two courses. This meant being away from home two nights each week but Chris kept the family going and gave me encouragement to keep going to school. I continued to attend the University of Maryland at night as long as we were stationed in Washington and had about 36 semester hours of college credit when we were transferred.

In the Spring of 1955 we decided we were not happy living in the apartment. We found a little three bedroom house under construction in a new area called Springfield, Virginia. We liked the area and decided to buy the house. The developer had gone out into the woods, knocked down most of the trees and started a new town. There were several hundred homes in the area when we moved there and they continued to build at a rapid pace. When we moved in 1957 it was beginning to take on the appearance of a city.

Sharon was never happy in the school in Falls Church but soon adjusted to her new school in Springfield. The area was growing so fast they could not build schools fast enough to stay ahead of the enrollment. Some of the children, including Sharon attended class in the Methodist Church next door.

We moved our church membership from Encinitas to the new Methodist Church in Springfield. This was the most dynamic Methodist Church we had ever seen. There were new members every week. Everyone was very active including the Graves family. The church had a continuous building program underway since the area was growing rapidly. Money was no problem. There were no rich members of the church but there were no poor ones either! Everyone was working and contributing to the growth of the church.

I had joined a "car pool" right after we moved to Springfield, however this did not work out very well since I was going to the University of Maryland Classes two nights each week. Parking for people working at Marine Corps Headquarters was a real challenge. The parking lot was on the back side of the Marine Corps Base, across the street which adjoined Arlington National Cemetery. Parking was on the northwest side of the base and a good long walk from our office. The parking permit was merely a hunting license. If the car pool was late, finding an open parking space was a real challenge.

A Navy Captain who lived in the area was being transferred and he had a small British car called an Anglia for sale for $300.00. We decided to purchase the car since there was a good possibility I could acquire his small car parking space under the back steps leading into our building. There were several small spaces of this type and not many people owned small cars at that time. After buying the car I applied for the parking space and since I was the only applicant, I was assigned the parking space. This proved to be very handy, especially when it rained. I did not get wet getting from the car into the building.

The little British car not only solved the parking and commute problems but by taking the rear and front passenger seats out it could be used to haul bulky objects. The trunk lid opened back to form a platform rather than opening up like most cars.

There was an Army Base called Cameron Station in nearby Arlington, Virginia where all of the household goods came in prior to being delivered to their owner. These items were shipped in large wood boxes about the size of a small bedroom. Instead of burning the boxes, they permitted military personnel to salvage the lumber for their own personal use. Most of the lumber was in good condition and those boxes from the Philippine Islands were made of mahogany wood. I hauled many loads of wood in the little car and built a walk-in playhouse for Sharon and Cathy in the back yard. I hauled slabs from a sawmill to finish the outside of the playhouse. When finished, it looked like a log cabin.

They were demolishing a World War II housing area at Cameron Station and I hauled in pieces of broken concrete from the floors of the houses. I obtained sand for a base, placed the broken concrete pieces in the sand and put fresh cement in the cracks between the pieces of concrete. When finished, we painted the pieces of concrete an alternate red and green with masonry paint and we soon had a very attractive patio.

In 1956 we traded the 1950 Buick in on a new Ford Station Wagon. I made a luggage rack inside the station wagon. By cutting slots on the inside of the tailgate the rack would extend from the tailgate to the wheel wells. We could place the luggage on the rack and put air mattresses on the floor of the station wagon and a person could stretch out and sleep while traveling.

In the summer of 1956, I managed to obtain a 30 day leave. We wanted to go to Texas to visit Mr. and Mrs. McDonald and my aunt and uncle. We did not have enough money to stay in motels on the way so as usual for us we drove day and night. We carried a small ice chest and Chris would buy food along the way and make sandwiches for us to eat.

We had the Station Wagon tuned up prior to leaving Springfield but after several hours of driving it started running rough. We decided to put up with it and have it tuned again when we arrived in Terrell, Texas. The second day on the road, we stopped at a beautiful picnic area at a large lake near Rockwood, Tennessee. When we finished our lunch and returned to the car it was smoking and making a strange noise. When I raised the hood I could see the wiring harness was on fire. I disconnected the battery and put the fire out burning my hand in the process. The car would not run and we were stranded!

A very friendly local resident came over to see what the trouble was and offered to help. It was Sunday and everything was closed but the friendly local guy said he knew where the man lived who drove the wrecker for the Ford Agency. He offered to take me into town and see if we could find the wrecker driver. I accepted his offer of help. We went into town, found where the driver lived. He and his buddies were involved in a poker game on his front porch. After I explained our situation, the wrecker driver excused himself from his poker playing buddies, took me down to the Ford Agency, unlocked the compound, obtained the wrecker and we were on our way to retrieve the Station Wagon, Chris, Sharon and Cathy. Neither the friendly local guy or the wrecker driver would accept any money for their help.

The wrecker driver took us to a Motel and assured me they would start working on the car as soon as the shop opened the next morning.

When I arrived at the Ford Agency the next morning they were working on the car and said it would be ready by noon. They called the local State Farm Insurance Agent. He came down and looked at the damage to the car and said it was fully covered under the Comprehensive part of my Insurance Policy. He noticed my burned hand and insisted that he take me to a local Doctor to have it checked. The Doctor put some ointment on my burned hand, bandaged it and by noon we were back on the road.

We were most thankful for the friendly people we came in contact with at Rockwood, Tennessee. I cannot think of any other place we have been where we were treated as well as we were there.

The car continued to run rough and when we arrived in Terrell I took it to the local Ford Dealer. They tuned it up but it was still missing. They could not figure out what the trouble was. Finally one of the mechanics said they had one in a few weeks earlier with the same problem. He said it was probably a faulty camshaft. This meant tearing the engine down. The Warranty was only good for 3,000 miles and since we were slightly over that I would have to pay for the labor cost. Ford would pay for any parts that were needed. I gave the go ahead to tear the engine down since we did not want to drive back to Virginia on only seven cylinders.

It turned out the camshaft had a faulty lobe that had not been properly hardened. It looked as though someone had taken a file and filed it down so it would not lift the valve, causing a failure to fire on one of the cylinders. They replaced the camshaft, valve lifter and two valves, put the engine back together and it ran fine. We never had any more trouble with the Station Wagon and when we traded it off seven years later it had more than 90,000 miles on the odometer.

Our trip back to Virginia was uneventful and by driving day and night we were back at home in two days. In those days all of the highways were two lane and went through all of the little towns. This made cross country travel rather slow.

In the fall, Sharon enrolled in Mount Vernon High School in Alexandria, Virginia and Cathy attended a new Elementary School in Springfield, Virginia. I enrolled in two more courses at the University of Maryland and Chris enrolled in a Tailoring Course offered by the Adult Division of the local School District. We were all in school at the same time.

My Marine Corps duties had settled into a predictable routine but I was not real happy. I was in a position to learn things I would have been much happier not knowing. Primarily the politics and in-fighting that takes place in the military Headquarters and in Washington in general. This was during the Eisenhower Administration. He was known as "Mr. Clean" but he spent most of his time playing golf and the government was run by his Chief of Staff, a crook by the name of Sherman Adams.

They were stealing briefcases all over town to try to find out what the other people were up to. I would be assigned Headquarters Duty on the week-end about every two months. One of my duties was to deliver messages to the Commandant who lived across town at the Marine Barracks at 8th and I Street in Washington. They would fasten the Briefcase to my arm with a handcuff so if someone should steal the Briefcase he had to take my hand along with it.

The most depressing thing I found out was that I could forget about being promoted to Major. Those of us commissioned at the beginning of the Korean War were for the most part former Senior Non-Commissioned officers with extensive combat experience in World War II. We were now senior Captains with sufficient time in grade to be promoted to Major. We were senior to a group of Naval Academy and ROTC Graduates. The Marine Corps Planners knew that with our military records, if we were to come into the zone for promotion, many of us would be promoted to Major. Their solution was to have a promotion zone from Captain to Major of one man each year for the next four years. They also established a policy that upon reaching 20 years of service, we had to either retire or revert to our permanent rank. My permanent rank was Chief Warrant Officer but many others would have to go back to their old rank of Master Sergeant.

The Marine Corps Planners could have accomplished their purpose by having a large promotion zone and letting our group compete on an equal footing with the Naval Academy and ROTC types in front of a promotion board. They were afraid that some of the "Mustangs" (this was a name assigned to officers who had been promoted from the enlisted ranks) would be promoted and some of the Academy and ROTC types passed over. Had I remained in the Fleet Marine Force, I would not have known about this policy until I had completed my 20 years of active service and would have been a much happier Marine.

By the summer of 1957 I had completed 17 1/2 years of service and was eligible for reassignment. I was looking forward to being reassigned to any place outside the Washington area. I concluded that duty at Marine Corps Headquarters should be reserved for a last duty assignment prior to retirement.

MARINE CORPS AIR BASE, CHERRY POINT, NORTH CAROLINA

My new assignment was as Officer in Charge of the Data Processing Installation at Cherry Point, North Carolina. I had never had a duty assignment with Marine Corps Aviation and was looking forward to my new assignment with pleasure.

There was an old saying in the Marine Corps that there are only two good duty stations in the entire Marine Corps, "The one you are going to and the one you just left". My view was the one I was going to had to be better than the one I was leaving. There were only two good things to remember about my assignment at Marine Corps Headquarters. One, it permitted me to earn 36 semester hours of college credit and two it gave me an opportunity to acquire knowledge of the IBM Punched Card Equipment. This was to prove to be most valuable at a later date. We sold our house in Springfield to a Marine Captain I had known for many years. We did not make any money on the house but we did have cheap rent for almost three years. We received $1,000.00 cash and the buyer assumed our loan. We were happy to be able to get out from under the loan. We still had the house in Encinitas and did not need another house to worry about. Trying to keep the one in Encinitas rented was all of the worry we needed.

Upon arrival at the Marine Corps Air Base at Cherry Point, we were assigned temporary quarters for a few days and by the time our furniture arrived we had been assigned quarters in a housing project near the main gate.

We received a warm welcome from the Aviators and were soon settled into a pleasant routine. It soon became apparent that Marine Aviators were different from "ground pounders" or "grunts" as they referred to anyone who did not fly.

By ground Fleet Marine Force standards, the Aviators were a "loose" bunch of Marines. They did their job and did not get caught up in a lot of trivia as so often happens in ground units. They worked hard and played even harder. They did not waste a lot of time on ceremony and called each other on a first name basis except on very formal situations. I decided I could live with that type attitude and settled in for a pleasant tour of duty.

About 20 miles from Cherry Point was Moorhead City, North Carolina and Atlantic Beach. This was a beautiful beach and we spent a lot of time at the beach during the summer and fall.

By fall we moved into quarters on the Base. Our Apartment was on the first floor of what had been a Bachelor Officers Quarters in World War II. It had been converted into family quarters after the War. Our Apartment was large and very comfortable as apartments go. There was a swimming pool nearby and the Air Station Bus would pick the children up and take them to the ten cent movie on base and bring them home when the movie was over.

Chris joined a group of ladies that had an exercise class in the Gymnasium on the Base two mornings each week. They had workouts, played Volleyball and had a lot of fun. North Caroline State University and East Caroline College offered college courses on the Base. I enrolled in two courses each semester as long as we were at Cherry Point. When we were transferred 2 1/2 years later, I had run my total up to 52 semester hours.

The Data Processing Installation was responsible for maintaining the Personnel Accounting Records for all Marine Corps Aviation personnel, both active duty and reserve personnel, stationed east of the Mississippi River.

We were responsible for about 90,000 individual Marines. As changes occurred that had an effect on the individual, this would be reported to us by means of a typewritten Unit Diary. The information reported on the Unit Diary would be coded and punched into an IBM Punched Card. These transactions were processed daily and at the end of the month, we would prepare a series of reports for Marine Corps Headquarters and other reports to go back to the individual units showing the accounting status of all personnel. There were about 25 people in the Installation. We were not overworked by any means, but did stay busy.

About every two weeks, I would be assigned duty as Officer of the Day for a 24 hour period. In this capacity I was responsible for the security of the Air Base and any unusual activity that took place from 5:00 p.m. until 8:00 a.m. the next day. Unit Commanders would take care of problems in their organizations during regular working hours. In addition, I was responsible for the Honor Guard for the Station when it was necessary to present honors for visiting dignitaries.

In addition to the Officer of the Day, there was a Colonel or very senior Lieutenant Colonel assigned duty as Staff Duty officer. In the event there was an occurrence the Officer of the Day could not handle, he would call the Staff Duty Officer for assistance. The Staff Duty officer could remain in his Quarters at night but was required to keep the Officer of the Day informed of his location if he should leave his quarters. I found it necessary to call the Staff Duty Officer on one occasion. I received a call one night around midnight that there was a disturbance at the Bachelor Officers' Quarters. I got into my assigned vehicle and proceeded to the scene of the disturbance, about two miles away. When I arrived at the Bachelor Officers Quarters I was surprised to find two Lieutenant Colonels engaged in a fist fight! I had never seen officers of any rank in a fist fight and was completely taken by surprise to see two ranking officers so engaged.

I stepped between them and ordered them to stop fighting. I fully expected one or both of them to punch me out but they had the good sense not to strike a junior Officer, under arms and wearing the brassard of the Officer of the Day. Everything was going quite well until each of them demanded that I throw the other one in the brig. I grabbed a nearby telephone and called the Staff Duty Officer, a senior Lieutenant Colonel and told him I needed his assistance. He wanted to know what was happening and when I explained the situation to him he said he would be there as soon as he could get dressed.

I assured him I could keep them from killing each other but could not determine which one should be placed under arrest. It appeared to me that both of them needed medical attention. One had a severe nose bleed and appeared to have a broken nose. The other one had some very loose teeth and was bleeding from his mouth.

When the Staff Duty Officer arrived, I turned the two Lieutenant Colonels over to him, excused myself and returned to my duty station at the Provost Marshal's Office near the Main Gate to the Air Base.

Several months later while assigned duty as Officer of the Day, I was making a routine patrol out near the runway. There were two Marine F4-D Fighters making an afterburner takeoff side by side on the wide runway. They were really rolling and just as they became airborne, one of them started rolling from side to side. The pilot could not control the aircraft and soon one wing hit the runway. At this point the plane cartwheeled several times and burst into flames. I was the first person on the scene and immediately got on my radio and called for an Ambulance and Fire trucks plus Military Police to keep spectators away. The pilot was thrown clear of the aircraft but was killed upon impact. I had witnessed many airplane crashes on the ENTER-PRISE but nothing as violent as this. The young Captain that was killed left a wife and two children, a modern tragedy.

Our tour at Cherry Point was not all violence and tragedy. There were many good days. In the summer we spent a lot of time at Atlantic Beach and I frequently went fishing with several others for Flounder. This was an unusual way to fish. The Neuse River that bordered the Air Base was a tidal river over a mile wide and you could wade out into it for 150 yards and not be in water over waist deep. We fished at night with a lantern in one hand and a steel gig about 4 feet long in the other. There was a heavy cord about ten feet long attached to the gig with a float on the other end. This served two purposes. First you would not lose the gig and when you gigged a Flounder you would slide the fish up the gig and onto the cord and then drag it behind you while you searched for another Flounder. This fish is normally larger than your open hand and about one inch thick. At night they lie on the bottom of the river in the sand. The Flounder is very tasty and contains only one bone.

I had purchased a small boat, motor and trailer. In the winter the Neuse River would freeze over. The sea going trout fish would come up the Neuse River and into a tributary that ended at the Air Base Power Plant. The Power Plant gave off a lot of hot water into the small tributary. The fish would swim into the warm water and become disoriented. They would flop around near the surface and we would catch them with a dip net. They would be frozen solid in a few minutes. Chris never participated in this activity since she was afraid of water. My job at the Data Processing Center had become more or less routine. I had good people working for me that were willing and eager to do a good job. I was learning more and more about the use and operation of the various IBM Machines and never gave any thought as to how this assignment would effect our lives at a future date.

The Marine Corps built a new housing area for officers on the base, called Capeheart Housing named after the Congressional Bill that authorized the new housing program. These homes were far superior to any other housing on the base. There were not enough senior officers to occupy all of the houses. We were offered a set of quarters designed for a Major or Navy Lt. Commander. We moved from the Apartment into the nicest home we had ever lived in up to that time. The house had three bedrooms, two baths, separate dining and living room, also a carport with a large storage area. Last but most impressive was a screened in patio or back porch. I have not mentioned the mosquitoes at Cherry Point. In the fall the first weather front that wraps around the area and blows from the northeast would blow mosquitoes into the entire area from the marsh land along the North Carolina Coast. These were the largest and meanest mosquitoes we had ever encountered. The only way to stay outside was on the screened in patio.

Cathy had acquired a marvelous kitten. He was solid black with long hair. He developed quite a personality. We sometime suspected that he thought he was a dog! He would jump into the bathtub with Cathy and run through mud puddles. Every time the car started the cat thought he was supposed to get into the car, which he did on many occasions. He would perch on the top of the car seat behind the drivers head and look out at the scenery. The cats name was Nikko which means cat in Japanese.

As Nikko was soon developing into a young "tom cat" he wanted to roam the neighborhood. We decided the best thing to do was to have Nikko castrated. There was a young Veterinarian in the small town of Havelock, near the Main Gate of the Airbase.

We agreed that Chris would drop the cat off at the Vets office in the morning and I would pick him up after work. Things got a little out of hand. When Chris dropped the cat off, there was a black man attendant. When he asked Chris what they were supposed to do to the cat, she was too embarrassed to say "castrate" him. Instead, she said she wanted the cat fixed. The black attendant took the cat and Chris departed thinking everything was taken care of.

After getting off work, I went to the Vets office to pick up Nikko. The Vet brought the cat out with a terrible pained expression on his face and started to apologize profusely. He said he had never made a mistake like this in his life. I did not know what he was talking about until he handed the cat to me. He had performed a Hysterectomy on our tom cat, then realizing his mistake, he proceeded to castrate the cat. The poor cat was in a state of shock with glassy eyes, stitches across his stomach and rear end.

Rather than getting mad, my sense of humor took over. Chris always said I had a peculiar sense of humor. Anyway I passed the cat back to the Vet and doubled over with laughter, completely out of control. The more I laughed the more embarrassed the Vet became.

He again apologized and stated that he would like to keep the cat for several days at no additional charge so he could take good care of the cat. He was afraid Nikko would catch pneumonia and die. I left the cat with the Vet and went home.

When I related the story to Chris, I had trouble explaining the situation because I was laughing so hard tears were running down my cheeks. We did not know how to break the news to Cathy and ended up telling her the Vet wanted to keep the cat a few days.

I made the mistake of relating the story to one of the neighbors and we might as well have published the story in the paper. The next day, the story was all over the Air Base and throughout the little town of Havelock. The Vet was the butt of many jokes and was so embarrassed I thought for a while he would leave town.

In a few days, Nikko was as good as new and was able to run all over the house. He provided many hours of family entertainment and right away wanted to ride in the car every time we went anywhere.

Soon after our arrival at Cherry Point, we decided we would move our Church Membership from Springfield, Virginia to the little Methodist Church in Havelock, North Carolina and try to become a member of the community. We were welcome in the little Church. Soon Chris and I were involved in all of the Church activities, including construction labor to build an addition to the Church. Chris did a lot of painting and I learned to lay floor tile and spent several hours on my knees laying tile. We made a number of friends and discovered that most of the people in the area worked on the Air Base. There were a few tobacco farmers in the area, a few commercial fishermen and several people employed in the local stores.

I continued to take two college courses at night that were offered by North Carolina State University on the Air Base.

The area around Cherry Point, with the exception of a few tobacco farms, was covered with Pine trees and various kinds of underbrush. Within these areas were many Deer. When Deer season opened, they had a peculiar way to hunt Deer. They would station the "hunters" in a line about 100 yards apart. They were armed with a shotgun using 00 Buckshot. Another group of men with dogs would spread out on the other side of the wooded area, make a lot of noise and chase the Deer toward the "hunters". When the Deer came within shooting distance of the "hunters", they would ambush the Deer. I had some difficulty calling this a sport. I thought it might be sport if the Deer could shoot back.

As soon as the first hunt of the season was over, the Deer that escaped the 'ambush would move onto the Air Base where no hunting was allowed. They were all over the Golf Course, in the ditches along side all of the roads and some even roamed into the housing areas on the Base. Fortunately the noise of the airplanes kept them off of the runways. I thought it was a smart move on the part of the Deer to move onto the Air Base. There was one undesirable point however, they were a traffic hazard, especially at night. If you were not careful, one of them would become excited and jump right in front of your car. One night one of the Military Police was responding to a call and was speeding. A Deer jumped out in front of him, was struck by the front of the pickup, came up over the hood and through the windshield causing serious injury to the Marine.

As soon as the hunting season was over, the Deer would move back into the woods and you would not see them again until the next hunting season arrived. It was a mystery to me how the Deer knew the hunting season was over.

Located on the Air Base at Cherry Point was an operation called 0 & R (meaning overhaul and repair). This was a large building, very much like an Aircraft Factory. This is where most of the civilians that lived in the area worked (close the Base and the O&R and the entire area would be a ghost town in no time). They would bring in the very tired, used up airplanes, strip them down to the skeleton, and rebuild them from the ground up. They would also modify them to include any late model modifications to that type aircraft. When they came out, they were as good as new. I made friends with a Captain who worked in the O&R operation and he was always willing to show me through the place. I was fascinated by what they were accomplishing.

When the airplanes had been restored to like new condition, it was necessary to give them a thorough flight test. They had a Master Sergeant pilot, a World War II survivor who tested all of the rebuilt airplanes. It did not matter if the plane was an old multi-engine transport or one of the modern Jets, the Master Sergeant flew all of them. Prior to and during World War II, both the Marine Corps and Navy had many squadrons of enlisted pilots. Many of them were commissioned during World War II and ended up a Major or Lieutenant Colonel if they survived the war. This Master Sergeant was one of the few remaining enlisted pilots in the entire Marine Corps.

The Air Base was commanded by a Major General. I had very little contact with him. The Chief of Staff was an old time, very senior Colonel and I worked closely with him. Whenever he wanted a job done such as Commander of the Honor Guard or other function that was common to ground type Marines as opposed to Aviators, he would call upon me for the assignment.

CUBA

In the late fall of 1958 I was working in my office and the telephone rang. It was Major Henderson the Air Base Adjutant. He said "a few of us are going on a trip down south and the Chief of Staff wants you to come along". He would not tell me where we were going but that I should take enough clothes for five days, no uniform but light weight civilian attire. Captains do not tell Colonels they do not want to do something. When I went home I told Chris that I would be leaving the next morning for four or five days and did not know where we were going! The next morning I reported to the Flight Line and observed we were to get aboard an RSD, a large 4 engine transport plane (the Airlines called this type airplane a DC-4). The passengers consisted of the Chief of Staff, Station Adjutant, Commander of the Military Police Unit, myself and two Majors from the Second Marine Air Wing. The Second Marine Air Wing was the major tactical unit stationed at Cherry Point. Other aviation units were stationed at Marine Corps Air Station at Jacksonville, North Carolina, near Camp Lejeune. Others were at the Marine Corps Air Station at Beaufort, South Carolina. I guessed that we were going to Beaufort Air Station for some sort of inspection. The Air Station at Beaufort was a small civilian airport when we were stationed at Parris Island, South Carolina in 1947 and 1948. This was where I learned to fly the Piper Cub and PT-19 airplanes. I thought it would be nice to visit the area again.

The aircrew of the transport plane consisted of two pilots, an engineer-navigator and a Master Sergeant Crew Chief, a total of 10 people. All of the seats had been removed except for 10 seats just aft of the Pilots Compartment. The rest of the plane was a large empty cargo area but did not contain any cargo.

After departing from Cherry Point, we soon passed over the Air Station at Beaufort, South Carolina at about 8,000 feet. By noon I recognized the city of Miami, Florida below us and we were still headed south. I finally asked the Chief of Staff where we were going, he said we were going to Havana, Cuba for a couple of days to observe the Cuban Military and then to St. Thomas, U.S. Virgin Islands for a couple of days of recreation and sight-seeing. We landed at Jose Marti Airport in Havana in the afternoon and received a perfunctory greeting from a few Cuban Officials. We were soon on our own.

Jose Marti Airport was a beehive of activity. Many of our old World War II C-47 Transport planes were coming in empty and going out loaded with Cuban Soldiers. They were being flown to the eastern part of the Island of Cuba where they were supposed to be fighting Fidel Castro and his Rag-Tag Army. There were a number of U.S. built World War II Fighters at the airport, mostly P-47 and P-51 types. The majority of them looked like they were not in a flyable condition for lack of maintenance.

In 1952, Fulgencia Batista had overthrown the Cuban Government and was the current Dictator. The people hated him and Fidel Castro had announced that his purpose was to overthrow Batista and bring true Democracy to the Cuban People. The Cuban people we had an opportunity to talk to were convinced that Fidel Castro was a true savior and they could not wait until he threw Batista in jail or hung him to a lamp post.

An observation of the Cuban Army Troops being flown out to fight Fidel Castro indicated they did not have their heart in the fight. They were a sorry looking bunch of troops.

The United States had obviously been furnishing all of the military equipment for the Cuban Army. The troops were armed with U.S. World War II M-1 Rifles, Machine Guns, Pistols and Uniforms, including Packs and Web Equipment. All of the aircraft were U.S. made.

We were told by some of the Cuban civilians that the United States had been propping up the Batista Dictatorship for many years and U.S. citizens were not very popular in Cuba. They tolerated us but were not very friendly.

Many of the Cubans claimed the United States had supported a number of Presidents and Dictators of Cuba since the turn of the century. The reason, according to them, was that United States big business interests owned all of the Sugar Mills, Oil Refineries and the Tourist Industry. The backbone of the Cuban economy was Sugar Cane. The American owned Sugar monopoly would pay the Cubans two to three cents per pound for their sugar production. This created deep resentment against the United States. Their belief was the United States would support any Dictator as long as he kept "hands off" of U.S. big business interests. They may be right.

I could not help but remember the stories told by the "old time" Marines when I first entered the Marine Corps in 1939. All of them had served in Nicaragua and Santa Domingo (sometimes called The Dominican Republic, depending upon which Dictator is in power). Their primary mission was to protect U.S. business interest and to keep the people under control while the United Fruit Company practically stole their Bananas. History referred to this as the Banana Wars.

As it turned out, the Cuban Troops Batista was sending out to fight Castro were merely reinforcements for Castro and his Rag Tag Army. Instead of fighting Castro, the Cuban Troops would desert and join the Castro forces. In a number of cases, entire units would desert and switch to Castro's Army.

We spent one day sightseeing in Havana and the surrounding area. There were many modern buildings and many others that were very old and in need of repair. The University of Havana had been closed by Batista because of student protests. We visited a very old Catholic Church in the middle of old Havana. It was well maintained and there were many Cubans milling around in the Church. We also toured a Rum Distillery. I did not know there was as much Rum in the entire world as we saw aging in a warehouse filled with very large Wooden containers. We were told they contained over seven million gallons of Rum.

We ate dinner in the Hotel Dining room and I was surprised to discover the steak and ice cream tasted like Rum! It seems they grind up the sugarcane stalks after the juice has been squeezed out and feed it to their cattle. By the time the cattle eat the ground up stalks, it has fermented causing the beef and ice cream to taste like Rum.

The next morning, we departed from Havana for St. Thomas, Virgin Islands. We flew over the eastern part of Cuba, the Island of Hispaniola (the western part of the Island is Haiti and the eastern part is the Dominican Republic) and Puerto Rico.

As we approached the Airport at St. Thomas, the Pilot in charge of the plane called the Captain in charge of the Military Police Unit at Cherry Point and myself to the cockpit to have a little fun out of us. The Pilot said, "see those two mountains down there with the little patch of green between them, that is where we are going to land". The Military Police Captain made a hasty departure for his seat and refused to look out the window. After dropping the landing gear and flaps on final approach, the Pilot told me to find a seat and buckle up. The Airport at St. Thomas at that time consisted of a sod runway that was barely large enough for a 4-engine Airplane. We landed without incident and the Pilots in the group really laughed at the Military Police Captain.

After securing the Airplane, we rented two Volkswagens and drove to a luxury Hotel overlooking the city of Charlotte Amalie. After everyone had checked into the hotel, we made a tour of the Island and the city of Charlotte Amalie.

The Island of St. Thomas was beautiful. There was one major drawback however, there was no fresh water on the Island unless it rained. They had scraped off the side of several small mountains and had paved the smooth area. At the bottom of the paved area was a catch basin to catch the rainwater. This was their only source of fresh water.

St. Thomas is what is called a "freeport" meaning no taxes on booze and luxury items. If a person could live on booze and perfume, he could really live cheaply on St. Thomas.

We stopped at a large Liquor Store and the Chief of Staff, Station Adjutant and the two Majors from the 2d Marine Air Wing went into the Liquor Store after telling us to come back and pick them up in about two hours. I still did not know what was going on but found it strange they would spend two hours in a Liquor Store. It turned out they had lists from other officers at Cherry Point showing the quantity and type of booze they wanted brought back on the flight. The price of booze on St. Thomas was a fraction of what it would cost in the United States.

The next morning we checked out of the Hotel, returned to the Airport and returned the Volkswagens to the Rental Agency. Upon boarding the airplane, I fully understood why the senior members of our group spent so much time in the Liquor Store. The airplane was completely filled with cases of booze of all types except for the area containing the few seats. The Station Adjutant (Major Henderson) had the largest bottle of Rum on record. It was a 7- gallon jug filled with dark Rum.

In the afternoon we landed at the U.S. Naval Station Guantanamo Bay on the southeast coast of Cuba for fuel and to kill time. Our flight was scheduled so we would arrive at Cherry Point at 1:00 a.m., the next morning. This arrival time was selected so very few people would observe the plane load of illegal, untaxed booze being unloaded.

On the return flight, it dawned on me that I had been a little slow in figuring out what we were doing. The trip to Havana to observe the Cuban Military was a cover for the main purpose of the trip, which was to haul back a plane load of illegal booze. This was another case where I would have been happier not knowing this type of activity existed.

When we were about 30 minutes from Cherry Point, the plane commander announced that he had a code worked out with the Control Tower and if the local Customs Agent was on the Base we would circle out over the Atlantic Ocean and the booze would be thrown overboard. He also stated that if anyone protested dumping the booze the protester would be thrown overboard also.

The local Customs Agent was not on the Base and we made a straight in approach to the airfield. We taxied to a remote area and were greeted by 40 or 50 people in casual dress, many of whom I recognized as senior officers. They started carrying cases of booze to the vehicles and I was reminded of the day in Leyte Gulf in 1944 when we tied the MONTPELIER to the Ammunition Ship with Kamikaze Planes in the area and the Captain announced that as soon as the ammunition was aboard and stored away we would pull away from the Ammunition Ship. It was amusing to see senior officers carrying ammunition. In this case, it was senior officers carrying cases of booze. In a few minutes the plane was empty and I walked over to the Control Tower and called Chris to come down and pick me up. We had quarters on the base and in a few minutes she arrived.

A few weeks after returning from St. Thomas the Station Adjutant (Major Henderson) had too much Rum from his giant bottle, got into a big fight with his wife, got into his new automobile, took off down the street at high speed, lost control of his car and smashed into a large pine tree. He was killed instantly. All of this in a 15 mile per hour speed zone on the base. So much for his illegal booze!

I continued to follow events in Cuba. By the end of 1958 things started to unravel rapidly. Large units of the Cuban Army began flip flopping over to Fidel Castro's side and in early 1959 Batista loaded all of the cash and gold he could lay his hands on onto a Cuban transport plane and "bugged out" to the French Riviera. It turned out the Cuban people, as happened so many times in their history, merely traded one dictator for another.

Chris continued to enjoy her exercise group and I attended night classes two nights per week. Sharon and Cathy liked living on the base and my job was going well.

In late summer of 1959 Captain Mitch Pawlik was assigned to the Data Processing Installation for "on the job training" under my supervision. I had mixed emotions about this assignment: flattered that I would be considered capable of training him into a new occupational field, but knowing in the back of my mind that as soon as he was qualified for the job, one of us would be moving on and it would probably be me!

In November 1959 the Station Adjutant received a hurry-up transfer. The Chief of Staff called me to his office and informed me that I was now the Adjutant, Marine Corps Air Station, Cherry Point, North Carolina and I would report directly to him. This was what I would call a plush assignment. I sat in on meetings with the Commanding General and the various senior commanders. I also worked with the Colonel in command of the Overhaul and Repair Facility (Airplane Factory). After more than three years as Adjutant of the 3d Shore Party Battalion, 3d Marine Division, this assignment was a "piece of cake".

In January 1960 my cushy assignment came to a sudden end! Going over the overnight message traffic from Marine Corps Headquarters, I was startled to see orders transferring me from Cherry Point to Marine Corps Recruit Depot, San Diego, California. My assignment was Officer in Charge of the Data Processing Installation at the Recruit Depot. Talk about mixed emotions! For my part, I was not too happy to leave my good assignment but the really bad part was that Sharon and Cathy would have to change school in the middle of the school year. I called Chris and broke the news to her. We were to move right away but were authorized a 30 day delay in reporting to San Diego. We notified the people that were renting our house in Encinitas to vacate right away since we needed possession.

After getting over the shock of the sudden change of station orders, we started looking forward to again living in our own house in Encinitas. This was about 25 miles from the Marine Base at San Diego and I could commute to work with no great difficulty.

We scurried around arranging to have our furniture packed and shipped, said good-by to our friends at Cherry Point and departed for California.

We stopped in Texarkana, Texas and spent the night with my cousin R.C. Graves and his family. We bought a new 1960 Volkswagen in Texarkana for $1,400 cash. I had wanted this type car for some time but could not justify two cars while stationed at Cherry Point. The assignment in San Diego would require two cars or leave Chris stranded in Encinitas most of the time. After closing the deal on the new Volkswagen, we departed for Terrell.

Chris drove the Station Wagon while I followed in the Volkswagen. We arrived in Terrell late in the afternoon and Mr. and Mrs. McDonald were expecting us.

We spent a few days in Texas visiting relatives and then left for California since we did not want to keep Sharon and Cathy out of school any longer than necessary. We bought a tow-bar and attached the Volkswagen to the Station Wagon and departed for California. Things went well until we were a few miles north of El Paso headed for Las Cruces, New Mexico where we had planned to spend the night. We started to pick up a few flakes of snow. After about thirty minutes, the snow was coming down in abundance and darkness had closed in. We were too far out of El Paso to turn around and we pushed on toward Las Cruces. The snow was falling so heavily I could not see the road. Chris rolled her window down and could see the side of the road. She guided us on into Las Cruces by watching the side of the road. We found a Motel in Las Cruces and spent the remainder of the night and most of the next morning. The snow accumulated to about 10 inches overnight and the next morning all roads were closed! Around 10:00 a.m., the Highway Patrol declared the roads open and we continued our journey to California.

The highway was in pretty good shape and things were going well. When we were about 18 miles west of Las Cruces, we hit a patch of ice. The Station Wagon started to skid and the more I tried to correct the skid the worse things became. The Volkswagen seemed to skid and cause the Station Wagon to skid out of control. We were meeting oncoming traffic and I don't know how we avoided a collision. Somehow we missed the oncoming traffic and both of our vehicles made a 180 degree turn. We ended up in a bar ditch headed back toward Las Cruces. We were all scared stiff, but no injuries. The Volkswagen jack knifed against the left rear bumper of the Station Wagon and had a bent fender and broken headlight. Fortunately the bar ditch was shallow. We decided to try to drive out of the ditch. Chris got into the Volkswagen and by using the power of both vehicles at the same time, we were able to drive out. We found a place to turn around and resumed our trip to California. The remainder of the trip was uneventful.

When we arrived in Encinitas, we were appalled at the condition of our home. The house needed paint inside and out. The hardwood floors were a mess and the grass in the rear yard was knee high.

Our furniture had not arrived and we decided to "camp" in the house and do as much work as possible before I had to report to San Diego for duty. We found a man to sand and refinish the hardwood floors while we concentrated on cleaning the house and yard.

The entire lot contained 1/2 acre and without our lawnmower (it was in the undelivered household goods), there was no way I could cut the grass on such a large area. There were thousands of snails under the Avocado Trees, and knee high grass everywhere.

I built a fence across the back yard, leaving enough space behind the house for a normal size yard. My next move was to purchase six ducks and four geese for the back area. The ducks would eat the snails and the geese would eat the grass. In about six weeks the grass and snails were gone. I had to buy food for the ducks and geese from then on, but they had earned their keep.

Our furniture finally arrived. Sharon and Cathy enrolled in School and I reported to my new duty station at the Recruit Depot in San Diego. This was where I started my Marine Corps Career in 1939.

The Marine Corps Recruit Depot was all "spit and polish". This required an adjustment on my part after spending three years with the "laid back" Aviators, most of whom referred to each other by their first name.

After a few days at San Diego, I started checking around to see how many old friends I could find on the Base. Warrant Officer Bud Elmore who had survived the 3rd Shore Party purge with me had retired about a month prior to my arrival at the Recruit Depot. There was not another person on the Base that I knew. Suddenly I felt very lonely! For the past 10 years, every time I transferred to a new duty station, it was like old home week. There would always be a number of people I had served with before. Even at Cherry Point, there were several Aviators that I had served with previously. I feel sure I developed a "crappy attitude" because I knew my days in the Marine Corps were numbered. I would be forced to retire or revert to Chief Warrant Officer by June 30, 1961. I spent my time in the Data Processing Center, served as Trial Counsel or Defense Counsel on numerous court-martials and was assigned as Officer of the Day for the Base at least every ten days.

I did not look forward to spending the next nine years as a lonely Chief Warrant Officer. Most of my friends were either dead or retired so I started looking around for another career. In 1960 there were a lot of "dead head, trouble makers" in the Marine Corps. In order to get rid of a deadbeat, it was necessary that he have three Special Courts-Marital. On the third conviction he could be separated with a Bad Conduct Discharge. This required an excessive amount of paperwork and administrative investigations. I could handle this, but the fund drive for the United Way really ticked me off. I did not mind working the tail off of my troops but I did not like to brow beat them to contribute their meager salary to the United Way. When we turned in our funds for the United Way Campaign, the Colonel commanding our Battalion checked the totals and instructed each of the Unit Commanders to return to our respective organizations and collect another $100.00 from our troops. With the advantage of "hindsight", I realize that I may have been overly sensitive, but the thought of brow beating my troops for another $100.00 was more than I could handle. I had been offered a job by State Farm Insurance Company and decided that I had had enough. I wrote out a check for $100.00 out of my own pocket and turned it in to the Colonel. On my way out of the Battalion Headquarters, I turned in my request for retirement.

My request for retirement was the first week of October and the Marine Corps did not waste any time approving my request. Within two weeks my orders transferring me to the Retired List had been received with an effective date of 30 November 1960. At the time, I was 2 1/2 months beyond my 38th birthday and had completed 21 years and one week of active service. I spent the remaining few weeks of my Marine Corps Career briefing the young woman Marine Captain who was to be my replacement on the various duties associated with the Data Processing Center.

On November 30, 1960 there was a small ceremony in the Commanding General's Office. Chris was present along with a few members of the General's Staff. Major General Victor H. Krulak presented my Retirement Orders and Retirement Certificate, shook my hand and wished me good luck. That was the end of my Marine Corps Career. I left the Marine Corps with a good feeling toward the Marine Corps and had no regrets. I was thankful to reach retirement eligibility.

STATE FARM INSURANCE COMPANY

On December 1, 1960 I started to work for State Farm Insurance Company as an Agent in Encinitas, California. I had studied their sales techniques and methods prior to leaving the Marine Corps. I soon learned I could sell the Automobile and Home Owners Insurance coverage but had great difficulty selling Life Insurance.

My greatest problem was in dealing with the public. I had dealt with Marines of all types for 21 years and thought civilians were just like Marines without a uniform. Was I ever wrong! Marines might take liberty with the truth when describing what they did on shore leave on a Saturday night but when dealing with anything of any substance, they always told the truth. Not so with civilians. They would look you straight in the eye and lie like a rug about any and everything. When selling Automobile Insurance, it was necessary to find out if the prospect had had any accidents or had his insurance canceled by another company. The same procedure applied to Fire Insurance. After signing someone up for coverage, the paperwork would be sent to the Regional Office for processing. They would run a background check on the individual and it frequently turned out that the person who had sworn up and down he had never had an accident had totaled out two or three cars and had one burned under suspicious circumstances. The same for Fire Insurance. Many times it turned out the customer had burned down a house in several states and had his insurance canceled more than once.

We had a District Manager who was responsible for 16 Agents. He would come by on occasion and needle me to sell Life Insurance. If I needed him for something he was always out of town.

Every six months the Company would have all the Agents in the Southern California area attend a meeting in Hollywood at one of the large nightclubs. They would feed us a steak dinner, have a well known Orchestra for entertainment and bore everyone to death with speeches. They would introduce the successful Agents and exhort everyone else to perform just like the successful ones. We were to return home and sell, sell, sell.

After six months with State Farm Insurance, I had a feeling that I would never be a successful salesman. This bothered me because the word failure was not a part of my vocabulary. However the thought of failure was continuing to persist in my deepest thoughts. Because I would not admit I was not going to become a successful Agent, I stayed with State Farm Insurance for a year and a half.

My experience with State Farm Insurance was not a total loss because it provided a valuable learning experience. I found out first hand that people would look you straight in the eye and lie.

It turned out my best customers were the average working man, especially the Mexican farm workers. When the Insurance Premium was due, they would come into the office and pay cash and thank me for taking their money. On the other hand, the so called wealthy people who lived in the exclusive Rancho Santa Fe area were a bunch of "deadbeats". It was necessary to chase them down to collect their Insurance Premium. They offered every excuse known to man and if you canceled their insurance for non-payment, they were totally incensed. They constantly demanded special treatment and favors and if they had a small accident there was no way to please them short of giving them a new automobile.

The event that finally convinced me to look for another line of work involved one of my best customers. I had insured his two automobiles, boat and a Homeowners Policy on his home and found out he did not have any life insurance. He had a wife and two children, drove to San Diego on the crowded U.S. 101 Highway and if any man ever needed life insurance he did. I gave him my best sales pitch for life insurance. He looked me straight in the eye and said "Look fellow, I ain't buying anything that I can't eat, smoke, drink or ride".

I went home that night and discussed the situation with Chris. She had known for some time I was not happy with my work and was willing to go along with anything I wanted to do. I had wanted to be a School Teacher for some time but believed we could not make it through college without a full time job. We discussed the problem at length and decided that with my $269.00 per month Marine Corps Retired Pay plus $160.00 per month on the G.I Bill we could make it if we were careful.

My applications for admission to San Diego State University and to East Texas State College in Commerce, Texas were approved. We decided to put our house on the market. If it sold, we would move to Texas. If it did not sell, I would enroll at San Diego State University and commute to school from Encinitas.

Our house sold right away and we made plans to move to Commerce, Texas. We would realize $1,000.00 cash and a monthly payment of $80.00 until the house was paid for. The additional $80.00 per month would help our chances of surviving for two years while I was in school. The Moving Companies wanted $600.00 to move us to Texas. We decided to rent a large U-Haul Van for $160.00 and move ourselves.

REVERSE GRAPES OF WRATH

Our move from Encinitas, California to Commerce, Texas in early July 1962 consisted of a convoy of a large U-Haul Van, our 1956 Ford Station Wagon and 1960 Volkswagen, all loaded to capacity except for passenger room. Cathy later referred to our move as the Reverse Grapes of Wrath, a rather fitting description.

Our niece, Beverly Fulton flew out to California and we took her to Disney Land before departing from California. She rode back to Texas with us.

Things started out great. We were towing the Volkswagen behind the Station Wagon. We encountered wet tar along the way that clogged the steering on the Volkswagen to the point where we could no longer tow it because it would not follow the Station Wagon properly. By the time we reached Yuma, Arizona it became necessary to disconnect the Volkswagen from the Station Wagon. Sharon had to drive the Volkswagen the rest of the way to Texas. We spent the first night on the road in a Motel in Arizona. Sharon smuggled our little dog Trudy into her room and let her sleep with her.

As an economy measure, we decided to spend the next night camped out on the road. Somewhere east of El Paso we stopped for the night at a Roadside Rest Area. Chris slept in the Station Wagon, Cathy and Beverly in the cab of the U-Haul Van and Sharon and I slept out on the ground near the Van. Around 2:00 a.m., I was awakened by a slight noise. When I opened my eyes, there was a Skunk about 6 inches from my face. I stayed very still, hoping he would go away. As the Skunk started to move away, I heard Sharon moving around. I whispered to her to be still and quiet! There is a Skunk nearby. The Skunk finally departed but I did not sleep very well the rest of the night.

We arrived at Mr. and Mrs. McDonald's home late the next afternoon, tired but happy that we had no serious difficulty making the trip from California.

We stored our furniture in the McDonald's Garage and turned in the U-Haul Van in Ardmore, Oklahoma. There were so many people moving from California to Texas at the time they would not permit me to tum the U-Haul Van into a Texas dealer since they were stacking up in Texas.

I enrolled for the Second Summer Session at East Texas State College in Commerce and started looking for a place to live in my spare time. Rental property in Commerce was hard to find. We found a neat little 3-Bedroom house for sale two blocks from the Campus. The house required $1,000.00 down payment and monthly payment of $38.00 per month. This seemed too good to be true and we bought the house and started moving our furniture right away. As soon as the water was turned on, the bottom fell out of the Water Heater. We called a Plumber and he put in a new one. When I tried to pay him he said no I will send you a bill at the end of the month.

We were really surprised to discover you could cash a check anywhere in town. Everyone was friendly and trusting. What a contrast with California, where no one trusted you for anything and it was almost impossible to pay for anything with a check.

In a short time, the Summer Session ended and I enrolled for 18 Semester hours for the Fall Term. Sharon had attended Palomar Jr. College in California. She transferred her credits to East Texas and enrolled for 18 Semester Hours for the Fall Semester.

We moved our church membership to Commerce and became a part of the community. Cathy was in Jr. High School and Chris kept busy taking care of things at home. She had to plan our meals very carefully because of our tight budget. One thing in our favor was the tuition at East Texas State College. Sharon and I could enroll in 18 or 19 semester hours for $50.00! We bought used books when we could and saved several dollars each semester by doing so.

Most of my classes were in the morning. I found a quiet place in a back corner on the second floor of the Library and did most of my studying in the afternoon.

The first winter in Commerce, we learned that our little house did not have any insulation. The temperature was 8-10 degrees for a few days and we were really cold. Chris spent most of several days in the bathroom since this was the only part of the house that was warm. Sharon and I would frequently go into the living room and wrap up in a quilt in order to watch the evening news on the television.

I concentrated on one semester at a time rather than looking at the eventual graduation date. My grades were A's and B's with one D in Government. The mid-term and final examination consisted of one question. If you stumbled, even a small amount, you were in big trouble in that class.

My Student Teaching was at Paris High School in Paris, Texas. I Graduated in May 1964 and immediately started looking for a job as a Business Teacher.

In the Spring of 1964 Chris started complaining that she had a viral infection since she was sick quite a bit. I kiddingly said "you will probably get over it in about nine months!" Chris finally went to a Doctor with her problem and came home with the news that she was pregnant and due to deliver in December. Soon after this news, Cathy came down with German Measles! We were concerned that Chris would catch them and had read some really bad stories of what terrible things happened to pregnant women who caught German Measles. The Doctor advised a complete round of Gamma Globulin shots for Chris. This was very painful for her, but it worked, she did not get the measles. My anxiety increased. I had a daughter in college, another in Jr.

High School and a pregnant wife. My job hunting became a serious business. I finally found a job at Mesquite High School, Mesquite, Texas. I had turned down a job at Las Vegas, Nevada. I did not care to have two daughters in Las Vegas.

My job in Mesquite did not start until September so we stayed in Commerce and I completed 12 Semester Hours toward a Masters Degree during the summer of 1964.

We spent every week-end looking for a house in Mesquite. We put the house in Commerce up for sale and it sold right away. We located a nice house in Mesquite in a good neighborhood that was a VA repossession. We were able to assume the existing mortgage and had to pay only the closing costs.

My salary at Mesquite as a beginning teacher would be $4,000.00 for nine months. This was not much of a salary but we had been getting by on less and I knew my salary would improve when I obtained my Masters Degree.

In our two years in Commerce, we had not purchased anything except bare essentials. Almost everything we owned was worn out or very near being worn out.

Our 1956 Ford Station Wagon was nearing 100,000 miles and I did not know how much longer it would last. I traded the Station Wagon and $300.00 for a 1959 Edsel Sedan. The Edsel was in near new condition and only had 30,000 miles on the odometer. It turned out the Edsel had spent its entire life in Greenville in stop and go traffic. When I started putting hard miles on it going from Commerce to Mesquite regularly, it started using oil and putting out a cloud of smoke. The Edsel automobile came along at the wrong time in history and as a result had a bad reputation. Truth of the matter was most people laughed at people driving an Edsel. This did not bother me, but Sharon and Cathy would lie down in the back seat when we went down town for fear someone would recognize them and kid them about riding in an Edsel.

We moved to Mesquite after the Second Summer Session ended. We found a small apartment in Commerce for Sharon since she needed one more semester and would graduate at the end of the fall semester. Cathy enrolled in Mesquite High School.

During the summer after I had signed a contract to teach business courses at Mesquite High School, I received a call from the Personnel Director of the Mesquite School District that he wanted to talk to me. During our meeting the High School Principal told me they had never had a High School Registrar but they had been authorized to create the new position. He offered me the job and I immediately accepted the offer. I would still teach two business courses. My financial condition was such that if he had told me I had to clean the restrooms after school I would have agreed to do so. As it turned out, this was to provide me with a very satisfying and successful future career.

My first day on the job at Mesquite High School was registration day. I also learned that registration was my primary responsibility. We used the procedures that had been used in prior years and it took three days to enroll the 2,000 students. I resolved to work out a different enrollment procedure before next registration day. The student records were in terrible shape. Two secretaries spent all summer transferring grades from the Teachers Grade Sheets to the students Permanent Record card. This was to be another of my responsibilities. I realized immediately there were not enough hours in the day to accomplish all of the things I was required to accomplish.

I remembered my Marine Corps Data Processing experience and approached the Principal about modernizing the registration and record keeping procedures. It turned out the Principal was a Navy Hospital Corpsman and had served with a Marine Unit in Korea. He was fond of Marines and we became good friends. He gave me a free hand to modernize the system and promised to support me all the way to the School Board. It was obvious the School District was too poor to afford their own Data Processing System and I started looking around for an alternative procedure.

Sharon was doing her Student Teaching in Terrell and staying with her Grandparents (McDonalds). On her Way to school on December 10 she hit some gravel on a curve and flipped the Volkswagen over. She was taken to the Hospital in Terrell and the Highway Patrol called me at the High School and informed me that Sharon had been involved in an accident and was in the Hospital in Terrell.

I went home and broke the news to Chris of Sharon's accident. We departed for the Terrell Hospital and upon arrival found out Sharon had some cracked vertebrae and bruises but she would survive. We spent most of the remainder of the day at the Hospital, the Nurses telling Chris to take it easy and rest. She insisted she was doing fine. We went home in time to pick Cathy up from school and Chris was doing fine when we went to bed. Shortly after mid-night she awoke with serious labor pains. We left immediately for the Air Force Hospital (Perrin Field) at Sherman, 80 miles from Mesquite. By the time we arrived at the Hospital her pains had subsided. The Doctor wanted to keep her overnight. I had to return to Mesquite since Cathy was home alone and I needed to do some things at the High School and then go to Terrell to check on Sharon.

Shortly after 9:30 a.m., December 11, 1964 the School Secretary called me and said I had a long distance call in her office. My office was some distance away in another building and I took off running, thinking now what? I was out of breath from running and "punchy" from lack of sleep. The person on the telephone told me he was an Air Force Doctor at Perrin AFB and my wife had just delivered a healthy, red headed, baby boy. I said a baby what? He repeated what he had just told me and said that Chris was doing fine. The

Secretary overheard the conversation and was laughing out loud. Until I left Mesquite, every time I saw her she would say "a baby what" and have a good laugh.

Sharon and Cathy were really surprised when I told them that they had a red headed baby brother. They wanted to know where the red hair came from. My grandfather was a red head and my grandmother had a red headed brother and several red headed sisters.

We named our son Wade Tyler. The Wade part was in honor of my best friend John Wade. We were in the C.C.C. at Wolfe City, Texas and enlisted in the Marine Corps together on November 24, 1939. John Wade became a Marine Aviator and was killed in 1944. The Tyler was my Great Grandfather, George Freemont Tyler.

Sharon had to wear a back brace for some time, however she was able to return to college and graduated from East Texas State College at the end of the Fall Semester.

I drove to Commerce every Saturday and took two courses toward my Masters Degree. I would get home around 3:00 p.m. on Saturday, totally exhausted. We would go to Church on Sunday and I would barricade myself in the back room on Sunday afternoon and work on my studies. I finally worked out a routine of getting up at 3:00 a.m., to study while everyone else was asleep and it was nice and quiet.

The Volkswagen had been repaired and it looked good, but I was never happy with it. In early 1965 we traded it in on a new 1965 white Mustang. The Mustang was equipped with all available extras including Air Conditioning and cost a total of $3,200.00. Sharon and Cathy were delighted that they no longer had to ride in the Edsel.

Things were going well at home and I was once again able to concentrate on the problem of modernizing the record keeping system at the High School. I found a company in downtown Dallas that had a medium size IBM 1410 Computer that was not fully utilized. They were anxious to take on the computer work for the High School. We worked out a contract that pleased all parties and were soon hard at work developing a Grade Reporting and Permanent Record procedure for the High School. The "old time" teachers were really skeptical. They could not believe they would be furnished a card for every student in each of their classes, make two marks on the card with a special pencil and the Grade Reports and Grade Sheets they normally slaved over would be produced for them. They would catch me in the hall and want to know "what is the catch". This procedure is too easy. There must be more to it than making the marks on the cards.

The computer used the same cards that were used for the Grade Reports to prepare a pressure sensitive label which was pasted onto an 8 ½ x 11 card that became the students permanent record. The labels could be attached to the student record card in two days rather than taking the secretaries all summer to accomplish the job under the old method. I was never as popular as the Coaches, however my stock took a decided jump with the teachers and secretaries. I received a 1,000.00 dollar salary increase for the 1965-66 school year. My new salary would be $5,000.00.

After receiving her degree in Home Economics, Sharon worked as a Dietitian at a small Hospital in Dallas. She obtained a teaching position in Sherman, Texas for the 1965-66 school year. She met Lieutenant Brian Mulrey who was stationed at Perrin AFB. They were married February 19, 1966.

Things were going smoothly at home and at the High School. I had completed my Oral Examinations and would receive my Masters Degree at the end of the Spring Semester 1966. In the middle of May, just prior to graduation at the High School they held what was called "College Night". Counselors from the many Universities and Junior Colleges talk to the graduating senior about attending their school. I was making small talk with one of the Counselors from Henderson County Junior College in Athens, Texas. He wanted to know what my job was at Mesquite High School. I told him I taught two business courses, was the High School Registrar and I took care of the Computerized Student Record System. He became very interested and told me they were looking for a Computer Instructor at Henderson County Junior College. He told me to call J.B. Simmons at the college Monday morning. I promised to do so and immediately dismissed the thought from my mind.

The following Wednesday (I now had my own telephone), I received a call from J. B. Simmons at Henderson County Junior College. He said "I thought you were going to get in touch with me". I said I thought his Counselor was "putting me on". He assured me he wanted to talk to me. I told him I could not get away until Saturday. He said the college was closed on Saturday, but he and the College President would be there to see me. I had never been to Athens, Texas but checked the map and realized it was 65 miles southeast of Dallas. I had no difficulty finding the Campus of Henderson County Junior College. I met with Mr. J.B. Simmons for a few minutes. He then took me in to see the College President. They made me an offer I could not turn down! They would pay $7,900.00 for me to teach 5 classes and $300.00 per class for more than 5 classes. I was to start work at Henderson County Junior College in July 1966. When I broke the news to Chris, she was both happy and sad. We decided we would sell the house. Chris, Cathy and Wade would live in an Apartment in Mesquite until Cathy graduated from High School at the end of the Fall Tenn. I would find a room in Athens and come home on Wednesday night and week-ends until we could find a house in Athens.

HENDERSON COUNTY JUNIOR COLLEGE

I received my Masters Degree in May 1966, resigned my job at Mesquite High School in June and reported to Henderson County Junior College the 1st of July, 1966.

When I reported to Henderson County Junior College, the President wanted to know where I was going to live. I told him I would find a room temporarily since my family would remain in Mesquite until Cathy graduated from High School. He told me he had a nice air conditioned room in one of the Dormitories he would like for me to use, no charge, just keep an eye on things. I should have been smart enough to realize what I was being conned into. The free rent clouded my better judgment! Things went well the first week. About 2:00 a.m., the middle of the second week I was awakened by a terrible noise. I jumped out of bed and discovered drunken football players riding a motorcycle up and down the stairs of the Dormitory. Using my best Marine Corps voice, I put a stop to the nonsense, took names and turned them into the President the next day. Since they were football players, nothing happened to them.

At Mesquite High School, football players were given grades and coddled all the way through High School. It soon became apparent that football was a "Sacred Cow" at Henderson County Junior College. With the beginning of the fall semester, classes were dismissed every Friday afternoon for a "Pep Rally". The students loved it. I couldn't believe my eyes. We were informed in no uncertain terms that all Instructors would attend every game on Saturday night. As at Mesquite High School, I had the honor of selling tickets at the gate every Saturday night. We bought a nice house in a good neighborhood in Athens for $17,000.00. This was the best house from a construction standpoint I had ever seen. It had been custom built by a local Doctor. All doors were solid wood with brass hardware throughout the entire house.

Our first grandchild Christine Anne Mulrey was born October 8, 1966. We were very proud of her, but somewhat shocked to realize that we were now grandparents!

My first semester at Henderson County Junior College was a real learning experience for me. One of my class assignments was to teach Data Processing to 30 Federal Prisoners that were bussed to the campus from the Federal Prison in Seagoville, Texas (near Dallas). This was a six semester hour course and was from 8:30 a.m. to 3:30 p.m. every Saturday. These students were all high class criminals. Among others, there was an Attorney, 2 or 3 Bankers, a Ship Captain, an Airline Pilot, some CPA's and an owner of a Blood Bank who had been convicted of selling blood from cadavers!

I asked my boss Mr. J.B. Simmons if we should be teaching Data Processing to these prisoners. My feeling was these people would be released some day and they would have knowledge that would permit them to really manipulate company funds and records. He told me my job was to teach and not worry about what they might do when they were released. One thing I would say about the prisoners, they were the most intelligent and motivated students I ever taught. All they did all week was study. I had the feeling by the end of the Spring Semester, that they knew more about Data Processing than I did.

As soon as we purchased the house in Athens, I moved out of the Dormitory. I would go to Mesquite on Wednesday night and Chris, Cathy and Wade would come to Athens for the week-end. As soon as Cathy graduated from Mesquite High School everyone moved to Athens and Cathy enrolled at Henderson County Junior College. The house in Athens was on a one acre lot. It seemed that I spent every Sunday (except time for Church) mowing the lawn. We decided we never wanted another one acre lot. It was too much to mow and not enough to graze. At 4:00 p.m., every Thursday we held a faculty meeting at the College. Frequently there would be little business to discuss but the Dean of the College always ended the meeting with the statement that he wanted to see all of us at the "Pep Rally" on Friday and at the game on Saturday night. His final comment was always, "Now look folks, don't worry about how those boys quote Shakespeare, you grade them on the way they carry the football Saturday night". I was less than impressed with this attitude.

There was another interesting development near the end of the Fall Semester. Our football team had defeated all competition and was selected to go to Pasadena, California for the Junior Rose Bowl. There were about 90 men on the football team, 90 girls on the drill team and a like number of men and women members of the marching band. They all went to the Junior Rose Bowl. With 270 students absent from a total of 1,400 there were not enough students to hold classes. As a result, the college was shut down for an entire week. If I had any lingering doubts about the purpose of the college being to educate students, my doubts were confirmed. I realized that football was the primary purpose of Henderson County Junior College.

While I was working at Mesquite High School, I applied for the job of Registrar at the new Community College in Denison. I met the President, Dr. Cruce Stark. He was very pleasant but informed me the job had been filled. The next year, the Community College was created in Dallas. I applied for the job of Registrar and was told the job had been filled by the Registrar from Grayson County College in Denison. On Saturday, I drove up to Grayson County College to see Dr. Stark again. He told me he had hired a man from Mississippi that he had worked with several years prior. I thanked him and told him he would hear from me again if the job ever became vacant.

In November 1966 the senior Counselor at Henderson County Junior College told me he had to attend a meeting of Technical-Vocational Advisory Committees at Grayson County College and wanted me to come along and keep him awake since it was about 120 miles away and we would be coming back late at night. I agreed to go with him and ran into Dr. Stark at Grayson County College. He remembered me and stated he would have hired me as his Registrar if he had not already made a commitment to his friend from Mississippi. I thanked him for his consideration and told him I would be back to see him if the job ever became vacant again.

The appeal of Grayson County College was partly that it was near Perrin AFB with Hospital, Commissary and PX privileges. The main appeal was that it was a new college and everyone worked as a team. At Henderson County Junior College the faculty was split four ways. The old faculty vs. the new faculty. The President and the Dean fought constantly. Each of them had their own supporters. Then there was the split between the Academic and the Technical-Vocational Teachers.

The Henderson County Junior College football team won the Junior Rose Bowl in Pasadena, California and Bob Baccarini, the Head Coach owned the town of Athens. He was offered numerous coaching positions at various four year Universities but since he was Mr. Big in Athens and owned the town, he chose to stay at Henderson County Junior College. His assistant coach, being somewhat smarter than Bob Baccarini, accepted an assistant coaching job at Kansas State University and eventually ended up many years later as the Athletic Director at the University of Oklahoma! Poor Bob Baccarini fell upon bad times two years later.

Our son-in-law Brian Mulrey received orders to Viet Nam for the spring of 1967. Sharon and Baby Chris moved to Athens and rented a little house to be nearby while Brian was overseas.

Things were going well at Henderson County Junior College and one morning in late spring during breakfast, the telephone rang. It was a secretary at Grayson County College who had been one of the secretaries at Mesquite High School when I was there, calling to tell me the Registrars job at Grayson County College would be vacant in a few weeks. Later that evening I received an additional call from a former classmate Neal Baker, a History Teacher at Grayson County College, with the same information.

On Saturday morning I drove up to Grayson County College to see Dr. Stark. 'When I arrived, I was told Dr. Stark was out of town but the Vice President, Ed Bullard would see me. Mr. Bullard told me that Dr. Stark said if this man Frank Graves shows up tell him he can have the Registrar's job with a salary of $9,600 for a 12 month contract. I knew Chris had had her fill of moving but I realized I would never be happy at a school that taught football and played school. I said "Where do I sign". Soon I was on my way back to Athens to break the news to Chris that we were going to move once again.

We put a for sale sign on the house and started looking for a house in Sherman and Denison on the week-ends. We were shocked at the prices of homes in the area. A house comparable to the one we had in Athens was $27,000 to $30,000. This was out of our price range and we finally settled on a rent house on Brown Street in Denison. We sold our house in Athens. Sharon moved into our rented house in Denison and we moved into the little house Sharon was renting in Athens. This was a lot of shuffling around, but things worked out.

By this time, Wade was a very active little boy. Before we moved out of our house in Athens, he found a bottle of black ink and poured it in the middle of the living room floor on the off white carpet! A few days later, I looked out to see what he was doing in the yard and he had a garden hose stuck in the gasoline filler pipe of the Mustang. When I yelled at him, he said "gas in car". Fortunately, cars in those days had a drain plug in the bottom of the gas tank. I did not start the car for several hours to let the water settle to the bottom of the tank, removed the plug and let the water drain out. No serious damage but it was a good thing I caught him in the act. I had to teach the 1st Summer Session at Henderson County Junior College and as soon as it was over, we moved to Denison. I reported to Grayson County College in July 1967.

DENISON, TEXAS

Upon my arrival at Grayson County College, I was warmly greeted by Dr. Stark, the College President. He informed me that the very efficient Secretary in the Registrar's office, I had met on one of my visits had resigned and moved to Lubbock. He was proud of the fact that he had taken care of the situation. He had hired a young lady with a College Degree as my Secretary and had two work-study students who would work with me part-time. His pride and joy was the new work-study student who was in her Sophomore year and had a 4.0 Grade Point Average. He informed me it was his policy that all full-time Secretaries must have a College Degree. I thanked him for taking good care of the situation. He departed and I busied myself getting organized.

The second day on the job, I discovered the very attractive Secretary with a College Degree could not find the home keys on the typewriter. When I asked her what her Major was in College, I was shocked when she told me she Majored in Interior Decorating and Design! My second shock of the day was when the 4.0 Grade Point student worker showed up. She did not know how to type and to make matters worse, she could not file! I tried to teach her how to file but it was a lost cause. I decided she was a "Book worm" and if she ever got caught in a rainstorm she would get wet, since she would not know to come inside. I soon found a replacement for her. The remaining student worker was excellent. She and I ended up doing all of the typing and the Secretary answered the telephone and tried to take care of the counter.

A few days later, I thought I had died and gone to heaven when I learned Grayson County College did not have a football team. They did have Basketball and Baseball and the faculty was invited to attend the games but no pressure applied to force everyone to attend all games. Dr. Stark believed our primary purpose was to teach students. He was what I would call a Benevolent Dictator. He treated everyone with dignity and respect. It did not matter to him if the Instructor taught Physics or Automobile Mechanics. As long as they did a good job they never had a problem with him. If someone goofed off he would be all over him in a hurry. He was fair but firm, my kind of guy.

In August 1967 we purchased on old two story house on Bond Street in Denison for $13,995. It was all we could afford at the time. The payments were 87.00 per month. We thought we would make do with the old house for a few years and when our financial conditions improved we would look for a modern house. I believed that if I did a good job as Registrar I could expect to be rewarded with an increase in pay. In addition to my $9,600 salary, I would receive 350.00 for teaching a night class each semester.

We moved into the old house on Bond Street near the end of August. Chris and I were exhausted and sat down on the screened in side porch for a few minutes to rest. After a few minutes, I asked her where Wade was. She said that she did not know. I went into the living room and found that he had dragged a hose in the back door and had hosed down the living room and was working on the kitchen when I found him. I yelled "God Almighty, tum that hose off".

A few days later we had a sewer line stopped up. The plumber that cleaned it out had thrown dirt upon the patio and was washing the dirt off with a hose. Wade spotted him and ran out yelling at the plumber "God Almighty, turn that hose off". The plumber was really startled to have this little boy yelling at him.

Before we moved from Mesquite I traded the Edsel for a 1966 Chevrolet sedan. The floor of the car was about 4 inches below the bottom of the door. One day I went out to the car to go to work and found 4 inches of water in the car. Wade had been using the hose again. After this incident, I removed the handle from all of the outside faucets.

Early in 1968 the husband of my Secretary was transferred from Perrin Air Force Base and the Secretary informed me she would be leaving Grayson County College in a few days. I wanted to shout "hooray" but managed to restrain myself. I thought I would now be able to hire someone I could get some work out of.

In those days, the fall semester did not end until the middle of January. There was a fine student in my Data Processing Class in her early thirties with extensive work experience. I asked her if she would like to work in the Registrars office and she agreed to do so. She was Mrs. Pat Briggs. Dr. Stark vetoed the idea because she did not have a College Degree. I argued that I needed someone who would work. I told him I had two Degrees and she could have one of mine. After about a week he relented and said I could hire Mrs. Briggs but it was against his policy. By this time I was desperate because I had been working late at night and on Saturday and Sunday trying to stay ahead of the paperwork.

Mrs. Briggs worked out extremely well. Dr. Stark was impressed with her work and this broke the ice jam. He never again insisted that a Secretarial or Clerical position be filled by a college graduate. My work load improved and I was able to stay home most nights and weekends.

I came home one afternoon and Chris announced that "Your Son" was up on the clothes drier doing something and the lights were flashing on and off! I said "Oh no, he was messing with the fuse box. There are 220 volts of electricity in that box". I went to town and bought two pad locks and put them on the two fuse boxes where they stayed until he was grown.

A few weeks later, we were scared out of our wits. Sharon and Chris drove up and went into the house to visit. I was working out in the little house and Wade was riding his tricycle. The tricycle was squeaking and I knew he was all right as long as I could hear him. I had early on learned that when things got quiet to look for trouble because he was sure to be into something. A few minutes later, I realized I could not hear the tricycle squeaking. I started looking for Wade and could not find him. I was afraid he would try to climb up into the garage attic and fall out. He was not in the garage and I was getting panicky! As I ran out of the garage, I had a fleeting view of something red in the window of Sharon's car. It was Wade hanging by his neck from the car window! Sharon had left the window part way down on the drivers side of the car. Wade had stood on his tricycle trying to get into the window of the car. The tricycle had rolled out from under him and he was hanging with his head between the door glass and the roof of the car. I screamed for Chris, she came out and held him in her arms. We took off at high speed for the Hospital at Perrin Air Force Base. Wade was not making a sound but was breathing. I think Chris and I were hyperventilating. As we made the final turn to go into the Hospital, Wade started yelling. That was the best noise I had ever heard. We rushed him into the Doctor who examined him carefully and said his neck was bruised but he thought he would be fine. He wanted to keep him overnight for observation to make sure he did not develop any complications. Chris stayed at the Hospital with Wade and I came on home after a few hours.

Wade continued to cause us many anxious moments until he was about 5 years of age. At that time, he settled down and has been a pleasure to be around ever since. We were apprehensive about him becoming a teenager but he slipped through those years without the slightest problem.

Our first grandchild Christine Ann Mulrey was born October 8, 1966 at Perrin Air Force Base. Our grandson Brian Mulrey, Jr. was born July 17, 1971 at Wiesbaden, Germany. Cathy married James G. Fielder July 23, 1976. Jim and his son, Michael were a welcome addition to our family. Our grandson William Bristow Fielder was born March 5, 1979 and John Austin Fielder August 2, 1980 at Corpus Christi, Texas.

When Wade was about 11 years old, I overheard him talking to one of his friends about school. He stated, "When my Dad talks about walking to school through the mud and snow, it gets longer every time he tells about it". I kept quiet, thinking that "I am going to fix you good one of these days". The following summer one Saturday morning I asked Wade if he would like to go for a drive in the country. He was willing but wanted to know where we were going. I told him he would know when we arrived there.

We drove to Windom, then 4 miles south to where the Flag Springs School once stood. I told him this is where my school was located. We drove east on the dirt road for 1 mile and parked the car. We got out of the car, crawled through the barb wire fence, down the hill, across a creek, up the hill, down the hill crossed another creek, crawled through another barb wire fence, up the hill through head high weeds and located the old well where our house stood. I told him, this is where I grew up.

We walked back to the car the way we came. Wade must have been convinced about how far his Dad walked to school because I have not heard him mention it since that day. In the summer of 1979 I managed to work in two weeks vacation. We went to Germany to visit Sharon and Brian. Brian took leave from his Air Force assignment and they took us on an interesting tour. We went to France and visited the World War I Battle area at Verdun. Some of the trenches are still visible, overgrown with trees. The land is unusable because of the many unexploded shells from French and German Artillery.

Our tour included Bavaria and the largest Beer Hall in the world in Munich where Hitler and his thugs got their start. There were visits to several Castles and Churches. I was most interested in Hitler's mountain retreat "The Eagles "Nest" in the Bavarian Alps. From Bavaria we went through Austria, across the Brenner Pass into Italy. Going from Austria to Italy reminded me of the contrast in going from San Diego to Tijuana. There were lots of trash and derelict buildings, even damaged buildings from World War II that had not been repaired. The Italians were in no hurry. They were waiting for the government to repair the war damaged buildings.

We spent 2 or 3 days in Venice, toured the city, swam in the Adriatic, gawked at the works of Art and the ancient buildings. We purchased a chandelier on the Island of Murano. It was necessary to disassemble it to be packed properly so we could bring it home without damage. The Italian could speak no English and I could not understand Italian. He told me how to reassemble it once we managed to get it home. If I had not watched him take it apart, it might still be in a box. We finally managed to put it together and wire it to take our electricity and bulbs. What a chore!

The Italians are fun to watch. If you were to tie their hands they would not be able to communicate.

We spent another day and night in the Italian Alps and then back to Germany by Way of Austria. Beautiful country.

I must say that I was very impressed with Germany and the Germans. They work hard and keep their country clean, no trash or junk cars littering the countryside. I looked for damage from World War II but could find no evidence of the war. They had repaired everything. Their Bread and Beer is especially good. I could probably live on those two items.

When we returned home, I was happy to learn my job at the college had been changed from Registrar to Vice President for Admissions and Records with a substantial increase in salary. Up to this point, we were getting by but we had to really save to make the trip to Germany. Things were now looking much brighter.

In 1969 with the help of Mr. and Mrs. McDonald, we purchased some depleted, brush covered, eroded farm land near Colbert, Oklahoma. Mr. McDonald as well as myself believed that the place had some possibilities and for $115.00 per acre we decided it was a good buy. It looked so terrible the Real Estate Agent that took me over there would not get out of his Jeep since he thought I would not be interested. Christene's Uncle Tom Grier took one look at the place and announced that he would not have it if they were to give it to him! We later purchased 14 acres of the old railroad right of way for $100.00 and 12 acres on the north side of the area for $6,000.00. We raised cattle on the place until 1990 when my health problems forced me to sell the cattle and lease the land to Bill Busbey.

It is our wish to pass the land on to our children and hope that they will keep it in the family. I believe the time will come when it will not be possible to buy land at any price. The place could be a quiet retreat to get away from the "rat race".

My job at Grayson County College was an interesting challenge. I kept busy and the years rushed by too quickly. In 1981 I was promoted to Executive Vice President and Dean of the College with a very substantial salary increase.

In 1982 Dr. Truman Wester Retired as President of the College. He was replaced by Dr. Jim Williams. Dr. Williams was not fond of my take charge, get the job done, no nonsense, let the Teachers Teach methods. He could not fire me without good cause so he reorganized the Administrative procedures. He moved me down the hall into a job called Vice President for Administrative Services. This job involved Computer Services, Campus Police, Transportation, Mail and Telephone Services. In other words, all of the "cats and dogs" that everyone else was able to "wiggle out of".

Wade stayed busy with his Scouting Activities and grew up much too soon. He graduated from high school in 1983 and from Grayson County College in 1985. He transferred to North Texas State University and graduated two years later.

In 1985 We signed up for a Cruise in Tahiti, paid our money and waited. A few days before we were due to depart, we received a letter stating the ship was still under repairs. They offered to refund our money, take the cruise a year later or spend 3 days in a Luxury Hotel on the Island of Tahiti plus a week at Club Med on the Island of Moorea and a cruise of the Islands the following year with the only additional cost, the air fare to Tahiti and return.

We opted for the Hotel and Club Med trip with the Cruise in 1986. The three days in the Hotel on Tahiti were great. The 12 mile ferry trip to the Island of Moorea was wild. They piled everyone aboard the ferry, no safety instructions or any emergency procedures discussed. I roamed around and found a locker containing life jackets. We stayed near the life jacket locker for the rest of the trip.

We were assigned a grass hut near the beach at Club Med. The hut had all necessary facilities. I would swim in the Lagoon every morning and evening. Too hot to swim during the day. They had all kinds of entertainment and the food was outstanding.

The entertainment at Club Med proved to be interesting. One unusual feature was that some of the dancing girls were boys. It seems in ancient times the King decreed that all boy babies were to be killed to eliminate competition for control of the Islands. To get around the decree the mothers raised their sons as girls. That tradition is still followed in some cases, thus the reason for the "boy" dancing girls.

The Islands were beautiful, even prettier than Hawaii. The only fly in the ointment is, they are governed by the French! The Tahitians hate the French and as a group they are a very unhappy bunch of people.

We returned to Tahiti in 1986 and visited all of the Islands in the group except one that did not have facilities for the ship. We would visit an Island during the day and sail at night for the next Island. Since the Islands are close to each other, the ship would spend the night cruising at 4 knots, not fast enough for the stabilizers to kick in. As a result, Chris was sea sick most of the time.

Our first trip to Tahiti was an air carrier called People Express. It was a reasonably comfortable trip. They declared bankruptcy shortly after our return from Tahiti. Our second trip was a charter outfit from Los Angeles. They would not let the outfit into the terminal area of the airport. After getting a look at the 747 parked about a mile and a half from the terminal I think I understand why. I would have canceled the trip except we had paid in full and would not be able to get our money back. The 400 passengers were transported from the terminal to the 747 about 100 each trip in something that could be best described as a "cattle car", standing room only. I was admonished by Chris when I started mooing like cattle do when they are confined in close quarters.

At last, all 400 of us were stuffed into the 747. We taxied the mile and a half to the terminal area, finally given clearance for the runway and were on our way. After reaching cruising altitude, I settled back in my seat to relax and the arm rest fell off. A short time later my foot touched the air vent cover near the floor and the cover fell off. My thoughts were, I wonder how the maintenance is on the critical parts of the aircraft. I reported the incident to the Flight Attendant and she said, "I reported that two weeks ago, and they have not fixed it yet". Sometime later I decided I was in need of some liquid stimulant and discovered they ran out of food and booze after two hours into a 10 hour flight!

On the return trip, when we checked in the attendant wanted to know if we wanted smoking or no smoking seats. I said "put us as far away from those damned smokers as you can". She put us in the first row of seats in the nose of the 747. It was fine with me but Chris was as nervous as a cat all the way back to Los Angeles. In the nose of the 747, there is a constant pitch and yaw that is not felt near the middle of the aircraft. In addition, every time they adjust the controls you hear the terrible hydraulic noises.

We landed in Los Angeles shortly after daylight and went through U.S. Customs. The Customs Agent wanted to know if we had anything to declare. I said I sure have, "I am delighted to be back in the U.S. and I will not ride a charter flight again. If I am not able to pay for a regular scheduled airline flight I will stay home". He got a big laugh out of my frustration and waved us on our way.

In 1980 I began to develop respiratory problems that became progressively worse each year. By 1986 I was having serious breathing problems almost every day and night. I was reminded by the ever-present lengthening shadow of time that if I was ever going to do some of the things I had always wanted to do I had better get on with it. With this thought in mind, I retired from Grayson County College after 19 good years on August 31, 1986.

In August 1988 the family gathered in Denison for the marriage of our only granddaughter Christine Mulrey. On August 6, she married Lt. Mark Koch, USAF and they left for duty at Clark Field in the Philippine Islands. Our first great-grandchild Sarah Catherine Koch was born March 27, 1990. They left Clark Field in 1991 when Mt. Penatubo erupted and covered everything with volcanic ash.

Our second great-grandchild, Kaitlin Taylor Koch was born November 10, 1994 in North Dakota. This gave us two great-granddaughters, one granddaughter and five grandsons. Our family Doctor, John P. Tyson loaded me up with antibiotics every time I had a serious breathing problem. Cathy promised to quit smoking if I would go to a specialist. I started going to Dr. Elaine Brown, a local Allergist. She gave me many tests and started giving me a shot every 10 days. All the shot did was make my arm sore. I left her after about a year and went to Dr. Habal.

Dr. Habal diagnosed my problem as Bronchial Asthma. He began to load me up with drugs. One of the drugs was a very powerful cortisteroid called Medrol. He did not inform me of any side effects of this drug. While visiting Sharon and Brian in Minot, North Dakota I came down with a severe bronchial infection. Sharon took me to the Air Force Emergency Room where an Air Force Doctor threw a fit when he found out I had been taking Medrol for several years. He told me about the bad things that would happen to me if I continued to take Medrol. He said "Never take that stuff more than seven, ten days at the most." This got my attention. When we returned home, I purchased a Drug Book that listed most drugs used and started reading about the side effects of any drug prescribed for me.

By the fall of 1989 my breathing problems were so severe Chris had to do most of the driving. I ran a low grade fever all the time, my Weight had dropped to 140 pounds and I was so weak I had difficulty getting out of my chair. I was unable to properly care for the cattle and we sold all of them in 1990.

In early 1990 my left arm became infected with bursitis. I had trouble sleeping and every time I tried to move the arm the pain was severe. Chris and Sharon were after me to try physical therapy. The Physical Therapy Center required a referral from my Doctor. When I talked to Dr. Tyson he said that ordinarily he would give me a shot of Cortisone to clear up the bursitis but I had too much medication already.

After a week of physical therapy, I had full use of my left arm. The therapist put me on the Treadmill and Aerobic Machines in his clinic which was called Health Trends. I would walk a few minutes on the Treadmill and cough for five minutes, do a little exercise on the Aerobic Machines and cough for another five minutes.

After several days of very mild exercise, I realized I could force myself to do a little more each day. I continued this routine 5 days per week and continued to make progress. After six months, I was able to discontinue the breathing machine I had been using 3 or 4 times each night and several times during the day. My health began to gradually improve and after one year of exercise I started cutting back on the Medrol. Dr. Habal said I was trying to play Doctor. I told him yes sir, I am going to get off of Medrol if I can. He did not care for my comments but I had decided I had to look after my own best interest. As my strength returned I increased my daily workout to the point where I was able to do two miles on the treadmill at 4 miles per hour and ran through 50 cycles on six different machines. It took me 2 1/2 years to get off of the Medrol but I was finally able to do so. Six months later I was able to get off of Theophylline. That left only the Proventil and Azmacort Inhalers. These are used on a daily basis. Most of the people who come to Health Trends come to lose weight. I gained weight, back to my normal weight. I told the lady that runs the Health Trends operation that I was her best salesman. I have made the exercise program a part of my life and will continue to exercise as long as I am able to do so. It is a lot more fun than going to the Doctor!

Wade married Julie Johnson January 6, 1990. Julie and her son, Nathan were a welcome addition to our family. Chris and I suddenly realized we were faced with an empty nest. We knew from now on we would only have each other except for visits.

In November 1991 we decided we would go to Hawaii for the 50th anniversary of the attack on Pearl Harbor. We stayed in a nice Hotel on Waikiki but were kept so busy with activities, Chris did not have an opportunity to see much of the Island. We agreed we would make a return visit someday.

There had been incredible changes made on the Island of Oahu since 1942. High rise buildings covered the Waikiki area as well as Pearl City. There were only two navy ships in Pearl Harbor. In 1940-41 there would be 70 to 80 ships in the harbor most of the time. They dumped their sewage into the harbor and it was like a large cesspool. In 1991 the water in the harbor was clear and clean. They required the ships to pump their sewage ashore to the sewage treatment plant and as a result, the harbor was clean enough to swim in. The visit to the ARIZONA memorial was an emotional experience for me. Almost half of those killed on December 7, 1941 were aboard the ARIZONA.

December 9, 1991 I was standing out on our balcony at the hotel admiring the scenery when I noticed the Battleship Missouri had cleared the Pearl Harbor Channel and was not too far from Waikiki. I knew she was headed for Bremerton, Washington to be decommissioned, not only the last Battleship in the U.S. Navy but the last Battleship in the world on active duty. I called Chris to come and look, I said "take a good look at that ship, you will never again see a Battleship underway in full commission".

Chris and I both realized that the time would soon come when we would no longer be able to live in our home on Bond Street. While the house was as comfortable as an old shoe, it required a lot of maintenance and it was a large area to try to keep clean. We were in no hurry to find a smaller place but decided to keep our eyes open in case we stumbled across something we liked that was not overpriced. We were determined we would not be an economic slave to a new expensive house at our age.

In December 1992 we learned of a VA repossessed house on Morrison Drive. We took a look at the place, more or less counted the rooms and submitted a bid of $38,000 to the Veterans Administration. We did not expect our bid would be accepted and were very surprised to learn four days later that our bid had been accepted. We then took a close look at the place and decided it needed major rehabilitation! As soon as the deal was closed, we started to work. Chris and I worked seven days per week (except time out on Sunday for Church) for three months. Wade and Julie helped every weekend. Except for some plumbing work, pipes broken off in the walls, reworking the counter tops and lower cabinets, tile in the kitchen and dining area, the four of us performed all of the work. We spent an additional $10,000 on the house. We rented the house to Wade and Julie since we were not ready to move. We had to have time to figure out what to do with all of the things we had collected over the years, not an easy task.

At the end of March, 1994 we took our promised return trip to Hawaii. It was a great experience until we decided to take a one day trip to the big Island of Hawaii. Our tour of the Island included a van trip around the entire Island, our mistake. Among other things, we visited Volcanoes National Park. The Volcano was spewing sulfuric acid fumes among several other things, including bubbling lava. I breathed a lot of the fumes from the Volcano that really gave me fits. We returned home two days later and I was in really bad shape. On the let down to the DFW Airport it felt like my head was in a vise. I managed to get in to see Dr. Tyson the next morning. He wanted to know what I had been doing since I had the worst sinus and respiratory infection he had ever seen. He said he was going to hit me with everything he had. With his most powerful drugs, it still took me two weeks to fully recover. I will not get near a Volcano as long as I live, unless one erupts in my neighborhood.

In October 1994 we took a cruise to the Caribbean and to Venezuela. Caracas was a very modern city with evidence of much wealth in the city. Caracas is about 30 miles up in the mountains from the coast. The hillsides are covered with poor squatters. The tour guide said they did not know how many squatters there were but they estimated about one million, mostly illegal. Some areas are so dangerous the police will not venture in. The guide stated "if things get out of hand the army will go into the area and restore order".

The various Islands were interesting. It was easy to tell the former French Islands, They were usually filthy dirty. The former British Islands were some better and the Dutch Island of Aruba was immaculate.

Our grandson Frank Tyler Graves was born March 21, 1995. He is the only one of our grandchildren who has been near enough to see on a regular basis and to spoil as grandparents often do. I am sure I will do a good job of spoiling him.

During September 1995 we took another Caribbean Cruise on a different Cruise Line. We visited different Islands but soon discovered they are very similar. We ate like pigs but I was surprised that neither of us gained weight.

In late May and early June 1996 we flew to Anchorage, Alaska and took a Cruise through the Inland Passage to Vancouver, B.C. Sharon and Brian joined us in Seward, Alaska where we boarded the ship. At Skagway, Alaska Sharon went out to inspect a Glacier, Brian made a bicycle tour and Chris and I took a bus tour into the Yukon Territory of Canada. We went through the area where the gold miners passed through on their way to the Gold Fields at Dawson City during the 1890s gold strike.

On the tour into the Yukon Territory we had lunch with a family that was trying to create a Frontier Type Village. They live there all year and I was curious as to how they survived the winter with only four hours of daylight. I asked one of the daughters how cold it gets in the winter. She said last year was pretty bad. The temperature was 60 degrees below zero but then it warmed up to only 40 below zero. She said it was a little bad when the power went out for two or three weeks! I could handle the summer weather up there but there is no way I would spend a winter in that area.

The Glaciers were interesting. When a large chunk of ice would break off it sounded like thunder. By large, I mean the size of three Super Wal-Mart Stores!

Our stop at Juneau, Alaska was an interesting learning experience. Juneau is the State Capital with a population of roughly 30,000. It is the only Capital in the world you cannot reach by train or motor vehicle. The only access is by air or water. We overwhelmed the place since there were five cruise ships in Juneau at the same time.

The last stop on our tour was Vancouver, B.C. a very clean and beautiful city. We had a non-Stop flight from Vancouver to DFW. As always happens, we were happy to be home. Alaska was very pretty but I feel we have seen all of it we care to see. All snow and ice looks pretty much the same.

In July 1996 we decided the time had come to move from our old home on Bond Street. We had lived there 29 years and had collected more "stuff" that would not possibly fit into the house on Morrison Drive. There are still things in the Garage, Attic and Work Shop that have not been moved. Perhaps at a later date.

During September and early October 1996 we decided to take our Travel Agent up on a special two cruise offer to visit both the eastern and western Caribbean.

Two days before the first cruise was over, I came down with one of my severe bronchial infections. I went to see the ship's Doctor and he gave me some antibiotics I had not had before. We should have canceled the second cruise, but I was feeling much better and thought everything would be fine. The second night on the Carnival Ship we were returning to our cabin from the show and I told Chris I had a terrible itch around my waist. When we reached our cabin, about 10:00 p.m., I took my clothes off and saw huge red splotches under my arms and around my waist. A severe reaction to the antibiotic!

By 1:00 a.m. I was covered with red splotches from head to foot. It felt like poison ivy and fire ant stings all at the same time. I cannot recall a more miserable night. Early the next morning I went to visit the ship's Doctor. He took one look at me and told me to not take any more of the antibiotic. He gave me a different medication and an ointment to rub on the red areas which was my entire body. Within 24 hours I was back to normal except for the bronchial infection. When we reached Cozumel, Mexico I found a Pharmacy that had Prednisone in stock that I could purchase without a Doctor's Prescription. I created my own dosage the same as that provided by Dr. Tyson. I made a promise to myself that I would not leave town again without some proper antibiotics and a Prednisone Kit.

In September 1996 Brian Jr. was transferred to Korea for one year of service. We do not know where he will go from there.

At Christmas 1996 Sharon and Brian visited from Albuquerque; Chris, Mark, Sarah and Katie Koch from Belleville, Illinois and Michael Fielder from North Carolina. The only one missing was Brian Jr. Cathy and her family and Wade and his family were also with us. A very happy time.

It looks like 1997 will be a busy year. We plan a trip to Oshkosh, Wisconsin for the Enterprise Marine re-union in June. We will leave a few days early and go by Belleville to visit the Kochs.

Our year started off with the purchase of a new car. After 50 years of owning white, beige, green, brown or blue cars, Chris said she was tired of "bland" colors. We opted for a fire engine red Mercury with all of the bells and whistles this time. We hope the rest of the year will be just as colorful. In October we plan to take a cruise leaving New York, going up the coast and up the St. Lawrence River to Montreal, Canada. We have almost run out of places we want to go.

I want to finish this document by saying that I have lived in an interesting time in History. From going to town in a wagon pulled by two stubborn mules, to watching men walk on the Moon, to leaving from DFW Airport and landing in San Juan, Puerto Rico four and one half hours later, is a remarkable change.

My life has been blessed with a wonderful wife, children, grandchildren and great-grandchildren. There have been rough spots to be sure. These have been far outnumbered by good ones. If I had my life to live over, I am not sure I would make many changes. I am prepared to meet my God with no regrets.

F.E.G. JUNE 1997

Frank and mother Ida Ethyl Culbreath-Graves 1924

Frank and Durward Graves 1926

1927   1937 CCC Uniform

Hawaii 1940   Sergeant   Lieutenant

On Board the USS Montpelier

Chris and Frank Graves November 1943

Meeting Admiral Halsey 1947   Iwo Jima 1953

Captain Graves   Frank in Japan 1953

EPILOGUE

In 2007 I took my father to New Orleans so he could be interviewed for a television documentary about the USS Enterprise entitled "Battle 360: USS Enterprise". Also present were several other men who had served in the Marine Detachment aboard the ship. I had heard their names for years but had never met them. The second night we were there, we all went to dinner. After dinner there was time to sit and listen as my father and his friends spoke openly about their time together on board the Enterprise. Some spoke about the Japanese ship that sailed along Oahu a few days before the Pearl Harbor attack, about the Doolittle Raid, Midway, and Eastern Solomons. Others talked about Santa Cruz and the later operations that Dad wasn't part of. I learned things that night I never knew, and I also realized how much the other men respected my father. They spoke frankly about the nightmares each had experienced after the war. I realized that I was witnessing a group session of sorts. As I sat there and listened, I learned that each of them carried with them experiences they relive periodically in their dreams.

About a month later, I asked Dad about the conversation around the table. I asked him why none of the men ever sought psychiatric help. He looked at me and said, "I have never met a 'talking doctor' who really understood and they haven't either. Unless you were there, you cannot understand. Besides, I would rather spend those doctor fees on good booze with my friends."

Dad lived a good life, taught me a lot of things, and gave me a lot of wisdom through his teachings. I was with him in the hospital each night as he waited for God. We talked, laughed, and reminisced during his lucid moments. He was very proud of me and told me so. We spoke about my sister Cathy and how proud he was of her and her family. Her sudden illness and death in 2012 had been almost too much for him to bear. He also talked about my sister Sharon, his pride in her family, and her work researching our family history. Although he never joined, he shared his delight in the fact that Sharon, Cathy, and I became members of both the Mayflower Society and the Daughters/Sons of the American Revolution to honor our ancestors. Dad said he learned things about the family that he didn't know because of

Sharon's research. He also said that knowing he had so many Patriot Ancestors in the family tree made sense in a way. "After all Wade, they were a pretty hearty lot who blazed new trails. You have to have grit, determination, and a little bit of stubbornness to do the things they did. I think some of those traits are genetic."

As hard headed as I can be at times, I have to agree with him!

Dr. Wade T. Graves (son)

Made in the USA
San Bernardino, CA
27 November 2016